GUARDED BY TWO JAGUARS

GUARDED BY TWO JAGUARS

A Catholic Parish Divided by Language and Faith

ERIC HOENES DEL PINAL

THE UNIVERSITY OF ARIZONA PRESS
TUCSON

The University of Arizona Press
www.uapress.arizona.edu

We respectfully acknowledge the University of Arizona is on the land and territories of Indigenous peoples. Today, Arizona is home to twenty-two federally recognized tribes, with Tucson being home to the O'odham and the Yaqui. Committed to diversity and inclusion, the University strives to build sustainable relationships with sovereign Native Nations and Indigenous communities through education offerings, partnerships, and community service.

© 2022 by The Arizona Board of Regents
All rights reserved. Published 2022
First paperback edition published 2025

ISBN-13: 978-0-8165-4702-9 (hardcover)
ISBN-13: 978-0-8165-5656-4 (paperback)
ISBN-13: 978-0-8165-4703-6 (ebook)

Cover design by Leigh McDonald
Cover photo: "A view from inside La Catedral, Cobán" by Carlos Germán Tarragó Hoenes, 1998
Typeset by Sara Thaxton in 10/14 Warnock Pro with Good Headline Pro

Parts of chapter 3 have appeared in "How Q'eqchi'-Maya Catholics Become Legitimate Interpreters of the Bible: Two Models of Religious Authority in Sermons." In *The Social Life of Scriptures*, edited by James S. Bielo. 2009. New Brunswick, NJ: Rutgers University Press.

Publication of this book is made possible in part by the proceeds of a permanent endowment created with the assistance of a Challenge Grant from the National Endowment for the Humanities, a federal agency.

Library of Congress Cataloging-in-Publication Data
Names: Hoenes del Pinal, Eric, 1975– author.
Title: Guarded by two jaguars : a Catholic parish divided by language and faith / Eric Hoenes del Pinal.
Description: Tucson : The University of Arizona Press, 2022. | Includes bibliographical references and index.
Identifiers: LCCN 2022014523 (print) | LCCN 2022014524 (ebook) | ISBN 9780816547029 (hardcover) | ISBN 9780816547036 (ebook)
Subjects: LCSH: Kekchi Indians—Religion. | Catholics—Religious identity—Guatemala—Cobán | Kekchi Indians—Social life and customs. | BISAC: SOCIAL SCIENCE / Anthropology / Cultural & Social | POLITICAL SCIENCE / World / Caribbean & Latin American
Classification: LCC F1465.2.K5 H73 2022 (print) | LCC F1465.2.K5 (ebook) | DDC 305.897/4207281—dc23/eng/20220414
LC record available at https://lccn.loc.gov/2022014523
LC ebook record available at https://lccn.loc.gov/2022014524

Printed in the United States of America
♾ This paper meets the requirements of ANSI/NISO Z39.48-1992 (Permanence of Paper).

For Nicole

CONTENTS

List of Illustrations — vii
Acknowledgments — ix

Introduction: Catholicism as Heteroglossia — 3
1. Por las calles de Cobán: Place, People, and the Dynamics of Conflict — 34
2. Contested Catholicisms: Social Movements and Catholic Theologies in Parish Life — 53
3. Catequistas y Predicadores: Constructing Religious Authority — 89
4. Están listos para cantar en Q'eqchi'? Ma nekeeraj xninqehinkil sa' Q'eqchi'?: Marking Ritual through Code Choice — 118
5. The Politics of Audibility: Language, Music, and Pious Noise — 145
6. Lo siento en mis manos, lo siento en mis pies: Embodying Piety — 175
7. Bearing the Collective Cross: The Body in Public Piety — 201

Conclusion: Leaving, Returning, and the Dialectics of Change — 223

Works Cited — 235
Index — 251

ILLUSTRATIONS

1. San Felipe's parish church — 29
2. (a) A village chapel; (b) Mass in a village chapel — 43
3. Santos in a procession — 51
4. Catequistas preparing for sermons — 99
5. Carismáticos praying over a predicador — 103
6. Carismáticos singing an alabanza — 162
7. Marimba choir band — 163
8. Carismáticos praying at a vigilia — 191
9. Mainstream Catholics praying at a Celebration of the Word — 194
10. Semana Santa procession — 203

ACKNOWLEDGMENTS

This book has been a long time coming and I have many people and institutions to thank for their support.

B'antiox eere exinkomoneb' sa' Cobán. Li tasal hu a'in nink'e chaq eere chan inmayej. Maak'a' waatin chi yehok chan xjala inna'leb' ut in yu'am xb'an naq xeewotz lee yu'am aawikin. Q'un inch'ool chi eeru. Ninb'antioxi mo ko jo' ta Carlos, Domingo, Enrique, Galindo, Gloria, Gumersindo, Hilda, Lucia, Magdalena, Mario, Manuel, Mynor, Natividad, Otto, Pedro, Raul, Victor, ut Zoila. Naq osob'esinbilee xb'aan li Qaawa'.

The original fieldwork upon which this book is based was funded by generous grants from Wenner-Gren Foundation and the Center for Latin American and Iberian Research at UC San Diego. A Faculty Research Grant from UNC Charlotte allowed me to conduct follow-up research a decade later that offered invaluable new insights. A Junior Faculty Development Award from my college allowed me to take a leave from teaching and thus finish writing this book nearly a decade after starting it.

At UC San Diego I benefitted from the mentorship of many incredible scholars. My biggest debt there is owed to Kathryn Woolard. Thank you for your steady guidance, encouragement, patience, and keen insights as this project first took shape. Joel Robbins, Nancy Postero, John Haviland, Thomas Csordas, Charles Briggs, Ana Celia Zentella, and Richard Madsen also helped to orient my work in ways both big and small. Thank you all.

I consider myself lucky to have found a congenial professional home in the Department of Religious Studies at UNC Charlotte. My thanks especially to Joanne Maguire, Sean McCloud, Will Sherman, Alex Kaloyinades, Letha Victor, Elise Berman, Gregory Starrett, and Becky Roeder for offering feedback on some very early drafts of parts of this book. Life in Charlotte has also been made immeasurably better by my friends outside of the university, too, so thanks are due to Tom and Carol, Kevin and Heather, Emily, Matt and Michelle, Erik and Lauren, and the rest of NoDa.

Since I first started this project, I have been fortunate enough share words, meals, and drinks with so many wonderful people who have shaped my work and outlook in both subtle and overt ways. I'm sure I'll kick myself for forgetting someone obvious once this reaches final print, but here goes. Thank you to JoAnn D'Alisera, Avery Dickins de Girón, Jon Bialecki, James Bielo, Jurgen Buchenau, Charles Mathewes, Omri Elisha, Kirstin Erickson, Erich Fox Tree, Naomi Haynes, Angie Heo, Jessica Johnson, Hillary Kaell, Marc Loustau, C. James MacKenzie, Oscar Macz, Melanie McComsey, Maya Mayblin, Kristy Nabhan-Warren, Valentina Napolitano, Kristin Norget, Kevin O'Neill, Elizabeth Peacock, Leighton Peterson, Kurtis Schaeffer, Bambi Schieffelin, Ryan Schram, Robin Shoaps, Ted Swedenburg, Brendan Thornton, Jakob Thorsen, Edward Wright-Rios, and Laurel Zwissler. If I have somehow managed to forget mentioning you here, please know this was by accident, and I encourage you to demand restitution from me when we next see each other—we'll share a beverage and a laugh at my expense for the oversight. If your name is on the list, I also encourage you to approach me and demand that we share a beverage and laugh in celebration of everything you've done for me.

I will, sadly, never have a chance to share a beverage and a laugh with the following people again (but maybe I'm wrong about that), they also deserve my thanks: Gerardo Botzoc, Mario Caal, Charles Goodwin, John McGraw, and Fidencio Yat.

Les debo mil gracias a los Hoenes en Cobán por darme una bienvenida tan calurosa a vivir con ellos. Gracias a Lis, Astrid, Marlon, Melissa y Marilis, Edson, Otto, y Giovanni por todos los bonitos momentos que compartimos. Esta labor jamás se hubiera podido hacer sin ustedes y les agradezco de corazón por todo el apoyo que me brindaron.

También hay que mencionar a Janina, Carlos, Alejandro, Luz María, Nestor, y Diego. Gracias pro aguantarme y hacerme ganas en Guate. Belén, Santí, y Kájo, a ustedes no los menciono no más porque no habían nacido para todo esto, pero no se enojen que ya la próxima sí los tomo en cuenta.

Acknowledgments

Merci à toi, Didier, Jean de Dieu, Konstantin, Maxi, Léon, Quiterio, et les autres missionnaires du CICM. Que vos œuvres soient bénis.

I am grateful to Allyson Carter at the University of Arizona Press for seeing promise in this book and for the efforts she made to move it to press swiftly.

My final round of thanks goes to my immediate family. My mother—Alice del Pinal—has my eternal thanks for the unwavering support she has offered me over the years, and especially for proofreading a whole draft of this book. Aleister Growley, Xanthippe, and Goose all deserve mention for their willingness to be petted and generally being good dogs. Although Aleister is no longer with us, he set the tone at the start of my writing. Xanthippe is to be commended for her willingness to chase balls so that I could take breaks from writing. Goose, well, I'm still trying to gauge what his contribution has been exactly, but I'm sure it's something.

My biggest thanks, of course, goes to Nicole Peterson, with whom I have shared the better part of two decades. She has seen me agonize over this project for far too long and has always been ready to offer feedback and encouragement. I love you, and I don't know what I'd do without you by my side. Here's to at least twenty more WrestleMania Sundays together.

GUARDED BY TWO JAGUARS

Introduction
Catholicism as Heteroglossia

It was neither the first nor the only letter of this kind that had been delivered to the parish, but it did happen to come into Padre Agustino's hands on a Saturday morning while several local lay leaders (*catequistas*) and I were sitting and chatting outside the church with the priest. The messenger who bore the letter had come a long way, traveling for perhaps two or three hours by foot and microbus from his rural community to the parish center of San Felipe in Cobán, Alta Verapaz, Guatemala, to hand over the letter to his clergyman. Having delivered the envelope to Padre Agustino, the messenger excused himself, saying that he would go pray in the church and wait for the priest's response before heading back to his community that day.

More so than a letter, the document was a record of the proceedings of a community meeting convened to discuss a pressing issue of significant local importance in the messenger's home village. Neatly handwritten in Spanish block print on a piece of yellow, college-ruled paper like the ones that make up legal notepads, the document constituted an official statement from the *comunidad* (community) of San Ignacio Tziib'ak.[1] This status was attested to by the presence of the community's official stamp and the names and

---

1. Following conventions of anthropological writing and the protections of privacy ensured by human subject research protocols that have guided my research, the names of individuals, communities, and the parish discussed in this book are all pseudonyms. I have also changed minor details about individuals and communities to ensure these entities some measure of privacy. However, the names of the city, country, and diocese in which they are located are accurate.

signatures or thumbprints of twenty-four of its members, which gave it the appearance of something like a legal writ. The text read as follows:[2]

> In the community of San Ignacio Tziib'ak of the municipality of Cobán of the department of Alta Verapaz. It being four in the afternoon on Wednesday October 19 of 2005. We are meeting in the village chapel of the aforementioned community to give record of the following.
>
> FIRST: Mr. Aroldo Xb'een, minister of the Catholic community gave a welcome to Srs. [nine names omitted], and the rest of the members of the Catholic Church to state the following—that those of the Charismatic Renewal always take us to a side of evil and not for the good of our church. Because of this I ask everyone—what can we say or express, because this is a conflict inside of the Church that these *Renovados* [renewed ones, i.e., members of the Catholic Charismatic Renewal] are bringing to us? I do not understand why they treat us badly, and [why] they have changed hearts.[3]
>
> SECOND: Mr. Baltazar Kaab' asked to speak and stated that the Charismatics have a doctrine that they sing the songs of other groups like Protestants. This is no longer one Church, which we do not understand. We are accustomed to the Q'eqchi' Religion because we are not *Castellanos* [i.e., Spanish speakers]. Because of this I say to everyone present in this meeting, let us raise our hand if we want to be told the truth by the priests—which is better: the Q'eqchi' or the Charismatic? We are not children, and we are not toys in the street. We are Christians, we are not animals.
>
> THIRD: Mr. Claudio Rox stated that when they [i.e., Charismatics] left the Q'eqchi' religion, they also left the village chapel open and all of the equipment of the congregation unattended. Some [of it] was taken and some was left, this was on the date of October 11, 2005. We Q'eqchi' Catholics do not understand their customs. In the days of September we met and we came in peace to celebrate God, and after this date they went again with their

---

2. The translation is my own. I have edited for clarity and to remove personally identifying information and have also included a few editorial comments in brackets to clarify its content.

3. The heart or *ch'ool* is the seat of both affect and cognition for Q'eqchi's, so this phrasing could read as an indictment of both the different affective religious lives of Charismatics as well as their adherence to a different set of doctrines.

mission. We are not fighting with them, but they always like the division within the church, and they always use lies to divide us and to be in conflict with the Church.

FOURTH: All of the members of the Q'eqchi' Catholic Church manifest this question to the *Padre*—what group is going to go forward: the Q'eqchi' or the Charismatic? Have him tell us the truth, and not to evade it, because we are Christians, and we want to know so that we can have calm hearts[4] and know who is going to heaven. With God all powerful we want to ask the Padre that he tell us the truth, because we will never leave our Q'eqchi' Catholic Church. We are used to praising God and preaching in Q'eqchi'. We do not want conflict. We want to be at peace and in harmony, not in a fight. We state, Padre, that the Charismatics do not just have problems in the chapel, they always have problems in the community. They no longer have respect for other people. Because of that we are afraid of them. We no longer understand the things they do in their groups or their customs. Moreover, they are identical to the Protestants. Because of that, we do not have any doubt in our heart.

FIFTH: Without anything further to do, the present meeting is concluded in the same place and date of its start, one hour later. All of those who participated leave the thumbprint of their right hand to sign this record.

This particular letter was part of a set of four such documents (two written in Spanish and two in Q'eqchi'—a Mayan language of the Quichean branch with about 700,000 speakers in Guatemala and Belize) that the parish received from the community of San Ignacio Tziib'ak over the course of four months in 2005. This document laid out in rather dramatic fashion the concerns of one party in a low-level, but often quite tense, conflict that preoccupied San Felipe's Catholics in the first decade of the twenty-first century.

Shortly after the dawn of the new millennium, a small but steadily growing number of members of this all Q'eqchi'-Maya Roman Catholic parish began self-identifying as members of the Catholic Charismatic Renewal. Members of *La Renovación*, as it was commonly referred to, practiced a

---

4. This is a transliteration of a Q'eqchi' phrase *"saa sa' ch'ool,"* which means to be tranquil in one's heart is to be well and at peace. So, the phrase here could be read as "to be at peace."

form of Christianity that could be described as pentecostalized, "pneumatic," or spirit-filled. They had set up parallel structures of religious authority to support these practices in their erstwhile Catholic communities, too. While San Felipe's parishioners had plenty of experience dealing with neighbors and family members who converted to non-Catholic Pentecostalism and left the parish to join other churches, the wrinkle here was that the members of these new congregations, despite their quite evident differences in comportment, also claimed that they were still Catholics and insisted on being recognized as such by the ecclesiastical hierarchy. That recognition entailed certain material benefits, not the least of which was a right to gather in the village's Catholic chapel. This was unprecedented. When someone became an *evangélico*—that is, a non-Catholic Christian, a Protestant—it was accepted that they would change their behavior, but they also stopped going to services at their local village chapel in favor of attending services at one of the many denominationally affiliated (Church of the Nazarene or Seventh Day Adventist, for example) or independent churches that dotted the streets of Cobán, and which were present in many of even the smallest rural villages. Becoming Pentecostal under normal circumstance meant completely breaking from one's former religious identity and entering into a new set of social relationships. These new *católicos renovados* or *carismáticos*, who so worried the lay leadership in San Ignacio, however, wanted to remain Catholic even as they stopped behaving in the ways that people generally expected Catholics to behave, and they wanted to do so with the consent of the parish hierarchy. Seemingly neither fish nor fowl (or rather, perhaps, fish who struck them as foul), the socioreligious position of these new carismáticos was not only paradoxical but also potentially dangerous.

Examining the text of the San Ignacio document offers a concise introduction to what worried the established Catholic lay leaders about these new Catholic Charismatics. It is striking how overtly the first person to speak (the village's head catequista and very likely the person who convened the meeting in the first place) accused the carismáticos of doing evil things in the community. To an outsider, little of what the carismáticos were accused of doing might be considered actually "evil." Yet, San Ignacio's lay leaders made it clear that the carismáticos' practices and beliefs were matters of grave concern, that they indexed the "changed hearts" of people who no longer treated their neighbors well and could thus no longer be justly considered members of the Catholic community in the village. Mr. Kaab' made clear that what he thought marked the carismáticos' divergence from the Catholic Church and gave evidence of their "changed doctrine" above all else was their use of Spanish-language hymns, which were those of Protestants. This in and of itself was enough to make them practitioners of something other than the "Q'eqchi' religion." If these troublesome others sang in Spanish, it must have been because they were practitioners of the *Castellano* religion.[5]

The collective authors of the document took the bold step of demanding definitive answers from their parish priest about this problem in their village. Mr. Kaab' wanted the priest to unequivocally state which of the two groups he endorsed as the true Catholics and thus settle the question of who could legitimately worship in the chapel. He framed the presence of the two forms of religion as incompatible with peace in the community. One form must be the correct one, and the other, seemingly by its very presence, had negative consequences. The authors of the letter were losing patience with Padre Agustino for not rendering a definitive judgement and, indeed, the purpose of the letter, more so than documenting the community's expressed grievances, was to prompt the priest to settle the dispute once and for all.

Although we do not have a record of how the Charismatics in San Ignacio framed the issue, the community leaders who authored the letter understood the Charismatics' divergent practices as calling into question the legitimacy of their own form of Q'eqchi' Catholicism, which they took to be the orthodox position. The letter's authors wanted the parish priest to clarify how their own institutional authority articulated with his and, presumably, with that of the larger institutional Catholic hierarchy, whom they felt they represented in the village. Receiving a positive answer, they hoped, would negate the Charismatics' growing influence and reaffirm their own position as the community's religious leaders. They did not understand why the competent clerical authority had failed to act to quash this insurgent movement, and perhaps feared that his silence was a tacit endorsement of the carismáticos'

---

5. It's not clear if he thought that all Castellanos were evangélicos, but he certainly seemed to think that Q'eqchi's speaking and singing in Spanish in church were not authentically Q'eqchi'. The Q'eqchi' word *kaxlan* as a noun means "chicken," but as an adjective is a generalized marker of foreignness. It may derive from the *Castellano/a* (see Bricker 1981, 5, although this etymology is cited unfavorably by Wilson 1995, 330n3). Things that are marked as "kaxlan," and thus potentially *Castellano*, are paradigmatically foreign and contrast with unmarked things that are inherently Q'eqchi'. For example, *wa* is a tortilla, whereas *kaxlan wa* is bread, or "foreigner's tortilla."

heterodox practices. If he was supporting the Charismatics, what did that mean for the status of the erstwhile mainline Catholics in San Ignacio? If Charismatics were in the right for singing in Spanish, what consequences did that have for the Q'eqchi' Catholicism that the letter's authors claimed as their own religion? Were Catholics like them being pushed out of the parish in favor of these upstart renovados? If so, was this an indictment of the sacred ancestral practices that their grandfathers and grandmothers had taught them? Or was the Catholic Church itself losing its way?

That afternoon in 2005 Padre Agustino was not particularly interested in dealing with the letter of complaint from one of the 122 communities under his pastoral care, no matter how official of a statement the presence of the village seal and signatures of its elder men made the document. He skimmed the text, shook his head dismissively, and handed it to me, saying that I should keep it since I was interested in these things.[6] The messenger from San Ignacio ended up waiting a couple of hours at the church[7] before Padre Agustino met with him again and told him to go back to the community with the message that he would address the problem when he next visited their *aldea* next month. No doubt this was not what the messenger had wanted to hear, and it is easy to imagine the disappointment that greeted this response back in San Ignacio.[8]

By the time this letter reached Padre Agustino, the parish had been caught up for several years in the ongoing conflict between Charismatic Catholics and their antagonists, whom I call "Mainstream Catholics" here in recognition of their numerical majority in the parish. As the majority group in the parish, Mainstream Catholics were typically an unmarked category there, but the carismáticos also sometimes called them *los catequistas* (the

---

6. I did not keep the original, although I did photocopy it with his consent before returning the document to the parish's secretary.

7. Visitors from distant communities on an errand to the church would often spend several hours waiting. Some would go into town to run other errands or to visit the central plaza; others would simply sit on one of the low walls surrounding the church courtyard and chat with anyone else who might be there. The parish's cook—Qana' Alberta—could usually offer them at least a cup of sweetened coffee and a *pan dulce* to make the wait more tolerable.

8. I didn't go with Fr. Agustino on that trip, so I don't know exactly how the meeting went. However, based on other experiences, I am fairly sure that people gathered to make formal statements about their grievances. The priest then no doubt offered an admonishment of the bickering and a plea for reconciliation, and the frustrations that all parties felt continued after he departed.

catechists), metonymically joining the group's formal lay leadership and its general membership.

The priest was tired of the fighting between Mainstream and Charismatic Catholics since, by his own estimation, he had been doing everything he could to put an end to it and foster rapprochement between the factions. Nonetheless, the conflicts had persisted because, as he once put it, "They have faith, but they don't understand it well, and so they get into fights for any reason." In his estimation parishioners were easily distracted by things that should not matter—like the language Catholics sang in—and he had come to see these local fights as more of a nuisance than anything else. Both sides were at fault, and both needed to change their attitudes.

> The Charismatics need to come to Mass, receive communion, and understand that they are católicos, [and] not evangélicos. They don't concern themselves with some [religious] things that they should as católicos, that's why sometimes there is danger that they can become Protestants.... [On the other hand], the catequistas need to understand that these aren't "separated brothers" [i.e., Protestants], but they have a mentality that things are this way and [have to be] just this way; [so] they get angry and start to fight. They all need to reflect on why we are Catholics and that we are part of one single church and realize that God doesn't want these fights [among us].

As far as he was concerned, so long as the carismáticos continued to proclaim themselves to be Catholics, showed up to Mass, and otherwise kept the sacraments, he wasn't too worried about what language they sang or prayed in, and neither should the Mainstream Catholics be.

Then again, Padre Agustino's understanding of what was important for Catholics to do, including how they should sing and pray, had been molded by much different life experiences than those of his parishioners. Padre Agustino was not Q'eqchi', nor was he a Castellano. He had been born and grew up in a multilingual urban center in Zaire. He was a member of a missionary order founded by Belgians who dreamed of bringing Christianity to Mongolia. Agustino had attended seminary in Cameroon before accepting his first post in the clergy in the outskirts of Mexico City the year his homeland was renamed the Democratic Republic of Congo. He was now in the unenviable position of serving as parish priest (and for a time the sole clergyman) to an underfunded, largely rural parish comprising 122 small communities spread out over mountainous terrain, each of which he was expected to visit somewhat regularly to perform the sacraments. It was challenging work, to say the least. The residents of those communities respected his authority as the parish priest and valued his ability to perform those special rites, but they also tended to hold very different views of what it meant to be Catholic than he did. Padre Agustino saw the local conflict in San Felipe as an unnecessary distraction from larger and more fundamental questions and concerns about the present and future of Catholicism. He thought that the catequistas needed to foster peace with the carismáticos so that the Catholic Church did not lose more people to the evangélicos' churches. Evangélico churches had been growing for decades in Guatemala, and that growth had seemingly only sped up since the signing of the peace accords that formally ended the Guatemalan Civil War in 1996. Padre Agustino felt that his catechists should focus more on ensuring that they were transmitting the Catholic Church's doctrine to their communities as faithfully as possible, not whether their neighbors were clapping along to hymns or singing in *kaxlan aatin* (Spanish). Indeed, he understood the matter as a false obstacle to community unity since many (though not all) of his parishioners were bilingual in Spanish and Q'eqchi' anyway. To him, the language one prayed in made very little difference as to whether a person's soul could be said to be in good standing with God. Padre Agustino was not particularly fond of Charismatic Catholicism himself, and he would occasionally join in with catequistas in making fun of their exuberant style of worship, but he also recognized that the institutional Church, including the region's bishop and his order's superiors, condoned the presence of La Renovación. Ultimately, the decision of whether to let carismáticos worship in the village's chapels under his supervision was not his to make (though certainly not all priests everywhere have taken this stance; see Althoff 2014, 156; Thorsen 2015, 32).

Padre Agustino's cosmopolitanism may have attuned him to the catholic dimensions of his faith, but it also led him to profoundly misrecognize why the terms of this conflict mattered so much in his parish. As someone conversant in Lingala, French, Spanish, and Q'eqchi', who also could get by in English, and had studied Greek and Latin in seminary, he embodied the polyglot character of the modern Catholic Church. For San Felipe's Q'eqchi'-Maya parishioners, however, the debate over language cut to the very core of what it meant to be Maya and Catholic. From their perspective, a choice of language indexed contrasting visions of what made one a Catholic. Whether one prayed in Q'eqchi' (and in doing so positioned oneself as a member of a specific ethnic community of faith) or whether one sang in Spanish (and in doing so positioned oneself as a member of a transnational community of *cristianos*), the language one used in church reflected certain fundamental claims about religious membership with significant social and cultural consequences. It was no wonder, then, that the language people sang in caused strains among neighbors, prompting some to write angry letters and in at least one case that I heard about leading to a fistfight between the heads of a village's two congregations (though this violence had also been precipitated by the fact that the son of the one and the daughter of the other had recently eloped).

Yet, for as high as the stakes were in 2005, a decade later these debates over language were largely a thing of the past. By 2016 San Felipe was a noticeably different parish from what it had been in the mid-2000s. Mainstream and Charismatic Catholics had more or less set aside the debates over language, but they were still—sometimes together and sometimes each in their own ways—grappling with new sets of questions about what it meant to be a Q'eqchi'-Maya Catholic (a point I will return to in the conclusion). I give away the ending of this drama now to make clear what this book is fundamentally about—namely, how Catholicism as a religion is formed and reformed through the words and actions of laypeople. In order to make this argument I adopt a perspective that frames religion as fundamentally dialogical, which is to say that it is constituted not by adherence to this or that principle, or by identification with this or that institution, or necessarily by participation in this or that set of practices, but rather by the constant and consistent interplay of voices debating, arguing, occasionally coming to blows over what those principles, identities, and practices mean to them in their own social world. Three narrower themes will help support this larger perspective.

First, this book is a study of religious differentiation, conflict, and change. The main subject of this book is how and why San Felipe's Mainstream and Charismatic Catholic parishioners who had been co-congregants came to view each other as religiously distinct and problematic "others." My work follows a trend in the anthropology of Christianity of examining how intergroup differences are produced through dialogue, contestation, and critique (see, for example, Garriott and O'Neill 2008; Bielo 2011; Handman 2015.) This line of research is concerned with the various ways that people's religious affiliations—through churches, denominations, or other similar groupings—are articulated not in isolation but through interaction with each other.

While studies of interreligious conflict and dialogue have often examined cases where the religions in question are different (as would be the case between Muslims and Jews or Sikhs and Hindus), it is also useful to look at how it is that different groupings of the "same" religion emerge. Processes of religious schism and change have been a constant theme in the history of Christianity. From the first century CE through the present day, differing interpretations over matters both great and small have caused internal fissures in Christian communities of practice leading to conflict, differentiation, and separation. To see this, one need only note that Peter and Paul both claimed Jesus's authority and arrived at differing guidelines for the nascent religion's membership. A brief glance at the history of Christianity offers a plethora of examples—from the suppression of Arianism in the fourth century, to the mutual excommunication of the patriarchs of the Eastern and Western churches in the eleventh century, to the European wars of religion that followed in the wake of the Protestant Reformation and Catholic Counter-Reformation in the sixteenth century, to the splits among denominations over the questions of slavery in the United States of America in the nineteenth century, to the emerging rift in the Anglican Church over the question of same-sex marriage in the twenty-first century, and so on. Much of Christianity's history has been made when people who at one time saw each other as co-religionists came into conflict over just exactly what it means to be a Christian by finding in this or that detail of their beliefs and practices a significant enough difference to produce dissension and division.

What makes the case of San Felipe unusual is that it illustrates these processes within a relatively homogeneous population and, therefore, highlights not just how religious differences are conceived and enacted but also how they are actively produced. That differentiation, as the story of San Ignacio's letter illustrates, was articulated not necessarily directly in terms that we might expect from religious conflict (i.e., over matters that could easily be labeled "theological," or otherwise related to core issues of religion), but rather through the idioms of language and communication. Both Charismatic and Mainstream Catholics came to attach specific meanings to a range of linguistic and embodied communicative behaviors (i.e., gestures and body postures), making these the key signs of difference in the representational economy of the parish (Keane 2007, 18). Both groups understood verbal language to be deeply consequential for what it meant to be a good Catholic, and especially for what it meant to be a good Q'eqchi'-Maya Catholic. Catequistas in San Felipe often said that carismáticos were "always yelling in Spanish" (although, in truth, the targets of this critique spoke more Q'eqchi' than Spanish when they gathered for worship and occasionally did so in sotto voce as well). Conversely, Charismatic Catholics often noted that Mainstream Catholics prayed with their shoulders hunched and seemed cold and joyless in church (although, in truth, the targets of this critique reported they felt a great sense of happiness and personal fulfillment from their participation in church). When parishioners said things like this, they were not just criticizing the linguistic competencies, preferences, or dispositions of that group of people; they were also making an evaluative claim about those people's religious and moral subjectivities. In effect, talk about talk (and gesture) was the medium through which both Charismatic and Mainstream Catholics articulated their contrasting visions of religious and moral personhood. In this regard they were engaged in what linguistic anthropologists describe as a language ideological debate—a sociocultural conflict that at least in part hinges on differing understandings about the nature and meaning of language (Blommaert, 1999) and/or gesture (Hoenes del Pinal 2011). But why should language and gesture have been so important for creating these differences? I will argue that in San Felipe, language was seen as both a resource for making claims about one's religious and social identities as well as ultimately a key component for establishing the grounds for shared religious experience. Language differences were not just useful symbols for talking about religious difference, they were necessary components for producing two different modes of being Catholic. Thus, my second aim in this book is to show how close attention to communicative practices and discourses about these practices advances the study of religion more generally.

Finally, while the conditions and stakes of this debate were fundamentally local, concerning in truth just a few thousand Q'eqchi'-Maya Catholics and a handful of clergy who worked with them, the debate itself offers us a way to address larger questions about social and religious change. What happened in San Felipe illustrates processes of change that at once concern the institutional body or bodies of the Catholic Church and the place of Mayas in the modern nation state. While much of the literature on religion and social change in Latin America has quite rightly emphasized the unprecedented growth of evangélico Christianity (i.e., the mostly Pentecostal-leaning Evangelical Protestant churches), less attention has been paid to the way that Catholicism has changed in response to that growth as well as due to shifts in its own internal makeup. By examining how the debate in San Felipe was motivated by local conditions and larger national and transnational movements within Catholicism, we can gain a better understanding of how change occurs within a religion.

Put another way, the three major themes that this book will address are (1) the dialogic construction of religious identity and practice, (2) the importance of language and embodied forms of communication in constituting religious identity and experience, and (3) how these dialogic processes generate change within a religion.

The Anthropology of (Catholic) Christianity (in Guatemala)

While anthropologists have for a long time produced works about communities of people who practice some form of Christianity and have arguably also relied on (often implicit) understandings of Christianity to build their models of religion (Asad 1993), it was not until the first years of the twenty-first century that a concerted effort was made to examine what difference Christianity makes for "how people at different times and in different places understand themselves in the world" (Cannell 2006, 1). Though "an anthropology of Christianity for itself" (Robbins 2003, 191) was a relatively late development within the anthropology of religion,[9] this area of inquiry rapidly became a major and highly productive enterprise that has yielded significant insights into both what Christianity looks like in its multiple guises around the world as well as important theoretical insights into religion's place in the modern world more generally.[10] There are by now also many review essays of

---

9. The reasons for this lack of attention are complex, having to do in part with the social evolutionist views of many of anthropology and sociology's founding figures and the resulting tendency to see religion as epiphenomena to other social and cultural dynamics (Cannell 2006, 3). The uncomfortable relations that anthropologists have often had with missionaries in the field seems to have played a part as well, although there is clear evidence that the two have often been more alike than not (see, for example, Salamone 1977; Cooper 2018). In any case, the tendency was to keep Christianity as such at distance from the discipline's core work to the point that Fanella Cannell has suggested that "Christianity has functioned in some ways as 'the repressed' of anthropology over the period of the formation of the discipline" (Cannell 2006, 4).

10. Some anthropologists now argue that if at one point the discipline had all but ignored Christianity, the pendulum has now swung too far in the other direction so that not only are

this literature (see, for example, Hann 2007; Bialecki, Haynes, and Robbins 2008; Bialecki and Hoenes del Pinal 2011; Jenkins 2012; Robbins 2014), as well as an ongoing bibliographic blog[11] that do a much better job of reviewing this ever-expanding literature than I can here, but I do want to situate my work within that larger literature in a few ways.

First, much of the anthropology of Christianity has been interested in the seemingly explosive growth of Pentecostal/Charismatic Christianity in the Global South. Although Africa and Oceania have been sites for some of the most important work done on this topic, in many ways Latin America presents the most dramatic site for tracking this global process. A full decade before the anthropology of Christianity coalesced as a subfield, David Stoll provocatively asked in the title of his 1990 book, *Is Latin America Turning Protestant?* Stoll, whose ethnographic work focuses on Guatemala, noted that a major shift was occurring in the region as growing numbers of people were leaving the Catholic Church, which had held a virtual monopoly on religion since the colonial period, and joining a proliferation of newly established Protestant churches. These former católicos were now identifying themselves as evangélicos or simply *cristianos* in Hispanic countries, and as *crentes* (believers) in Lusophone ones. Although mainline Protestant denominations saw some modest growth as part of this Protestant turn, it was really Pentecostal and neo-Pentecostal churches, some with denominational affiliations but many acting independently under the guidance of charismatic leaders, that saw the most growth. People were converting to these new churches in the wake of political revolutions and periods of violent state repression that followed closely in their tracks, and seemingly at the expense of reformist trends in Catholicism that liberal observers saw as augurs of a turn toward justice in the region (Burdick 1993). This shift in the region's religious demographics continued into the twenty-first century and, as the number of evangélicos has grown, they have increasingly taken prominent positions in the public sphere and helped drive social changes both large and small.

---

anthropologists of religion overwhelmingly focused on Christianity at the expense of examining other religions, but anthropologists of Christianity increasingly are also only talking to each other and not taking sufficient stock of how their work informs the larger "comparativist anthropology of religion" (Csordas 2017, 302).

11. AnthroCyBib: The Anthropology of Christianity Bibliography Blog. https://www.blogs.hss.ed.ac.uk/anthrocybib/.

Anthropologists of religion often point to evangélico Christianity's critical role in helping people manage their place in the region's changing social and political landscape as its primary attractor. Pentecostal Christianity offers people an alternative moral imaginary that allows for, among other things, reconfigurations of gender roles (Brusco 1995; Thornton 2016) and racial identities (Burdick 1998; Selka 2007). Additionally, Pentecostal churches offer symbolic and material resources such as new corporate identities (Gómez and Vásquez 2001), spiritual and physical healing (Wightman 2007), and a kind of sanctuary from the pressure of street life (Wolseth 2011) that make these religious institutions appealing to people living on the margins of social and economic stability.

Guatemala, where Protestant Christianity went from about 3 percent of the population at midcentury (Stoll 1990, 337) to at least 42 percent as of this writing (U.S. Department of State 2018) and is thus Latin America's most Protestant country, has provided rich ground for exploring Pentecostal Christianity's role in the changing social, economic, and political climate of the region. Kevin Lewis O'Neill, for example, has shown how the ethical and moral imaginaries of this form of Christianity help support new models of citizenship and discourses about security that accompanied the neoliberal structural changes the country experienced at the start of the twenty-first century (O'Neill 2010, 2015). Much attention, too, has been paid to how Maya people's adoption of Protestant forms of Christianity facilitated transformations in household economics (Annis 1987), helped to mitigate the effects of the political violence they experienced during the country's Civil War (Garrard-Burnett 1998), and provided new venues for ethnopolitical mobilization (Samson 2007).

The scholarship on Guatemala is exemplary of another trend in the anthropology of Christianity—namely, that the apparent novelty of Protestantism in the region has drawn most of scholars' attention, leaving the continuing social and cultural importance of Catholicism underexamined.[12] While important anthropological works examining changing Maya ethnic identities in

---

12. The same has been said about anthropological studies of Orthodox Christians elsewhere in the world (Hann 2007), though that is beginning to change as well (see, for example, Hann and Goltz 2010; Boylston 2018; Heo 2018). Orthodox Christianity's presence in Latin America has historically been negligible, but that has changed in the last ten years as several thousand Guatemalan Mayas (including some in diaspora) have begun affiliating with a new Orthodox Christian church led by an excommunicated Catholic priest. Interestingly, both the church's

the wake of the Civil War all emphasized the role that the Catholic Church's social and evangelizing programs played in laying the groundwork for the country's new social and cultural dynamics around race and ethnicity (see, for example, Warren 1978; Falla 2001; Wilson 1995), their tendency was to treat Catholicism more as background context than as an object of analysis in its own right.[13]

If there is an aporia there, however, we might well ask what, besides adding to "the consultable record of what man has said" (Geertz 1973, 30), do scholars gain from examining Catholic Christianity specifically? As Maya Mayblin, Kristin Norget, and Valentina Napolitano put it in the introduction to *The Anthropology of Catholicism*, "Catholicism's strength seems to be based as much on its rhetorical toleration of locality and difference as on its universalizing, and highly centralized, 'infallible' core" (2017, 7). The peculiar combination of a strong transnational institutional core which nonetheless allows for a great deal of diversity in the "lived" expressions of the religion itself may well be what makes Roman Catholicism unique among the world's religions, or at the very least may be one of its most characteristic features. The Catholic Church may seek to promote the impression of being a singular, centralized, and, hence, relatively homogenous institution, but the religious lives of Catholics around the world readily give evidence to its internal heterogeneity. This variability in the way that Catholics practice and experience their religion is, of course, in part the result of how local cultures interface with this purportedly universal faith, but equally important are the various ways in which Catholicism itself seems to foster internal heterogeneity. San Felipe's Mainstream Catholics and Charismatic Catholics, after all, represent two distinct institutionally sanctioned

---

leader and most of these new Orthodox Christians seem to have found their way to this new religious identity via Charismatic Catholicism (Hager 2019).

13. Ethnographic studies of Catholicism elsewhere in Latin America are likewise scarcer than one might expect given the religion's historical import in the region's colonization. Important monographs that are exceptions to this include Andrew Orta's examination of Ayamara Catholicism in Bolivia (Orta 2004), Maya Mayblin's study of Catholicism and gender in Brazil (Mayblin 2010), Ruth Chojnacki's study of indigenous catechists in Chiapas (Chojnacki 2010). Valentina Napolitano's book on the "Atlantic return" of female religious moving from America's southern cone to Italy likewise stands out as an examination of the transregional implications of Catholicism in Latin America (Napolitano 2015). Anthropologically inflected historical studies have done a much better job of examining the vicissitudes of the religion in the region (e.g., Hughes 2010; Wright-Rios 2009; Hanks 2010).

forms of Catholic practice. The Catholic Church thus poses something of a conundrum insofar as it is a global ("universal" in its own discourse) institution with a centralized governing hierarchy, but it is also manifestly quite internally variable.

Returning to the case of Guatemala, this point seems to be borne out by several recent works that highlight intra-denominational conflicts and changes like those I describe for Cobán. As Andrea Althoff has argued, the dynamics around conversions within Catholicism are as complex as those around conversions between Catholicism and Pentecostalism, and thus these internal conversions need to be factored into our accounts of the country's contemporary religious landscape (Althoff 2014, 34). Jakob Thorsen's theologically informed ethnography of Ladino (i.e., Guatemalans of mestizo or mixed descent) Charismatic Catholics in a Guatemala City suburb, argues that these kinds of internal conversions are leading to an "incipient pentecostalization," which somewhat paradoxically seems to be increasing people's sense of denominational commitment to the Roman Catholic Church (Thorsen 2015). As C. James MacKenzie has shown in his nuanced examination of religion in San Andrés Xecul, however, the move toward a pentecostalized or "enthusiastic" form of Catholicism is not the inevitable outcome of contemporary social conditions, nor is it the only kind of religious change happening; rather, they are part of a larger field in which the very question of what it means to be Catholic is being contested at the local level (MacKenzie 2016).

The larger question of how to theorize the internal heterogeneity of Catholicism in relation to its strong institutional core was taken up by the German political philosopher Carl Schmitt who in 1923 (ten years before he joined the Nazi party) proposed the idea that Catholicism constitutes a *complexio oppositorum* (complex of opposites), enabling it to encompass disparate, even seemingly incommensurable elements under a single institutional logic (Schmitt [1923] 1996, 7). For Schmitt, the incorporation of opposites and the tensions these seemingly produce even lend the institution a particular kind of vitality. Anthropologists of Catholicism have found Schmitt's idea to be a productive one for thinking through the ethnological variability of Catholics' practices in the contemporary world (e.g., Muehlebach 2009; Napolitano 2015; Bandak 2017; Norget 2017; Mosse 2017; Abreu 2021), and it certainly helps explain why Padre Agustino and his superiors in the Catholic hierarchy in Alta Verapaz seemed unbothered by the co-presence of two forms of Catholic practice.

Schmitt's theory, however, does not adequately account for all the complexity of the situation I encountered in Cobán. First, the theory does not engage with questions about how the oppositions within the larger complex are experienced from within it. That is, the complexio oppositorum does not help us address why San Ignacio's lay leaders were so perturbed by the sounds they heard coming from their chapels. To note that the institution can hold opposites in productive tension does not explain what it was about the language of songs that made San Ignacio Tz'iib'ak's catequistas write a letter demanding that the priest condemn their neighbors. To fully grasp what was going on in San Felipe, or for that matter in any ethnographic context, we need to also interrogate how differences are produced and experienced as problematic by local communities.

Second, not all of the plurality we see within Catholicism need be understood necessarily as oppositional. There are certainly other kinds of relationality—parallel, orthogonal, asymptotic, nested, and so on—that might better describe what is at stake when a group of Mesoamerican indigenous people living in a diocese that was founded as part of the Spanish colonial project in the 1540s draft a letter to a priest from central Africa who belongs to a missionary order founded in the 1860s by Belgians who had hoped to evangelize Inner Mongolia for advice on how to handle an emergent new form of spirit-filled religiosity that originated in both Pittsburgh, USA, and Bogotá, Colombia, in the 1960s. The very fact that that letter was written by those actors at that time implies a much larger history marked by contestation, but also by various forms of crosscutting interactions. The letter from San Ignacio Tz'iib'ak sought to document a drama that was profoundly local to that village but that also fractally indexed similar debates and conflicts occurring throughout their parish, diocese, and country. To do justice to the complexities of the case means bearing in mind the wider translocal and transtemporal dimensions of Roman Catholicism impinged on it in a way that takes seriously various articulations of the religion.

Less so than modeling the overarching institutional logic of Catholicism, then, I am interested in examining how Q'eqchi'-Maya parishioners debated among themselves what it meant to be Catholic, and how they did so in dialogue not just with each other but also with the African clergy, non-Maya Guatemalan Catholics, foreign observers, and a whole range of others. When turning our gaze toward debates such as this one, we must inevitably grapple with how Catholic "natives" navigate the monumental, magisterial institution of the Catholic Church because the reality of that institution is an important part of their lived religion. Yet it is no easy task to balance the intimate frame of the ethnographic encounter and the imperial extent of the Roman Catholic Church as a global institution.[14] If one of the key things that separates Catholicism from other forms of Christianity is precisely its catholicity—its claims to universality, which of necessity must encompass a great deal of variability—then how do we adequately model that dialectic? How do we, in other words, simultaneously bear in mind the catholic while closely observing the particularities of specific communities of Catholics?

Because language was such a crucial part of the conflict in San Felipe and because I take Catholicism to be inherently heterogeneous, I would like to propose that a dialogic approach inspired by Mikhail Bakhtin's concept of "heteroglossia" offers us a way to mediate between these frames.

Catholicism as Heteroglossia

Mikail Mikhailovich Bakhtin (1895–1975) was a linguist, philosopher, and literary critic who became the central figure of a group of Russian intellectuals (which also included Pavel Medvedev and V. N. Vološinov) interested in language and literature.[15] Together they developed a theory of language that emphasized the social and interactional nature of discourse. While this is not the place to review the entirety of the "Bakhtin circle's" oeuvre, I do

---

14. I borrow the language of the intimate and the imperial from Valentina Napolitano (2017b).

15. State repression under Joseph Stalin ended the meetings of Bakhtin's circle in the late 1920s. Some members were arrested, others exiled from major centers of Soviet intellectual life, and still others tragically consigned to an early grave. It was while he was in internal exile that Bakhtin produced his signature works of theory, although these did not become influential or well-known until they were reprinted in the 1960s. At that point scholars outside of the USSR— notably Tzevtan Todorov, Julia Kristeva, and Roman Jakobson—began to take notice of his ideas and brought them to the attention of scholars in the West. The full impact of Bakhtin's work would not come until after his death, but since then his ideas have been influential in literary and film criticism, cultural studies, philosophy, history, and the social sciences (for examples of this, see Mandelker 1995; Brandist and Tihanov 2000). Medvedev and Bakhtin's *The Formal Method in Literary Scholarship* ([1928] 1978) and Vološinov's *Marxism and the Philosophy of Language* ([1929] 1986) are often discussed alongside Bakhtin's writings due to the close similarity of their approaches. Some scholars have attributed those works' authorship to Bakhtin himself (see Clark and Holquist 1984), but it seems likely that any similarities are due to the close working relationships these authors cultivated (Brandist 2002).

want to briefly discuss three key ideas that emerged from their work and that shape my approach to the anthropology of Catholicism—*heteroglossia, voicing,* and *dialogism.*

Bakhtin begins his famous essay "Discourse in the Novel," by noting that "verbal discourse [i.e., language as it is spoken] is a social phenomenon—social throughout its entire range" (1981, 259). Bakhtin reasons that because societies are always stratified and heterogenous, then any adequate description of language must begin from the premise that its concrete uses reflect social stratification and heterogeneity. National languages such as Spanish, English, or Q'eqchi' are not monolithic or unitary but are rather internally stratified "into social dialects, characteristic group behavior, professional jargons, generic languages, languages of generations and age groups, tendentious languages, languages of authorities, of various circles and of passing fashions, [and] languages that serve the specific sociopolitical purposes of the day" (262–63). Bakhtin argues that this fact of language is evident in novels, which he describes as a literary form that is fundamentally characterized by the way that various characters' (including the narrator's) ways of speaking are linked, interrelated, and otherwise combined to simulate social realities. He coins the term "heteroglossia" (*raznorečie* in the original Russian) to describe how a diversity of socially marked ways of speaking (what he calls "voices") are artistically combined into the higher discursive unity of the novel. In other words, the speech of tsars and the speech of peasants (or of the petit bourgeoisie and proletariat, or of Q'eqchi'-Mayas and Ladinos, etc.) do not exist in isolation of each other but rather derive their meaning precisely from their interaction with and among each other within a larger social system.

Bakhtin notes that "the living utterance, having taken meaning and shape at a particular historical moment in a socially specific environment, cannot fail to brush up against thousands of living dialogic threads . . . ; it cannot fail to become an active participant in social dialogue" (1981, 276). Every utterance is thus part of an ongoing and open-ended system of interactions among voices that reflect distinct social positionings. The larger system of heteroglossia is meaningful precisely because of, not despite, the way that the multiple voices present within it both represent distinct points of view and struggle to make themselves heard over others. Language as a social reality is not just polyphonic (i.e., made up of distinct voices), it is also dialogic in the sense that its component voices speak to, alongside, and against each other.

According to Bakhtin there are two opposing tendencies or forces constantly at work in heteroglossia that help produce meaning—a *centripetal* force that tends toward centralization, standardization, and the creation of a unitary language; and a *centrifugal* force that tends toward decentralization, increased variation, and the creation of novel forms of language. The interplay of centrifugal and centripetal forces is constantly bringing social positions together and simultaneously also tearing them apart, and it is precisely the tension between language varieties that gives the larger system a semblance of order and coherence. While the representative institutions of the centripetal force (e.g., nations, schools, and churches) may seek to consolidate language into a singular authorized form—a monologue—their efforts are always met by resistant centrifugal forces evinced in, for example, verbal art, play, and improvisation that trend toward disintegration and decentralization.

These opposing tendencies are not just abstract features of the larger system, Bakhtin argues, they inhere in every instance of speech so that "[every] concrete utterance of a speaking subject serves as a point where centrifugal as well as centripetal forces are brought to bear" (1981, 272). To explain why that should be, we need to understand that language is rarely if ever monologic; it always represents multiple viewpoints simultaneously. In this system, "there are no 'neutral' words and forms.... All words have the 'taste' of a profession, a genre, a tendency, a party, a particular work, a particular person, a generation, an age group, the day and hour" (293). That is to say that all concrete uses of language always already index some social reality external to the speaker. "[Language] becomes one's own only when the speaker populates it with his own intention, his own accent, when he appropriates the word, adapting it to his own semantic and expressive intention" (293). As a word enters any given context, it is already "permeated with the interpretations of others" (Bakhtin 1984, 202). Rather than being a wholly creative act of invention, then, speech is rather a "voicing" whereby social actors appropriate each other's words and refract them to their own ends, and in doing so, necessarily invoke their previous and parallel uses. Of course, because speakers are beings embedded in stratified society, their languages are not equal, and so the degree of effort required to appropriate certain forms and the efficacy of those appropriations can vary significantly.

Nonetheless, when we voice someone else's words, we also refract their meaning. With our use of another's words, they accrue our meanings and intentions, and in doing so they can become "double-voiced." This means that words come to carry both our own intent as well as those of the parties from whom we have borrowed them. Thus, multiple voices or points of view are constantly in dialogue through the creative (and not so creative) appropriations of each other's idioms and meanings. Every voicing presupposes others that may be to greater or lesser degrees opposed, orthogonal, or in some other angular relationship to it (182), and thus, "each word . . . is a little arena for the clash and criss-crossing of differently oriented social accents" (Vološinov [1929] 1986, 41). Voices can thus be described as dialogic insofar as they can be said to interact with each other, but they are also characterized by *dialogism* insofar as they are internally variegated reflecting complex social dialectics, which are sometimes quite evident and sometimes hidden but nevertheless always present.

This is all well and good for thinking about Dostoevsky's poetics, but to paraphrase Tertullian, what has Moscow to do with Cobán? What utility does this theory about novelistic language offer for the study of contemporary religion? Linguistic anthropologists and sociolinguists have found in Bakhtin's dialogic model of language a useful tool for theorizing the multiple, heterogenous, and hybrid ways that speakers with overlapping but distinct linguistic repertoires interact with each other (Woolard 1998, 4; see also Duranti 2009, 20; Hill 1986, 89). They have found this approach amenable to the goal of understanding linguistic practice as something that is inextricably tied to larger social and cultural dynamics, too, because of the way that it emphasizes the ideological dimensions and power differentials implicit in linguistic heterogeneity (see, for example, Pujolar 2000; Rampton 2011; Tsitsipis 1998). Heteroglossia, in short, offers a model for thinking through the complexity of language as a social phenomenon that simultaneously evinces structures of regularity and normativity as well as a constant efflorescence of improvisation and idiosyncrasy that pushes back against those structures. Similarly, I would argue, if we allow that Bakhtin's conception of language and discourse can be metaphorically extended to be any form of symbolic practice, such as religion, his model works well for examining the heteroglot reality of Catholicism in contemporary Guatemala. To illustrate this, let us return to the ethnographic vignette that opened this chapter.

The authors, subjects, and recipient of the letter detailing the supposed abuses committed by the carismáticos in San Ignacio Tz'iib'ak each saw themselves as Catholic and yet understood what that term meant very differently. The polemical letter, which spelled out one party's position only made sense because it implicated other voicings of Catholicism—most evidently those of the carismáticos as clear antagonists and of Padre Agustino as a presumptive, if not yet confirmed, ally. Implicit in the discourse of the document were also the voices of evangélicos, of Castellanos, of the institutional Catholic Church, and of previous generations of Q'eqchi'-Mayas who had practiced their religion according to their own norms and expectations. The text—which presented itself as an authentic record of speech from a specific meeting, was formatted as a legal writ, and had been handled like a letter—was filled with "sideward glances" (Bakhtin 1984, 196) at the other's putatively hostile words; words that, in this case, were in Spanish and thus indexical of "changed hearts." This relatively short text evoked a larger social reality in which language—both as code and as performative praxis—served as a touchstone for negotiating orthodoxy, orthopraxy, and ultimately religious identity. To be sure, each of these parties had vastly different possibilities for enforcing their own voicings of Catholicism as orthodox, but the document suggests that each potentially sought to do so even as they were also aware that they would meet resistance from others. My argument, then, is that it was through the interaction of their voices (meant here both literally and as a metaphor for their respective practices) that Catholic Christianity was realized as a living religion in San Felipe parish.

The San Ignacio letter entextualizes the social drama of Catholic neighbors competing among themselves to put forward an authoritative vision of their religion. The events in San Ignacio were just part of a larger story that was unfolding throughout the parish as La Renovación's songs and prayers began to be heard in more villages and hamlets across San Felipe parish. If we zoom out even further, we might well recognize, too, that although the specifics of the conflict in San Felipe were shaped by the confluence of social, cultural, and historical peculiarities of that place, the stakes of these debates were the same ones that have animated religious factionalism and schism elsewhere.

A chief effect of the Bakhtinian theory of heteroglossia is that it forces us to see that what at first blush may appear to be a singular and monologic form (an institutionally sanctioned form of ritual language, for example) is only one component of a larger overarching system that encompasses it as well as any number of oppositions and resistances to it. In that light the apparently unquestionable authority of a monologic voice is rendered one stance among many, even if it can also be said to be one with special affordances of power and prestige. Applying the heteroglossic model to Catholicism (or really any religion or social institution) allows us to decenter our understanding of its structure and to more readily recognize the extent to which even marginal positionalities within that structure help shape its "living infrastructure" (Napolitano 2017b). Loud singing in Spanish and the complaints it elicited were not just social problems specific to a highland village; they were in fact religious debates about how to be Catholic. In this perspective, the conflicts in San Felipe were not simply episodes occurring at the fringes of a Guatemalan diocese but rather something that would fractally be representative of the larger processes through which Catholicism is practiced, imagined, and experienced. There was no less at stake in defining Catholicism in what was going on in San Felipe at the start of the twenty-first century than there was during the debates over birth control in Vatican II or over the use of vernaculars at Trent, even if we also recognize that cardinals in European metropoles wield a much greater degree of influence within the institution than do indigenous catechists in Guatemala. The model of Catholicism as heteroglossia, thus, allows us to address the problem outlined above about how we might better integrate the wonderfully diverse array of interpretations of Catholicism around the world into our understanding of the larger transnational institution.

There is a fourth Bakhtinian term that informs my writing about San Felipe—*chronotope*. Bakhtin borrowed the term from theoretical physics as a way to name "the inseparability of space and time" in novelistic discourse (1981, 84). He argued that space and time are necessary parts of human cognition and experience, and that, hence, meaning is always already mediated through chronotopic relations. I invoke the idea here to reflectively position this study, my findings, and ultimately the text that you are reading within discrete spatiotemporal bounds.

The book is focused on the activities that occurred in a single parish during a specific period of time. As Susan Bigelow Reynolds notes, scholars of Catholicism have not tended to pay enough attention to the parish as a unit of analysis and, as a consequence, have missed some of the crucial ways in which Catholics make the sacred local (Reynolds 2019). The dynamics of conflict between the catequistas and carismáticos I encountered in San Felipe did not seem to hold for other parishes in Cobán, and while I have no doubt that people in other parishes disagreed on what constitutes good

Catholic practice and am sure that factions in those places sometimes also found Charismatics to be problematic, the problem as it emerged in San Felipe was essentially unique to that population. The events I observed and the things that people said to me and each other were colored by the tensions of that particular moment in the mid-2000s when La Renovación was growing at unprecedented rates in the parish. By the time I returned to Cobán after a decade-long absence, the debates over Spanish and Q'eqchi' had abated and religious life in the parish had taken a different turn. While those changes are not the subject of this book, they necessarily color my perception and interpretation of what I observed while living in Cobán between 2004 and 2006. To note that the linguistic differences that were a cause for heated debate and broken relationships at one point were largely forgotten later is not to say that they did not ultimately matter but rather strengthens my larger argument that Catholicism is a heteroglossic and dynamic system that only appears stable and unified from certain vantage points and at certain times.

Nonetheless, I don't want to give the impression that the reach of this book begins and ends at the ecclesiastical borders of the one parish over the course of just a little over a decade (most of which I wasn't there for.) Rather, my point is that while the drama of San Felipe is played out at a unique moment and place, its underlying dynamics are like those that have played out in other places and at other times. At any given moment in any given parish there are sure to be debates both big and small that are local and historically contextual responses to the larger problematics the religion raises. Examining how one set of voices articulated Catholicism dialogically in one place and at one time helps us see the fundamental processes through which religious imaginaries are formed, contested, and changed.

Outline of the Book

This book is divided into three sections. This chapter and the two that follow it contextualize the conflict in San Felipe. Through the San Ignacio Tz'iib'ak letter, I have introduced the terms of the conflict and offered my theoretical approach to Catholicism as a form of heteroglossia. Chapters 1 and 2 situate the conflict within the larger social world of Cobán, Alta Verapaz, and the changing ways in which the Roman Catholic Church has conceived of its work among Guatemala's Maya people.

Framed by a description of a procession held annually in honor of Cobán's patron saint, chapter 1 introduces the city and the parish. This chapter is largely descriptive and meant to give the reader a sense of the social landscape that San Felipe's parishioners inhabit. Its discussion of the parish's history and organization offers an entry point to explain why the conflict between Mainstream and Charismatic Catholics was experienced as a local problem of community disintegration and why lay leaders in these communities felt the stakes to be so important.

The historical background that led to the differences between the two congregations is the subject of chapter 2. There I trace out changes in Catholic theology and practice in Guatemala since the twentieth century, emphasizing how global, regional, and national theological turns and pastoral initiatives variously transformed Catholic lay participation. I focus especially on the consequences that these movements had on how the Catholic Church has understood its work among indigenous people in Guatemala. Understanding the religious situation in San Felipe, I argue, requires recognizing the way that various strands of Catholic theology conceptualized the relationship between the institutional church and the laity. Knowing the history of those strands of thinking allows us to more fully appreciate the extent to which Mayas' experiences of Catholicism have always been an exercise of positioning themselves in relation to the institutional church's shifting discourses.

The book's middle chapters focus on the linguistic practices of San Felipe's parishioners to show how members of the two congregations "voice" their own understandings of Catholic piety in contrast to each other. Taken together these chapters establish how and why communicative practices became central to the conflict between catequistas and carismáticos in San Felipe. Through these chapters I argue that it is theoretically useful to apply the methodologies of linguistic anthropology to examine how interpersonal interactions undergird larger processes of social and religious differentiation.

Chapter 3 focuses on how Mainstream and Charismatic lay leaders were legitimized as religious authorities within their respective congregations. By examining how individual laypersons achieved and maintained their positions as *catequistas* and *predicadores* (preachers) as well as how they enacted their authority through speech, this chapter demonstrates the two congregations' contrasting ideas about the source of religious authority. Mainstream Catholic catequistas' authority to preach depended on their position within the institutional religious hierarchy. Maintaining that position required that they perform a kind of studied submission and faithfully reproduce its authorized discourse. Charismatic Catholic predicadores operated independently of the Catholic hierarchy and instead claimed the authority to preach on the notion that the Holy Spirit regularly inspired people to interpret the Bible. I show how those ideals were ritualized and examine the ideological underpinnings that supported each one as a way of framing them as contingent positions within a larger system.

Chapter 4 takes up the questions of why carismáticos' use of Spanish was such an important part of the debate. I argue that as a publicly available index of congregational difference, code choice was readily taken up as an object of cross-congregational critique that parishioners understood as indexing of fundamentally different visions of what it meant to be Catholic and Q'eqchi'-Maya. I argue that the defining difference between the groups' linguistic practice—Mainstream Catholics' code consistency in Q'eqchi' and Charismatics' code alternation between Spanish and Q'eqchi'—were motivated by key theological principles that differentiated the congregations. By analyzing transcripts of recorded speech taken from the openings of ritual events, I argue that we can see how each congregation established distinct ethics of comportment to go along with ritual space and time, and that as such, linguistic practice was a constitutive part of establishing their forms of religiosity.

Chapter 5 examines the two congregations' musical media and aesthetics of singing. I argue that hymn singing was a crucial technique through which the congregations promoted participation in Catholic ritual and thus a cornerstone of how each built the religious subjectivities of its members. However, because the sounds of their songs carried beyond the walls of the chapel, music also became ripe as a site for conflict between the groups. I focus especially on the role of the singing voice as an uncanny reminder of the growing rupture in the community to explain why music became such a problem. This insight allows us to reevaluate why the debate in San Felipe became acrimonious. Far from being just about ritual differences, the conflict grew because those differences were constant reminders of a break in community solidarity, which called into question the shared project of Catholicism in a country where other forms of Christianity had become increasingly socially influential.

The book's latter chapters focus on the body's role in religious practice. Chapter 6 examines how the gestures, postures, and bodily movements of Mainstream and Charismatic Catholics differed as well as why those differences became the subject of cross-congregational critique. By examining gesture and body movement across several genres of speech in ritual settings, I propose that each congregation developed a distinct style that built on and reinforced the underlying communicative ideology that they understood as governing their interactions with God.

Chapter 7 takes up the question of how and why bodily actions might have been so significant in the first place for people's religious subjectivities. I do so through a discussion of how Holy Week processions are organized and performed. I interpret the organizing logic of these rituals as well as my experience as a participant-observer in them in light of literature on intersubjectivity and intercorporeality. I argue that the collaborative nature of embodied ritual action served to forge intersubjective relations that were the bedrock for producing collective religious subjectivities. Discussing how these rituals were performed as public testaments of their faith also allows me to contextualize San Felipe's parishioners' Catholicism within the larger contested religious landscape of contemporary Guatemala.

The conclusion opens with a discussion of an unusual event I witnessed at the very end of my stay in Cobán in 2006 that recapitulated what seemed to

FIGURE 1   San Felipe's parish church

be an intractable conflict between the two kinds of Catholics at the time. Yet, as it turned out, a decade later things in San Felipe had changed and what was once a problem of great concern had ceased to be one. Through a brief discussion of what happened in the parish in the intervening decade that led not only to greater reproachment between Charismatic and Mainstream Catholics but also generated some new disagreements and debates, I return to the argument for seeing Catholicism as heteroglossic.

A Note on Positionality

I don't remember the first time I visited the church I call San Felipe in this book, though this is not surprising, since I would have been quite young then. Some of my earliest memories are of going to Cobán with my father to visit family there, and I remember walking up the steep stairs to this church with him. I remember visiting it again after he had passed away, after I had become a resident of the United States, and well before I knew what an ethnographer was. On my (almost) yearly trips to Guatemala during summer vacations, I would go with my aunt and cousins for a weekend to visit my grandfather don Samuel Hoenes Chocooj, who lived in Cobán most of his life. We would often take a walk up to San Felipe, stopping on the way back to buy *café con leche* candies wrapped in little squares of wax paper and smoky pork *salchichones*—two delicacies that to this day are as tied to my sensory memories of Cobán as anything else.

Those visits to the church were not reverent. My cousins and I would try to race up the steps joking and lamenting that we were there instead of somewhere "cool" like Antigua Guatemala with its colonial buildings and throngs of tourists, or Panajachel on the shores of Lake Atitlán where the hippies hung out. Back then the inside of the church held little interest for me, though I recall peering into the little niches that dot the walkway up to the church, curious to see what manner of offerings had been placed there— candles, flowers, copal incense, coins, feathers, a tuft of hair. Sometimes we would see a *sacerdote Maya* performing a ritual for someone on the patio of the church, but these were not the things that interested me much at the time. Even the story about the miraculous image of Jesus who had appeared on the hill and been jealously guarded by two jaguars seemed like a silly fable at the time. Little did I know that these things would eventually become the genesis of a book about two Q'eqchi'-Maya Catholic groups' efforts to safeguard their voicings of Christianity.

Don Samuel passed away before I had a chance to learn Q'eqchi', and I regret that I never got to speak it with him. It had been his first language since he was born and raised on a *finca* where everyone, save his father—Samuel Hoenes Fetzer[16]—had been Q'eqchi'-Maya. His children (that is, my father and his siblings) never learned more than a couple of phrases of Q'eqchi' and a few choice "bad words." During my fieldwork tenures, I have lived in don Samuel's house, with his second wife, their daughter, and her family (that is, my step-grandmother, aunt, and cousins). I learned a great deal about life in Cobán through them, too.

Quite a few of my interlocutors knew members of my family either personally or by reputation. Although the social circles that my Ladino family members and my Q'eqchi'-Maya interlocutors travel in can sometimes seem quite far apart from each other, at other times they have overlapped in surprising ways. Several parishioners had known my grandfather, and at least one had been his student at the local *Instituto normal* secondary school. My aunt Astrid had worked as a primary school teacher in the village I call Sa'xreb'e a decade before my fieldwork and thus knew some of the prominent residents of that village and several of them remembered her as well. Perhaps the most surprising connection, though, came the time I offered to drive a couple of Sa'xreb'e's carismáticos to a regional conference only to find that my cousins' paternal grandfather was the person checking everyone in. I had visited with don Otto and his wife several times at their home in Santa Cruz and knew them to be active members of their parish, but until that day I had no idea they were involved in La Renovación at all. Those connections and others located me in a particular way in Cobán's social geography as someone with roots there, but they also implied certain kinds of social separations between me and San Felipe's parishioners.

---

16. Samuel Hoenes Fetzer was born near Göttigen, Germany, and arrived in Guatemala in 1893 as part of a large migration of Germans that began in 1864. He and his brother Otto came with their cousin Ernest Fetzer and settled near Cobán, where they bought land and set to work cultivating coffee and cardamom. He spent much of his life in Guatemala living at his finca, which he reputedly rarely left (Terga Cintrón, 1991, 32). Josefa Chocooj—the second woman with whom he had children—was my great-grandmother. I am sad to say that I know almost nothing about her life.

Being Guatemalan, albeit Ladino (what elsewhere in Latin America would be called *mestizo*), having family connections in Cobán, and speaking Spanish natively each presented certain benefits and challenges to fieldwork. Members of minoritized populations the world over know all too well that sharing a nationality on paper with someone does not necessarily make you intimates or equals. My interlocutors and I may all have been born in Guatemala, but our ethnicities, class positions, and geographical locations each ensured that our subsequent experiences of membership in the nation were significantly different from each other. This is to say nothing of the fact that I emigrated as a child in the 1980s, whereas my interlocutors had to face the violence and uncertainty of those times more proximately. Any claims I can make to shared national origins with my interlocutors in Guatemala can easily be countered by the evident ways I am marked as a foreigner there. This is all to say that the place I am writing about here has multiple interconnections with my own biography. And yet, it is also distant in ways that are hard to fully articulate.

My ability to speak the local variety of Spanish with an unmarked accent made it easier to begin conversations in Cobán, but it was also a crutch insofar as I was never as fully immersed in Q'eqchi' as I might have been otherwise. I took lessons in and studied the language independently to the point where I achieved enough competency in Q'eqchi' to understand what was being said at religious services and occasionally contribute to them. However, during interviews and casual conversations it was always easier for me and my interlocutors to switch to Spanish than it was to try to muddle through them in Q'eqchi'.

It has become a normal practice for anthropologists of Christianity to also address their faith or lack thereof (I think we must have borrowed this practice from the confessional booth, since anthropologists of other religious traditions don't typically engage in this kind of self-disclosure), and so I feel I should also address that here. I am not now, nor have I ever been, a practicing or even nominal Catholic, nor have I ever really considered myself a Christian of any sort. Over the course of my field research there were a few instances when my interlocutors asked me about my religion, and I tried to answer them as frankly as I could that I was there to try to understand what it meant to be católico even if I wasn't one myself. Because I was a foreigner and spent a great deal of time at the parish center, people generally slotted me into the role of a seminarian or perhaps a visiting priest. I was always quick to correct them about this when I could. Being a foreigner, I did have the advantage that the clergy of the parish recognized that we shared something of the same sense of being both of a place and not from it. I often ate lunch with the priests when they were at the parish center, and Padre Agustino was always ready to offer me a cold Gallo beer when it was time to relax in the afternoons. I would like to think that over time my close interlocutors understood pretty well that I was an interested and neutral, but also sympathetic, observer.

My experience of life in Cobán and San Felipe are quite different from those of the people who are the main subjects of this book, and it is ultimately to their experiences that I hope to do justice. But I think that it is also important to acknowledge my connections to these places both because it is unlikely that I would have ever embarked on this project were it not for them, as well as because a scholars' subjectivity marks their work in ways both big and small. I write from a position of long-term familiarity with Cobán and San Felipe, even though for most of that time my familiarity has been hopelessly shallow. Like all ethnographers, I am trying to render into writing the disorienting experience of finding the strange familiar and the familiar strange, and yet my own biography complicates the categories of familiarity and strangeness in unusual ways.

CHAPTER 1

Por las calles de Cobán
Place, People, and the Dynamics of Conflict

On the morning of the third day of August the *santos* (saints) who make their homes in and around Cobán congregate in the central plaza to pay their respects to the city's patron saint—Santo Domingo de Guzmán (St. Dominic of Osma). At noon church bells ring and fireworks explode, announcing that Santo Domingo is ready to exit the city's main church (*La Catedral*) and diocesan seat of Verapaz. Accompanied by La Virgen del Rosario (Our Lady of the Rosary[1]) and a coterie of local dignitaries, including members of the saint's sodality, politicians, and the city's reigning indigenous beauty queen, Santo Domingo circles around the north side of the plaza until he reaches the end opposite the church. There, Santo Domingo and La Virgen turn around to receive the santos who have come for the festivities. As the santos are carved out of wood and otherwise immobile, their human bearers aid them in performing the greetings by tilting the biers on which they stand—first to the right, then left, and forward for their final bow. Each of the nearly three dozen santos who have come will perform

---

1. This epithet of Mary purportedly commemorates her appearance to St. Dominic in early thirteenth-century France. According to Catholic tradition, Mary bequeathed the Rosary prayer to Dominic on that occasion to help him evangelize and combat heresy (Mitchell 2009). In subsequent centuries she was honored for aiding Christians in several military battles, with Pope Pius V dedicating a feast day to her following the Battle of Lepanto in 1571, in which a coalition of Christian forces defeated the Ottoman Empire. Given her propensity for helping Christians attain both religious and military victories, it is perhaps no surprise that this version of Mary was an important one in colonial Latin America.

these actions called *"cortesías"* (which means both "courtesy" and "curtsy," neatly capturing the sense that this is an interaction governed by politeness and hierarchy), first to Santo Domingo and then to La Virgen, both of whom reciprocate the stylized greeting. San Francisco de Asís (St. Francis of Assisi) is the last saint to come in the line, and because Santo Domingo and San Francisco are said to be close friends, their greeting is particularly warm. The trio then leaves together, with the male santos flanking La Virgen. Musicians and masked dancers accompany this procession of santos around the plaza and the adjacent block on which the city's main market and the church stand. They then walk to a small chapel dedicated to Santo Domingo, about one kilometer away. The three principal saints will spend the night in that chapel surrounded by the sounds of prayer, the glow of candlelight, and the sweet pungent scent of *copal pom* incense. The people holding this vigil will also visit with each other and drink cups of warm cacao.

The humans and santos of Cobán honor Santo Domingo on that day because the city was founded by members of the religious order that bears his name. Dominican priests first came to the part of Guatemala now known as Alta Verapaz in the late 1530s under the auspices of the famous conquistador-turned-missionary Fray Bartolomé de las Casas, who was charged by the Holy Roman Emperor Charles V to evangelize the region after military incursions had failed. Pleased with the priests' early work "pacifying" a land that had heretofore been called *Tezulutlán*—which meant "the land of war" in Nahuatl—Charles V renamed it *La Verapaz*, or "the true peace." He declared the settlement of Cobán an imperial city and placed it under the administration of the Dominican friars, giving it a measure of autonomy from the rest of New Spain's colonial regime. Because of this designation and the privileged role that Catholic clergy took in governing it, colonization proceeded under somewhat different circumstances in Cobán and its environs than it did in the rest of the country, and the region remained somewhat isolated from the rest of Guatemala well into the nineteenth century (King 1974).

Today residents still call Cobán *"La ciudad imperial de Carlos V"* (the imperial city of Charles V), and the legacy of its founding as an experiment in conquest via evangelization remains an important part of Cobaneros's discursive elaborations of what makes their city unique. My aim in this chapter is to give a brief introduction to Cobán and its people, highlighting the religious institutions that shape the lives of San Felipe's parishioners.

Life in Cobán

Cobán is the *cabecera* (capital) of the department of Alta Verapaz in the north-central part of Guatemala, sitting close to where the country's highlands give way to the lowlands in the north. At the time of my fieldwork the *municipio* (municipality, which contains both the central urban area and surrounding countryside) had a population of about 146,500, with about 80,000 of them living in or near the city center, making it one of the five most populous in the country (Instituto Nacional de Estadística de Guatemala 2002).

Like other cities in Latin America founded during the colonial period, Cobán was built around a central plaza where religious and secular authorities as well as commercial interests met. At the heart of Cobán is a plaza (usually called *el parque central*, or "central park," in Guatemala) surrounded by buildings that include city hall, the old palace of arms (which now houses several governmental and NGO offices), the department's principal courthouse, and the city's main Catholic church along with the remnants of the Dominicans' monastery (which now houses the offices of the Diocese of Verapaz). There are also several shops and restaurants, a children's playground, a colonial-style inn, and the city's old theater where formerly plays were staged and films screened, but which is now mostly shuttered except when Pentecostal evangélicos rent it to hold revivals. The central plaza is located on a small ridge, where the Dominicans chose to settle in the sixteenth century, supposedly because the location offered them a good vantage of the immediately surrounding area in case any nearby Maya settlements decided to turn hostile toward them (King 1974, 44). The rest of the city occupies the shallow valleys around that ridge, so that some of the streets on its grid are surprisingly steep. The Cahabón River passes by the city to the south, flowing eastward toward the Caribbean, and mountains ring the city in all directions.

Beyond the plaza there are few remnants of colonial architecture, and the city's buildings tend to be more modern and utilitarian. Houses are typically built of concrete blocks covered with plaster. In older parts of the city, the front walls of residences and businesses abut the city's narrow sidewalks, and whole blocks may share a single street-facing wall with metal doors and different colors of paint marking where one begins and its neighbor ends. Homes there typically don't have exterior windows but rather feature an interior patio that opens to the sky, around which bedrooms and other living areas are arranged. In parts of the city that have recently been incorporated into Cobán's urban core, however, one also finds freestanding houses with small fenced-in front yards.

Regardless of their architecture, the homes of devout Catholics typically have an altar somewhere in them. Sometimes this is a table in a corner of a shared room, but in some larger homes, especially among those who take formal leadership positions in *cofradías* (Catholic sodalities dedicated to caring for santos), there may be an entire room set aside for an altar upon which multiple saints' images reside. Members of the household provision the altar with votive candles, flowers, and other small offerings. Besides being a space for personal and family devotion, these rooms are also sometimes used for gatherings of lay religious groups.

As the capital of the department of Alta Verapaz, Cobán is a commercial as well as political center. There are two large markets that trade in agricultural products brought in on buses or pickup trucks by small and medium-scale farmers starting in the early hours of the morning each day. While some of these products (especially corn and vegetables) are sold for local consumption, others are sold to warehouse consolidators for export. Coffee, cardamom (of which Guatemala is the largest exporter in the world[2]), and red chili peppers have traditionally been key cash crops in the region, and more recently okra and Hass avocados (which are hardier but blander than the domestic *aguacates criollos* that locals prefer) have also become important exports.

Cobán is a relatively vibrant commercial center by Guatemalan standards. There are a plethora of shops selling new and secondhand clothing, electronics, toys, and other manufactured goods. One can also shop for everything from fresh produce and meat to dry goods and spices, traditional clothing and jewelry, and religious paraphernalia, at bustling indoor and outdoor markets. Diesel trucks and pickups begin rolling into town every day before dawn to supply these shops. By the time they arrive, several street vendors are ready to sell them breakfasts of *pan dulce* (sweet breads), coffee, and fresh-squeezed orange juice, and others take their place later in the day selling a variety of sweet and savory snacks well into the night. The women who sell fresh produce out of handmade baskets begin to set up their portable shops on the peripheries of the formal markets early in the morning as well. Shoppers come throughout the morning to purchase food for the day, and

---

2. AGEXPORT Guatemala. "Comité de cardamomo" https://export.com.gt/publico/comite-de-cardamomo. Accessed March 15, 2021.

although business slows after lunch, trade continues into the mid-afternoon. Alongside more traditional goods, market stalls display manufactured goods both simple and complex, imported from China, as well as CD-ROMS bearing less-than-legal copies of popular music and the latest Hollywood blockbusters. Several US-based food and retail chains including Payless Shoes, Domino's Pizza, Taco Bell, Subway, and McDonald's, as well as Walmart-owned Paiz grocery store, operate franchises at a modern shopping mall built in what a few decades ago was considered the far outskirts of town.[3]

While not approaching the amount of business done in more well-known places like Antigua Guatemala, Lake Atitlán, or the classical Maya ruins of Tikal, Cobán is a minor stop along the tourist trail in Guatemala since it is a good waypoint for travelers headed to ecotourism sites farther north in Alta Verapaz and Petén. Few foreigners spend much time in Cobán, but Cobaneros living elsewhere in the country travel back frequently, often making it a point to be in town for Santo Domingo's fiesta and the accompanying fair, which features a dance dedicated to *el Cobanero ausente* (the absent person from Cobán) each year. There is also a major influx of visitors on the last weekend of May when the city hosts a half-marathon that draws tens of thousands of runners from around Guatemala and as far away as Kenya.

Life in *las Aldeas*

While its core is urban, the municipio of Cobán is largely rural. From most anywhere in the city one can see the verdant mountains that surround it, and

---

3. Following a pattern that anthropologists have observed elsewhere, the uncanny seems to have followed the expansion of late capitalism in Cobán (see, e.g., Taussig 1977; Ong 1988). When the shopping mall opened in 2003 there were persistent rumors that it was haunted. People said that shop workers would find goods, especially children's clothing, taken off the racks and scattered on the floor when they opened in the morning even though nothing had been stolen. Some people attributed this to the shopping center's construction along riverbanks known to be haunted by *La Llorona*. This spectral figure—who appears throughout Mesoamerica and as far north as the southwestern United States—is the ghost of a woman condemned to wander at night crying out in search of her lost children. She, of course, will never find her children since they were drowned by her own hands in a fit of madness. Those who hear her wails say that they are terrifying and unlike any natural sound. Perhaps the eeriest thing that people said happened at the mall, though, was that the life-sized fiberglass statue of Ronald McDonald that sits on a bench in front of his temple of fast-food consumption has been seen uncrossing and then recrossing his legs.

although Cobán's urban area has grown steadily over the years, it doesn't take much time traveling along major roads before the bustle of urban street life subsides and the distinctly different feel of the countryside takes over.

Life outside of the city is arranged into *aldeas* or *k'aleb'aaleb'* (villages, singular *k'aleb'aal*) of several dozen to a hundred or more households. The structure of aldeas varies somewhat depending on its history and locale. K'aeb'aaleb' closer to the city and those founded during the Guatemalan Civil War (1960–96) feature houses that are relatively close to each other with hard-packed dirt roads wide enough to be navigated by motor vehicles (if not always comfortably); they also typically have a small complex that includes a church and schoolhouse at their center. Aldeas farther away from the city core and those founded well before or well after the war (and hence less likely to have been structured around a rationalized organization that made surveillance easier) tend to not have clearly defined village centers and the homes that make them up can be quite far from each other and connected only by meandering footpaths.

Houses in rural areas are typically made of wood slats, roofed with corrugated tin sheeting, and have dirt floors. The simplest houses consist of a single room where all family members sleep, rest, and store personal belongings, with a second partially open structure that is used for both cooking and eating. Households with more means may have internal walls that break up the main house into separate living areas and will add screens to windows to help with insect control. As a family grows or finds new access to money, they may extend the size of existing structures by adding rooms or building a new freestanding house to accommodate newly married couples. If they are entrepreneurial, they will also build structures dedicated to the household's economic production, such as a shed for storing excess maize or firewood, a coop to raise chickens or turkeys, or a small store where people can buy essentials like cooking oil, sugar, beans, matches, firecrackers, as well as snacks and drinks. Some wealthier families in large villages have built cinderblock houses with tile floors, too. Access to running water and electricity varies greatly, both village by village and from home to home, but as a general rule the closer a house is to a major paved roadway, the better its chance of being connected to the utilities grid.

People in rural areas make a living from agriculture, producing some food for subsistence and some for the market, and men may migrate to work seasonally at plantations on the coast or as security guards in the capital city. All but the absolute poorest have small *milpa* plots on which they grow maize, beans, squash, chiles and a selection of herbs, although in some cases these can be quite far away from their house, and people will need to walk long distances to tend to them. Households with larger plots of land also maintain small gardens or orchards and keep chickens to supply them with eggs. Provided they have access to enough surplus maize and land, a household may also raise a few turkeys, pigs, or even cows intended either for the market or for use in a major life event celebration such as a wedding or the head of household's investment as the head of a cofradía. If there are streams or ponds nearby, people may catch fish and freshwater crustaceans to supplement their diets.

Besides houses, a k'aleb'aal typically has two other kinds of buildings—schools and churches. The size of a school will depend on the size of the village. Small villages farther from the city may only have a single-room wooden schoolhouse with a small play field, while larger villages might have small complexes of two, three, or four concrete block buildings with multiple classrooms. Similarly, the size and complexity of the local Catholic chapel will vary in size depending on the village's size and resources. While some larger villages have set aside land specifically for the chapel, in others this may be an extension of a person's house. Evangélico (i.e., Protestant, typically Pentecostal) churches can also be found in most villages, with some being freestanding buildings and others operating from the pastor's home. Because this land is essentially nonproductive, residents will sometimes keep a plot near the church and school clear to use as a soccer field and some also hold small weekly markets there.

There are also places in the municipio that straddle the urban/rural divide. In these peri-urban areas, clusters of houses with small agricultural gardens exist interspersed among commercial and residential development projects. Here homes are as likely to be made of wood as of cement block and may be hooked into municipal water and electricity grids (especially if they are along major thoroughfares) but nonetheless retain the feel of rural life. This is due, in part, to the fact that these had been villages that were subsumed by the urban environment and, in part, to a deliberate strategy of maintaining elements of rural economic life, like growing some of their own food, to supplement household incomes. Nonetheless, members of peri-urban households, especially younger men and women, are more economically oriented to the city than the countryside and much more likely to work some sort of service or professional job rather than depend on agriculture.

In any of these contexts, the basic unit of Q'eqchi'-Maya social identity is the household or *junkab'al* (one home), which, though based primarily on consanguinity, may also include other members (for example, adopted children and occasionally domestic employees), and is primarily defined through co-residence and participation in the household's productive activities (Kistler 2014). As Richard Wilk has argued, the junkab'al is a flexible unit capable of adapting to varying economic conditions and political pressures, and because of this they can vary in size from a single nuclear family of three or four people to much larger, multigenerational kin groups of over a dozen (Wilk 1991). Ideally a married couple (who may be betrothed either legally or customarily) will establish their own residence and junkab'al as soon as they have children so that they have some material assets to pass down to them (Kistler 2014, 112). Marriage and having children are the markers of maturity and adulthood, and it is after those life-stage thresholds are crossed that individuals are considered full participating members of the community.

San Felipe Parish

The parish church of San Felipe sits atop a steep hill on the northern side of Cobán, from which one can see much of the rest of the city. There has been a church building on that site since the early 1800s (Villacorta 1977), but it was not until 1961 that it became the seat of a parish. Until that time there had been only one parish in Cobán based out of the cathedral in the center of town, and San Felipe was initially conceived of as a parish that would help support the city's growing population on the west side of town. However, this plan changed within a decade as Guatemala's Catholics began to grapple with the reforms called for by the Second Vatican Council (1962–65) and the Episcopal Conference of Latin America's second general meeting in Medellín (1968; see chapter 2). Following a conference on indigenous people and evangelization held in 1973, plans were set in motion to fundamentally rethink how the Diocese of Verapaz would carry out its work (Melgar 2003, 23).[4] Part of this involved designating certain parishes as explicitly mission-

---

4. The workshop was organized by Juan José Gerardi Conedera (1922–98), who served as bishop of the Verapaz from 1967 to 1974. Gerardi is most well known for being one of the lead voices in the National Reconciliation Commission and the Recovery of Historical Memory (REMHI) project that documented human rights abuses during the Civil War in Guatemala. He was assassinated two days after the presentation of the REHMI report *Guatemala, nunca más* in 1998, which implicated the Guatemalan military in the murder and disappearance of

ary and oriented toward the region's indigenous populations, and San Felipe was meant to serve the municipio's Q'eqchi'-Maya population.[5] Echoing Catholicism's first forays into the region, Dominican clergy were the first to staff San Felipe, but in 1976 the Congregatio Immaculati Cordis Mariae (CICM, or the Congregation of the Immaculate Heart of Mary[6]) took over its administration and have continued to staff the parish until the present with the explicit aim of evangelizing the Q'eqchi'-Maya people of Cobán and "accompanying" them in their spiritual lives.[7]

---

thousands of civilians. During his tenure in the Verapaz he initiated many of the reforms that sought to bring indigenous people more fully into the Catholic Church and expanded the institution's use of Maya languages, including overseeing the production of the Q'eqchi' translation of the missal and the first song books in the language. His successor—Gerardo Humberto Flores Reyes—would largely continue that work, overseeing similar projects for Poqomchi' and Achii'.

5. That year, a third parish was also established to continue serving the urban Ladino population. Other parishes in other municipios were likewise designated for Achii'-Maya and Poqomchi'-Maya populations. In its present organization the Diocese of Verapaz categorizes its parishes as serving these three distinct Maya ethnolinguistic "pastoral zones" as well as a fourth that is coded as *Urbana* (urban) and intended for congregations that are primarily "Ladino" (i.e., non-Mayas or mestizos) or a mix of Ladinos and Mayas (see Hoenes del Pinal 2016b).

6. Congregatio Immaculati Cordis Mariae CICM, also sometimes known as the Missionaries of Scheut (after the town where they originated) was founded in Belgium in 1862 by Father Theophile Verbist who dreamed of doing missionary work in China, where he died doing just that (Verhelst and Pyke 1995). The order later conducted missionary work to Africa, beginning with the Belgian Congo in 1888 and expanding to Cameroon, Senegal, and Nigeria in the 1960s and Chad in the 1970s. In the twentieth century, CICM also established strong missionary presences in Asia (in the Philippines in 1907, Singapore and Indonesia in the 1930s, and Japan after World War II) and Latin America (beginning in Guatemala, Haiti, and the Dominican Republic in the 1950s, Brazil in the 1960s, and Mexico in the 1970s). Because of CICM's global presence, the priests who have served at San Felipe have been from many different parts of the world. The earliest CICM missionaries in Cobán were Belgian and Dutch, but to date, brothers born in the Philippines, Cameroon, the Democratic Republic of Congo, the Dominican Republic, and Haiti have also served there.

7. Even though the rationale for making San Felipe a Q'eqchi' parish was rooted in modernizing Catholic reforms, the practice of creating and maintaining ethnically exclusive and homogenous parishes actually has a precedent in the colonial period when *parroquias de indios* were formed and served to reinforce the separation of indigenous people and Europeans (O'Hara 2009). This had the unintended consequence of creating semiautonomous spaces in which indigenous people (or at least indigenous elites) could exert some influence and control over their religious lives (Early 2006; Baker 2008). As we will see in more detail in the next chapter, there is a complex history to how varying theological and political interests have shaped parishes, but for now it suffices to note that San Felipe embraced the idea that it is the city's

FIGURE 2 (a) A village chapel; (b) Mass in a village chapel

San Felipe's church is within the city bounds of Cobán, but the parish's jurisdiction primarily covers the municipio's rural areas, though the city's growth since the parish's founding has changed what exactly this means. The parish's territory covers roughly 160 square kilometers and includes both cooler highland areas near the urban core in the southeastern corner of the municipio as well as some of the warmer lowlands to the north and northwest of it. At the time of my fieldwork (2004–6), parishioners were organized into 122 communities, which were grouped into five geographic "sectors." The central sector was largely peri-urban communities, but the others were overwhelmingly rural, and many of the communities in three of these were not accessible by automobile. This meant that when Padre Agustino went on his weekly rounds to the aldeas, he would typically drive in the parish's Suzuki Samurai to one k'aleb'aal, celebrate Mass there, and then proceed on foot to the next one, where he would again celebrate Mass, and so on, following a loop that eventually brought him back to the first village to pick up his car on the third or fourth day. On these excursions he would also take care of any baptisms, weddings, last rites, or other sacraments the community might need. Padre Agustino traveled almost every week and stopped at anywhere between four and a dozen k'aleb'aaleb' on each trip; ideally, he would visit each community under his care quarterly, but heavy rains and other unexpected events could throw a wrench in those plans.

Parishioners in remote communities had an even harder time coming into town, since for them this would potentially mean walking for hours to reach a road and waiting there for a passing pickup truck to hitch a ride on into town or at least to a highway where they could board a bus headed to Cobán. Those living closer to the parish center were expected to attend Sunday masses at San Felipe on a somewhat regular basis; however, even for those living along major roads, the expense of paying for transportation into Cobán for Mass could still be a significant burden and kept all but the most dedicated and relatively affluent from attending every week. In practice, then, most parishioners attended Mass primarily on feast days, special occasions such as baptisms or weddings, or when their community was tasked with animating the service.[8] Nonetheless, even during the times that church

---

Q'eqchi' parish, and this impacted how parishioners conceive of their own place within the larger Catholic Church.

8. Responsibility for "animating" Sunday Mass is rotated among the CEBs in the central region of the parish. The CEB charged with this task is expected to provide a catechist to deliver

attendance was at its nadir between June and September—which coincided with a period of Ordinary Time in the liturgical calendar with no major feast days (save the Cobán's patron saint's day, which in any case was celebrated in La Catedral parish), as well as the middle of the corn production season when money was scarce—about two hundred people attended Sunday Mass at the parish center. That number would double in October and November, and close to six hundred parishioners would attend regularly as Christmas drew close. That number dipped a bit again after New Year's Day (which was the parish church's busiest day of the year owing to a tradition in which it is seen as auspicious to visit churches high atop hills to offer prayers for the coming year) and the parish's patron saint's day two weeks later when people came to venerate El Señor de Esquipulas. Attendance slowly ticked up during Lent and there was a flurry of activity around Holy Week as well, but church attendance would wane again after Easter Sunday.

In practical terms what all of this added up to was that most parishioners' primary point of contact with the Catholic Church was their local Ecclesial Base Community, or CEB going by Spanish *"comunidad eclesial de base"* and usually referred to simply as *la comunidad* (community) or *li ch'utam* (which roughly means "a group that meets regularly" in Q'eqchi'). CEBs have been a common feature of Catholicism in Latin America since midcentury (see chapter 2 for their origins), though their form and function vary depending on location.[9] The Diocese of Verapaz took the first organizational steps to instituting CEBs in 1968, and fully launched the system in 1975 (Wilson 1995, 173); they have been a fixture of Q'eqchi'-Maya Catholic religious life since then. In San Felipe, CEBs were groups with memberships of at least thirty but potentially several hundred people who met in small chapels and sometimes in private homes to hold a weekly lay-led ritual called *La celebración de la Palabra* or *Xnimqehinkil li Raatin* (Celebration of the Word or Liturgy).

San Felipe's CEBs typically mapped onto specific villages and bore their name, unifying the place of residence with the religious community (as we

---

the sermon, lectors to read Bible verses, a prayer leader, people to pass the collection basket, and a choir and musicians to play music.

9. For example, in urban Brazil in the 1980s, CEBs were small-scale groups that met in homes with the express purpose of political "conscientization" via Bible study (Burdick 1993). In Nicaragua, those organizations became more explicitly political and thus fell from favor in the eyes of the clerical hierarchy (Williams 2000). Not all CEBs act as progressive political spaces, however (Napolitano 1998).

saw in the case of San Ignacio Tz'iib'ak in the Introduction), although some larger villages had more than one CEB. There were also a few CEBs in Cobán's peri-urban areas that broke with this model and that were instead organized around extended social networks without reference to a particular place (although in practice the home of one member became the group's seat). The core of the Santa Eusebia CEB, for example, was an extended kin network. That group had been founded after members of a prominent family decided to split from an existing CEB tied to the peri-urban neighborhood (*colonia*) of the matriarch's home. This family made up a large portion of the colonia's ch'utam, but they did not like the group's leadership and felt that the lead catechist was prone to behavior not befitting a religious leader. The straw that broke the camel's back, I was told, was that their head catechist got drunk and danced with several young women at a party, after which several members decided to formally ask permission to establish their own comunidad. Though effecting the split and gaining legitimacy in the eyes of the parish was a long and difficult process that required them to persistently petition the priest for nearly two years, Santa Eusebia managed to establish itself as a separate entity and grew by recruiting people with whom they had fictive kinship relations (*compadrazgo*) as well as by attracting members of other comunidades who were likewise dissatisfied with their home community's leadership. As this case suggests, although the CEBs formally were under the jurisdiction and supervision of the parish clergy, their members had a degree of agency to direct their activities as they saw fit.

For a CEB to be effective it needed several things: a gathering space; a core membership who could organize and perform the duties required for the celebraciones, and a leader (or leaders) to officiate these rituals. As discussed above, most villages had a chapel, which was the preferred place to meet. Depending on the resources that a comunidad could muster, the chapel may have been a simple wood structure or a more formal concrete building. CEBs in peri-urban areas might not have access to a chapel, and they would instead meet at a member's home. That was the case for the Santa Eusebia ch'utam, where the large multipurpose room that held the household altar at the family's compound was readily pressed into service as the group's unofficial chapel.

Each ch'utam had a core membership of anywhere from a few dozen to a hundred or more adults and adolescents who met at least weekly but ideally semi-weekly to hold a Celebración de la Palabra. Additionally, each had a proportional plurality of two to five times that many people who were not regularly active with the CEB, but who nonetheless self-identified as Catholics and attended services occasionally. Each comunidad generally set up a small directorate (*junta directiva*) to manage the group's activities and finances.

A catechist (*catequista* or *aj tzolotij*) was the person most responsible for leading the Celebrations of the Word, though. These services mirrored the Catholic Mass's Liturgy of the Word but did not include the rites associated with the Eucharist. Celebraciones de la Palabra were the main type of religious service that parishioners attended. This was especially true for those who lived in rural k'aleb'aaleb' and thus only attended Mass when the priest made his quarterly visits, but even Q'eqchi'-Maya Catholics living closer to Cobán's urban core were more likely to attend their CEB's weekly services than Sunday Mass at the main church. Each group had at least one catechist, but ideally there would be two or three people who had gone through the catechist formation program and could actively exercise the office. A catechist's main task was to deliver sermons at Celebrations of the Word as well as at Masses, either when a priest visited their village or, in the central sector, when their community was called on to "animate" Sunday Mass at San Felipe's main church. Catechists were selected from among married parishioners who headed their own households, and thus met local cultural criteria to be of sufficient maturity to exercise the office. They also had to be people of good moral standing in their respective communities and have the necessary literacy skills to read and interpret the Bible for their communities (although there was a wide range of what constituted literacy, especially among older parishioners who may not have had as ready access to formal education as their offspring). The catequista also played an important role in preparing members of the ch'utam to receive the sacraments of first communion, marriage, or the baptism of a child.

In addition to the catechist, several other roles needed to be filled at the Celebrations of the Word. These rituals were built around Bible readings and followed a schedule prescribed by the Roman Catholic Church that included passages from the Old Testament, Epistles and Gospels, and typically a different person acted as the lector for each reading. Additionally, one person led the group in collective prayer after the Gospel readings. Adolescents and young adults were often called upon to be lectors, as this was understood to be a good way for them to begin to take on responsibilities for running the ch'utam and allowed the group to identify who might be well suited to the role of catequista in the future. Music was also a crucial part of these services, and CEBs supported small choir bands of musicians and singers to lead hymns.

Up to this point I have been describing the practice of Catholicism among Mainstream Catholics, which was essentially an unmarked category in the parish. As we will see in the next chapter, their "Mainstream Catholicism" drew from a wide range of theological orientations, including Catholic Action, Liberation Theology, the Theology of Inculturation, and a creolized or syncretic version of Maya Catholicism often dubbed *Costumbre* (lit. custom or tradition). Due to the history of those multiple influences, there was a range of beliefs and some variation in the practices of individuals who would be classed as Mainstream Catholics. The differences among them, however, had been somewhat muted in response to the recent establishment and growth of the Catholic Charismatic congregations who made up La Renovación in San Felipe.

A more detailed account of the Catholic Charismatic Renewal Movement's global development and its impact in Guatemala can be found in the next chapter, but for now it suffices to say that the first group of carismáticos in San Felipe was established in 2000 in the village of Rub'elchaj.[10] The founder of that group came into contact with La Renovación while visiting relatives in the neighboring town of San Pedro Carchá, where Catholic Charismatics had first been active in the early 1990s. As part of that experience, he felt compelled to "convert" to Charismatic Catholicism and furthermore felt that he was being called by God to preach and lead a new group in his home village. He went on to establish a group in Rub'elchaj, which began meeting at his house. The group grew quickly over its first few years and attracted a significant portion of its new membership from a large neighboring village of Sa'xreb'e. Within two years more than half of the congregation were residents of the second village, traveling several kilometers to attend weekly services. When one of the Sa'xreb'e converts eventually felt the call to preach himself, it was decided that a new congregation should be estab-

---

10. The Catholic Charismatic Renewal has a longer history and much broader participation among Ladinos in Cobán. In that population, the movement seems to be much less controversial and treated more as one among other interest groups like the Legion of Mary or *cursillos*. I suspect that this is due to the fact that among urban Ladinos, attendance at weekly Mass is the primary way of participating in Catholicism rather than through CEBs, as it is among Q'eqchi'-Mayas.

lished in that village, effectively splitting the group in two. La Renovación spread through the parish in the early 2000s by following this basic pattern in which a group was established in one village, grew in part by attracting people from neighboring villages, and subsequently split once residents of other villages had the numbers and leadership to establish and sustain their own congregations.

By the time I first met them in 2004, the Sa'xreb'e congregation's membership had grown to about 120 parishioners who attended services weekly, and a little more than twice that many who attended less frequently but who could nonetheless be counted to be there for major events such as all-night *vigilias* (lit. "vigils," although "revivals" might better capture the feel of these events). It was without a doubt the hotbed of La Renovación in the parish and the group through which I would learn the most about this form of Catholicism. Comparatively, there were four Mainstream Catholic CEBs in Sa'xreb'e, each of which was at least as large as the Charismatic group. The original Rub'elchaj group of carismáticos was still active with about fifty core members, and thus no more than a third the size of that village's sole Mainstream Catholic CEB. As far as I was able to tell, there were about a dozen other active Charismatic groups in the parish in 2005; however, it was hard to get an exact count of them for a few reasons. First, the insurgent and enthusiastic nature of La Renovación meant that new groups were formed when individuals felt the Holy Spirit moving them and so could be established from the bottom-up and rather quickly, unlike new CEBs, which were only established after long processes of study and reflection and required the official consent of the parish priest (as illustrated by the Santa Eusebia case discussed earlier). Second, carismáticos perceived the parish's interest as aligned with those of their most vocal critics—local CEBs' established catechists—and because of that, some of them preferred to not make their activities widely known, or at least not until their numbers were large enough to be able to make strong claims to their rightful place in parish life, lest they be censured by the priest. Finally, while some Mainstream lay leaders, like those from San Ignacio, would write to Padre Agustino to complain about Charismatics, others preferred to simply ignore the carismáticos, treating them as though they were evangélicos and thus separate from and not subject to the administration of the parish. Evangélicos were a presence in just about every village that San Felipe parish covered, and many católicos' strategy for dealing with them was to simply ignore them. I suspect there was more Charismatic activity in the parish than I was privy to, especially in rural areas, but I was not able to accurately gauge exactly how much. Though it was steadily gaining members, La Renovación remained a minority within the parish, and my best estimate is that less than 10 percent of parishioners identified with it. Even so, La Renovación's growth was cause for concern for CEB leaders. Why was that?

All of San Felipe's Charismatics would have been members of Mainstream Catholic CEBs prior to their "conversion" (a term which they themselves invoked to signal their changed religious outlook) to La Renovación. Despite the discursive moves to describe themselves as "renewed" Catholics and to distance themselves from the forms of religiosity promoted by the CEBs, the structure of Charismatic Catholicism religious life remained organized in terms that would have been familiar to Mainstream Catholics. The carismáticos still came together in groups that they described as a ch'utam or comunidad. They met regularly at times that echoed those of Mainstream Catholics. In Sa'xreb'e, for example, La Renovación met in the village chapel on Sunday mornings from eight to about ten o'clock and on Wednesday evenings from seven to nine o'clock. The Sunday morning timeslot mirrored the weekly Mass at the parish center, and weekday evenings at seven o'clock was when Mainstream Catholic CEBs typically held their Celebraciones de la Palabra. Like Mainstream Catholics, Charismatics preferred to meet in the village chapel[11] but would also use individual members' homes if needed. Most often it fell on one of the predicadores to offer up space in their home for such a meeting, similar to how a catequista's home could serve as a gathering place for a Mainstream Catholic CEB. Finally, as we will see in chapter 3, predicadores played an analogous role to that of catequistas, acting as both erstwhile community leaders and religious specialists tasked with performing key parts of their respective communities' (semi-)weekly religious services. In essence, then, Charismatic Catholicism introduced a parallel structure of religious praxis and authority that functionally displaced the equivalent social organizations, forms of leadership, and time commitments

---

11. Village chapels were more often than not under the care of the local catequista. In the case that two groups wanted to use the chapel at the same time, it was Charismatics, rather than their Mainstream brethren, who would have to make alternative arrangements. Likewise, if a chapel's caretaker wanted to prevent the carismáticos from using the chapel, all he had to do was arrange to not be at home when La Renovación's representatives came looking for the key to the building.

that Mainstream Catholicism entailed. As the San Ignacio letter that I discussed in the introduction shows, Mainstream Catholic lay leaders understood La Renovación's growth as coming at the expense of their own CEBs' numbers, and thus framed the new movement's success as a direct challenge to their own position within the religious hierarchy of their communities. The tensions between the congregations were thus a result of the way that Charismatic Catholicism presented an alternative model for being Catholic in these communities.

The santos who come to pay their respects to Santo Domingo on August 3 are an eclectic bunch. Some are tall and others are short, some male and others are female, some have light eyes and others dark, some have flowing locks, and the hair of others is molded closely to their head, some are dressed in velvet finery and wear triumphant silver crowns while others are dressed simply, and some are nearly naked. Each santo visually tells a different story of what it means to lead an exemplary and pious Christian life. For some,

FIGURE 3   Santos in a procession

like poor San Bartolo, who stands hunched over, holding his own flayed skin draped over his arms, it is a story borne of pain and persecution. For others, like San Calixto Papa, who is dressed in brocade, wears a tiara, and holds the papal *ferula* (i.e., staff of office) in his left hand, it is a story about ambition and cultivating a place for oneself in an imperial institution. For others like Santa Catalina, who holds a rapier with one hand and a martyr's palm with the other, it is a story of violent conflicts that produce both victors and victims. And for still others, like La Virgen de Candelaria, it is a story of care for God leading to spiritual illumination as symbolized by the infant Jesus she carries on one arm and the candle she holds in her other hand. This is to say that the santos visually represent the myriad ways that Catholicism can be lived. Taken singly in their own chapels and through the attentions that each is given by its cofradía, each santo has something to teach us, but when they come together in the parque central's public sphere, and especially when we take note of how they interact with each other, we can better see the rich texture of religious life in Cobán.

This chapter's peregrination through Cobán introduced the larger social world in which Mainstream and Charismatic Catholics clashed over what it meant to them to be Catholic. The next chapter examines in more detail the historical development and ideological underpinnings of their voicings of Catholicism in the context of both global and local developments of the religion.

CHAPTER 2

Contested Catholicisms
Social Movements and Catholic Theologies in Parish Life

About five meters from the church courtyard at San Felipe, amongst the pine trees and not very far from some of the old graves that partially encircle the church, there is a stone ring where *aj iloneleb'* (ones who see) or *sacerdotes Mayas* (Maya priests) perform *mayejak* (offering) ceremonies. The ground between the stones looks almost like obsidian; it is dark and glossy thanks to residue left by innumerable candles and balls of fragrant *copal pom* that have been burned there as offerings to the spirit world. Sugar and cane rum are also poured in the circle when the aj ilonel says his prayers over people who have contracted him to help them with some problem or secure good fortune in a new project (e.g., the building of a house, starting of a business, or a child going off to study in the capital city).

One morning, Qawa' Luis[1] and I were sitting on one of the low walls on the opposite side of the courtyard as one of the ceremonies was happening. He pointed toward the place with his chin and asked, "What do you think of all that?" As any novice anthropologist would, I launched into a boilerplate answer about how it was good that Maya traditions were still practiced because it meant that the culture was very much alive. Knowing that Qawa' Luis was a very dedicated catequista who had devoted years of his life to

---

1. Qawa' is a Q'eqchi' honorific that roughly translates to "señor" or "mister." The equivalent term for women is Qana'. In Q'eqchi' one refers to adults by using the honorific plus their first name, as in Qawa' Luis and Qana' Esperanza. I use this formula to refer to my Mainstream Catholic interlocutors in deference to their standing in the community and how they would have addressed each other.

service in the parish and was one of the handful of people who Padre Agustino depended on to help keep the parish running, I added that, "God must have something to do with those ceremonies, right?"

Qawa' Luis nodded in what seemed like agreement to my statement and looked up from under the brim of his gray trilby hat. "Some years ago," he began, "someone did something bad to me." Back then, he said, life was going very well. He had had good luck planting potatoes and broccoli and managed to save up some money to buy a calf to raise. The calf had grown big, and he had been able to sell it for a good price, so he continued to practice small-scale husbandry buying one animal at a time, raising it, and selling it for slaughter. The profits from the cows, his crops, and the small store that his wife ran from their home accumulated. Qawa' Luis eventually had enough money to buy a used car—a rare mark of financial success in his village. Like all the other parishioners I knew with cars, the vehicle was not primarily intended for personal transportation but was instead another source of income. Qawa' Luis used it as a taxi, driving people and their cargos between Sa'xreb'e and Cobán and occasionally elsewhere in the Verapaz region.

This was all to say that at the time Qawa' Luis was doing quite well financially. But then things took a very bad turn. First, the car broke down and the repairs were prohibitively expensive. Money to fix the car might have come from the sale of a full-grown cow, but his one calf became sickly, withered away, and died. Insects infested part of his potato crop, causing him to lose half of it (luckily, the broccoli and, more importantly, his corn were spared). As if that had not been enough, he himself got sick and had to spend almost a month in near-bedridden recovery. As a result, Qawa' Luis had to sell the broken-down taxi at a loss to make up for some of the revenue lost from his other unsuccessful enterprises that year.

One might be tempted to interpret this rash of misfortunes as the play of a capricious wager made between a divine master and his adversary over the faithfulness of the former's servant, but that was not Luis's framing of why this all had happened to him (though one could imagine, too, that the thought might well have crossed his mind.) Instead, he interpreted that series of unfortunate events, in part, in terms of the material realities and precarities that befall people as part of life—people and animals get sick, car parts wear down as rough roads take their toll on them, and while a judicious use of pesticides can help ensure that crops make it to market, even the expensive ones sometimes fail—and, in part, in terms of supernatural causes. Qawa' Luis saw a medical doctor to cure his illness, but he also consulted with an aj ilonel about it and his other concurrent misfortunes. What the latter specialist could tell him that the former could not, was the root cause of it all—namely, the envy that someone felt toward him. That envious other, who was probably a neighbor, had cast the evil eye and perhaps done more to harm Qawa' Luis. This was clear from the fact that all of these misfortunes seemed to pile on so quickly, one after the other. The medical doctor had prescribed medicines and rest, and these had worked to heal Qawa' Luis physically, but the aj ilonel also counseled that he should perform a mayejak ceremony to call forth blessings and get rid of the evil influence on his life. Qawa' Luis agreed, and since then, *gracias a Dios*, things had been better. His crops were doing well again and, though he hadn't gone back to raising calves or been able to buy another taxi, his store was doing well. In fact, he had recently purchased and installed a large oven so that his family could bake bread to sell. Moreover, his children were all flourishing. Within six months of our conversation, Qawa' Luis also officially became a member of the parish's first cohort of extraordinary ministers of communion and a grandfather, too. God's blessings were accruing in his life again, and it had been in part due to the *aj ilonel's* successful intervention against an envious neighbor.

When a party came with an aj ilonel to perform a mayejak, they first entered the church to offer some prayers to the santos inside. They did so once again before heading back down the hill to go home. As Qawa' Luis's story suggests, there was no apparent contradiction for many Q'eqchi'-Maya—even for highly devoted Mainstream Catholic lay leaders—between faithfulness in Catholicism and the belief in and practice of Maya religiosity. Yet, this was not simply a case where the two religions, or even the two interpretative frameworks of Catholic Christianity and Q'eqchi'-Maya spirituality, sat side by side or even came together into what anthropologists sometimes call syncretism, creolization, or hybridization (Stewart 1999). Qawa' Luis's initial question to me belied the fact that not everyone in San Felipe saw the Maya and the Catholic logics as compatible, or at least not compatible in the same ways. Charismatic Catholics tended to view the aj iloneleb' with suspicion, seeing them as more likely to cause harm than offer protections against it. Not every Mainstream Catholic was as sanguine about those religious specialists, either—some sought them out to help solve problems, but many also preferred to ignore them, and others wanted to actively discourage them from doing their works on church grounds. For example, Qana' Esperanza, who was a few years younger than Qawa' Luis, but otherwise his peer in terms of involvement in the parish, tended to steer clear of the aj iloneleb'.

She said that the mayejaks done there during the day were usually fine, but the problem was that some of the same people came back at night to do bad things. You never knew with those people, according to her, because they could just as easily do you harm as good and all they wanted was your money anyway. It was better to trust in God with your prayers even if it meant that your problems wouldn't be so quickly resolved. Qawa' Hugo, on the other hand, wanted to see the parish do more to welcome the aj iloneleb'. He saw them as guardians of his ancestors' sacred knowledge about God and the cosmos. For him, what they could reveal about how to live a pious life was as valid as what the Bible said, and he wanted to see them more fully integrated before that sacred knowledge was lost.

Although the Catholic Church in Alta Verapaz had adopted and adapted the mayejak and a few other elements of Maya religion as legitimate expressions of local "inculturated" Catholicism (see below), they stopped short of making a wholesale endorsement of Maya religiosity. A small but telling detail that illustrates this lies in the fact that the space for mayejaks has progressively moved farther away from the front of San Felipe's church. I remember seeing some of these ceremonies held in a corner of the church patio in direct sight of the church door when I visited San Felipe in the 1980s and 1990s. During my fieldwork in the mid-2000s, a small patch of the patio retained the telltale signs of the fires, but the ceremonies had been moved off the pavers and onto the dirt of the churchyard. When I returned in the 2010s, the site had moved yet again into the woods amid old grave sites and farther away from the church doors.

Understanding how the Catholic Church has negotiated the place of Maya spirituality within its institutional structure is critical to understanding how it was that someone like Qawa' Luis made sense of his identity as a Q'eqchi'-Maya Catholic since it allows us to see how and through what conceptual frames "Mayaness" (or perhaps indigeneity more broadly) is allowed to be expressed within Catholic Christianity. Tracing the way that the institutional Catholic Church has shifted its approach to evangelizing Maya people helps us to explore another aspect of Catholicism's heteroglossia—namely, the extent to which its doctrines and policies themselves evidence the dialogic tensions of disparate subject positions within the larger whole. This chapter explores some of the internal dynamics of Catholicism and Maya identity in Guatemala that created the context in which San Felipe's Mainstream and Charismatic Catholic parishioners took up the question of how to be Catholic and indigenous. Rather than being a comprehensive account of how multiple voicings of Catholicism have been practiced in the parish, however, this chapter should be understood as an exploration of the variegated ways that the discursive fields of the Catholic and the Maya have been articulated since the twentieth century, illustrating how the Roman Catholic Church itself prompts and facilitates heteroglossia.

Mayas and the Politics of Belonging in Guatemala

Mayas have lived under conditions of internal colonialism since the sixteenth century. This has not always meant the same thing or always had the same results in all places and times, but generally it has meant that Maya people, despite comprising at least 40 percent of the country's population (Instituto Nacional de Estadística de Guatemala 2002), have been socially marginalized and excluded from major centers of political and cultural influence (though, to be sure, exceptions can be found). The social and political repression of Mayas was arguably at its worst during the Guatemalan Civil War of 1960–96, reaching its apogee from the late 1970s through the 1980s when the conflict was primarily centered in Guatemala's highlands (See Carmack 1988; REMHI 1998). Almost paradoxically, though, it was during this period of state repression targeting indigenous people that a new articulation of Maya cultural identity emerged.

The rise of the pan-Maya movement (PMM, also known as the *Movimiento Maya*, Maya movement, or Maya cultural revitalization movement) changed the face of cultural politics in Guatemala in the 1980s. Taking shape as a diffuse network of activists and organizations, the PMM sought to gain state recognition of cultural rights for Guatemala's Maya population in the wake of state violence. Since the 1990s scholars have been keen to understand this unprecedented form of political mobilization and the new articulations of ethnic identity it implies (e.g., Fischer and Brown 1996; Bastos and Camus 2003), and there is a robust literature examining the implications of pan-Mayanism for electoral politics (Warren 2002), educational policy (England 2003; Maxwell 1996; Garzon et al. 1998), and cultural revitalization more generally (Wilson 1995; Warren 1998; Montejo 2005; Konefal 2010). Less often examined, though, have been the ways in which these new articulations of Mayan identity have taken root in institutions less directly linked to the state.

During roughly the same period in which the ideological foundations of pan-Mayanism coalesced and early forms of Maya cultural mobilization started to make an impact in Guatemala, the Catholic Church began implementing a series of ideological and organizational reforms that would change the ways that its pastoral agents conceptualized their role in relation to the laity. Driving these changes were discussions about how the Catholic community should be configured and what role the Church should play in "this world" to facilitate movement into the "next world" of Christianity's afterlife. Far from being simply organizational questions, these concerns were driven by new evaluations of the religious subject, salvation history, and the responsibility that the clergy had to the laity. The effect of these reforms was especially salient in Latin America.

As C. Matthew Samson has pointed out, while "religion seems to play a supporting role in Maya activism and Maya nationalism . . . [it] is largely absent from the discussion" of pan-Mayanism as a social movement (Samson 2007, 49; see also LeBaron 1993). There are two reasons for this absence. First, pan-Mayanism is largely predicated on the ideal of rescuing and reinvigorating a pre-invasion version of Maya culture in the modern world, and Christianity was most certainly not a part of pre-invasion Maya life. Thus, when religion is activated as a part of the broader pan-Mayan discourse, it is usually in the guise of "traditional" Maya religion, figured as relatively "pure" autochthonous practices that distinguish Mayas from Ladinos. For example, pan-Mayanist literature often lists ensuring that Maya priests have free and open access to ancestral religious sites (which would include state-run archaeological parks of classical and postclassical Maya ceremonial centers) as an important cultural right (e.g., Cojtí Cuxil 1994, 1996). Likewise, events sponsored by pan-Mayan organizations or others sympathetic to their goals commonly open with a traditionalist Maya ritual, so that development project inaugurations and Maya studies academic conferences often begin with a sacerdote Maya calling upon the ancestors and *Nahuales* (the spirits governing the Maya calendrical system) to watch over the event and ensure its success. The elevation of these forms of religion as an emblem of "real" Mayan identity of course belies the fact that Christianity plays an important role in the quotidian lives of many Mayas.

Second, part of the success of the pan-Maya movement "lies in the fact that its ideology appeals to individuals across religious boundaries," (Fischer 2001, 101) and dwelling too much on religion thus "presents the greatest threat to Maya unity [by] highlighting ideological differences with the weight of religious fervor" (189). As an organizational principle, then, activists have tended to suppress the importance of religion in the development of a pan-Mayan identity as a way of eliding the conflicts between (and among) Maya

Catholics, Protestants, and proponents of pre-Colombian Maya religion (not to mention Mormons, Jehovah's Witnesses, and others). Thus, the significant role played by Christian ideologies and organizations (especially Catholic ones) in shaping the basis of the PMM has been downplayed from within the movement itself.

Nonetheless, the historical and ethnographic record makes it clear that Christianity has long had an important role in constituting Maya identity in Guatemala and has had an impact on the political lives of Maya at a number of levels. Writing in the mid-twentieth century, Eric Wolf described the cofradías as the key institutions that sustained Maya "closed corporate communities" by organizing social relations and mediating between local communities and the state (Wolf 1957). Several decades later, as political and economic changes were destabilizing these traditional communities and as anthropologists began critiquing the idea that there were such things as bounded, homogeneous Maya communities in the first place, scholars began documenting the important role that Catholic social programs played in creating less locally circumscribed visions of Maya ethnic identity (Warren 1978). Following on this observation, Richard Wilson suggested that it was precisely that shift away from local identification that facilitated Mayas seeing themselves as national citizens, and thus as political actors with stakes in the state (Wilson 1995). This is to say nothing of the strong influence that Protestant forms of Christianity had on Maya life beginning in the 1970s (Annis 1987; Garrard-Burnett 1998; Samson 2007).[2] Likewise,

---

2. Protestant churches have been active in Guatemala since the nineteenth century. In 1832 President Mariano Gálvez issued a decree that guaranteed freedom of religion and conscience as part of a larger project of modernization that invited Protestant missionaries to work in the country and functionally ended the Catholic Church's hegemonic status in the country (Garrard-Burnett 1998, 4). Although there were small pockets of converts to Protestantism in various places, it wasn't until the second half of the twentieth century that their churches saw much growth, especially among Mayas. The major earthquake that shook the country on February 4, 1976 seems to have been an important catalyst for the explosive growth of Protestantism in Guatemala, as it both created massive displacements of Maya people and offered an opportunity for foreign missionaries to offer aid and evangelism. (Annis 1987, 79; Garrard-Burnett 1998, 120–22; Stoll 1990, 12). The fact that around this time Catholic lay organizations came to be linked to "subversive elements" by the state also benefitted Protestant churches by making them a relatively alternative religious space. Since then, Protestantism has grown significantly so that shortly after my fieldwork, Guatemala could be characterized as Latin America's most Protestant country.

Virginia Garrard-Burnett has shown that the intersection of new articulations of Christianity—be they Protestant, Catholic, or Costumbrista—and pan-Mayanism have served to further the larger strategic goal of promoting Maya self-determination and autonomy (Garrard-Burnett 2004). Thus, new visions of ethnic identity, forms of social mobilization, and arrangements of religious belief and practice often overlap. This chapter builds on that work by examining how a certain subset of lay-centered visions of Catholicism, which have brought to the fore questions of the relationship between spirituality and social identity, have affected the lives of Maya Catholics by variously promoting valuations of what it means to be indigenous. Understanding those various articulations helps us better see how the practice of Catholicism among Mayas constitutes a dynamic field in which they are in dialogue not just with each other but also with larger national and transnational discourses about religion and culture, as well as the complicated ways that each of these positions might be in concert or conflict with each other.

Guatemalan Catholicism in the Twentieth Century

Although ethnic categories such as "indigenous," "Q'eqchi'," and "Maya" were important to San Felipe's parishioners' identities, being Catholic was central to their sense of self. The lay church leaders, who were my closest consultants, expended a great deal of energy and resources in being Catholic by, for example, spending much of their free time engaging in serious study of religious texts, attending workshops and seminars to further their religious education, and organizing community rituals. To understand what it meant for them to be Q'eqchi'-Mayas in postwar Guatemala, then, we also need to understand the religious foundations of their identities. My consultants' engagements with Christianity were shaped by the complex historical changes that occurred in Latin American Catholicism in the twentieth century. In the next sections I trace out four theological movements—Catholic Action, Liberation Theology, the Theology of Inculturation, and the Catholic Charismatic Renewal Movement—that fed into these regional articulations of Catholicism.

From Costumbre to Catholic Action

The Second Vatican Council led to major reforms in the practice of Roman Catholicism worldwide. However, as Daniel Levine has pointed out, a number of independent reform movements that started in local churches throughout Latin America arguably laid the groundwork for Vatican II's major rethinking of the laity's role in the Roman Catholic Church (Levine 1992). In the 1940s various dioceses and missionary orders in the region began setting up programs to encourage lay participation and, thus, Vatican II may be best understood not as a wholly new project, but rather as a confirmation of work that was already underway in myriad local churches. Along with the emphasis on lay participation came increased tolerance for organizational innovations that would help the programs achieve this goal.

Those developments would have likely seemed implausible at the start of the twentieth century—a time when the Catholic Church's status in Guatemalan society seemed particularly weak. In 1871, the liberal government of President Justo Rufino Barrios issued a series of decrees that severely curtailed the role of the Catholic Church in the country's public and political life.[3] Under these new laws the state seized many of the Catholic Church's assets, dissolved religious orders, nationalized the schools that those orders ran, and expelled foreign missionaries. Although successive governments were less anti-clerical than Barrios's, the Catholic Church was a relatively weak social institution from the late nineteenth through the early twentieth century. The Catholic Church's own records show that there were only eighty priests serving Guatemala's population of 2.3 million in 1926 (Hernández Sandoval 2018, 33). The state's presence and influence in many Maya communities had also been historically weak, though, and in many places the Church had assumed some of its functions organizing and managing society. Consequently, the effect of the Barrios government's anti-clerical policies was felt most acutely there. Isolated from the ideological apparatuses of both the Catholic Church and the state, these communities became largely autonomous Maya spaces. This isolation fostered the conditions under which Costumbre became the preeminent form of religion among Mayas.

Costumbre can be described as a creolized religion that combines elements of Catholic Christianity and a pre-Columbian Maya cosmology.[4] In

---

3. The previous president (José Rafael Carrera Turcios, who had claimed the right of office for life) had largely sought to keep the Catholic Church close and signed a concordant with the Holy See in 1852 (ratified in 1854), guaranteeing the government's patronage of the Church and guaranteeing "Rome the protection of its flock within the emerging nation" (Sullivan-González 1998, 114).

4. Allen J. Christenson offers an exemplary explication of this in his analysis of Holy Week rituals in Santiago Atitlán (Christenson 2016). John D. Early has written a nuanced and thoughtful account of how the ideational systems of Catholicism and Mayan religiosity have historically been integrated (Early 2006).

Costumbre, Catholic santos, who are often identified with regional earth spirits (like the Q'eqchi'-Maya *Tzuultaq'a*), are cared for and venerated by members of cofradías according to a ritual cycle that maps on to both the annual agricultural seasons and the Catholic liturgical calendar (Reina 1966; Gossen 1976; Watanabe 1992; Wilson 1995). The cofradía system, which had been imported from Europe in the colonial period as a means of organizing the religious life of the New World's Indigenous communities, became the core organizational feature of Costumbre,[5] and in many places went on to become an all-encompassing civil-religious hierarchy that governed many aspects of day-to-day life (Holleran 1949). If cofradías ostensibly existed for the veneration of saints' images, in practice they also wielded significant social and economic power, and effectively regulated the individual's integration in the community. Full participation in the cofradía's ritual life meant significant investment of material resources to pay for offerings to the santos—*pom* (an incense made of tree resin), candles, and turkey or chicken blood—as well as for the food, drink, and music necessary for the accompanying *fiesta*. This material commitment paid off in the form of social and moral standing, though; and so, as a man divested himself of material capital, he accrued symbolic and social capital in the form of religious authority and influence in civic matters (Bourdieu 1977). In this worldview, material poverty was transformed into a sign of piety, and not just an inevitable consequence of a small-scale agricultural mode of production or of Ladino exploitation of Maya labor (Annis 1987, 61). Being poor while participating in Costumbre could potentially be interpreted as a desirable trait that signaled a person's high standing in the community and the cosmos.

With few priests overseeing religious ceremonies in Guatemala in the latter half of the nineteenth century, the men who fully invested themselves and their resources in the cofradías became their communities' de facto religious and civic leaders, and these organizations came to take on a power all their own in Maya life. The catalyst for this situation to change lay in the Vatican's reassessment of its governance over local churches in the region.

---

5. In his study of Catholicism in the colonial period, Adriaan Van Oss says it is impossible to discern the exact moment when the cofradías were instituted, but that they were likely part of the process of *reducción* by which indigenous people were settled into towns as the colonial governments and churches were first instituted. This would place their origin in the early sixteenth century. Importantly, he also notes that from the beginning the pattern was that cofradías were segregated so that Ladinos and Mayas belonged to different groups (Van Oss 1986).

Beginning in the 1920s and 1930s, the office of the Holy See sought to reform national churches throughout Central America to a more "Romanized" vision of Catholicism, and it employed an increasing number of diplomats to mend church–state relationships in the wake of the previous five decades of anticlericalism. This project at once sought to emphasize the sacramental works of the church as a counter to local syncretic practices, and to place greater oversight on the country's secular clergy so that the latter did not once again inflame tensions between church and the state as they had in the nineteenth century. The Vatican's diplomats eventually secured the state's permission for foreign-born missionaries to come to Guatemala and carry out this mission of Romanization (Hernández Sandoval 2018, 33).

In the 1930s Archbishop Luis Durou y Sure—a French-born priest who had risen through the ranks of the Vincentinian Fathers and come to Guatemala in 1912—undertook a large-scale project of church reform that aligned with those Vatican interests. His primary concern was to establish a more sacrament-based practice of Catholicism that would counter what he deemed to be the religious ignorance and superstition that plagued the country, but he was also concerned with stemming the growing influences of Protestant missionaries and leftist political parties. This would not be an easy task, however, given the relative institutional weakness of the Catholic Church in Guatemala's rural areas. Durou instituted programs to recruit local people to help in catechizing their peers and promote sacramental Catholicism to circumvent the continuing shortage of clergy in the country (Hernández Sandoval 2018, 49).

Durou's successor—Guatemalan-born Archbishop Mariano Rosell y Arellano—embraced these projects during his tenure and further expanded the tactic of recruiting lay catechists to spread Catholicism. Among Rosell y Arellano's major accomplishments was the implementation of a program called *Acción Católica Rural* (or Rural Catholic Action) that grew out of various initiatives in what was then the Diocese of Verapaz y Petén. Acción Católica Rural sought to establish Catholic orthodoxy in Maya communities (Bendaña Perdomo 2011, 208; see also Warren 1978; Falla 2001), and its agents saw eroding the power of the cofradías as a prerequisite to laying the groundwork for establishing its own structures of spiritual and moral authority. It was clear that this task could not possibly be carried out by the few Guatemalan priests remaining in the country, most of whom lived in relative comfort in the cities and few of whom had a taste for the kind of work this project would entail. Foreign missionaries who were more disposed to working in rural areas would need to be recruited,[6] as would lay people who could act as liaisons between the clergy and local communities. These laypeople would be trained in the more orthodox version of Catholicism and serve as proxies for the clergy in their own home communities, and their task would largely be to promote a more universalistic or cosmopolitan vision of the faith that emphasized the sacraments administered by clergy over the cycle of *cargos* and *fiestas* that sustained the geographically circumscribed cofradías' influence.

Beyond these religious goals, Acción Católica Rural also sought to keep Mayas away from leftist political organizations that were beginning to have an influence in the region in the wake of the Mexican Revolution, as well as from Protestant missionaries who had successfully filled the niche that Catholic clergy had left empty in the wake of the nineteenth-century Liberal reforms discussed earlier.[7] Economic and social development projects were packaged with religious orthodoxy as a means of counteracting these "outside" influences. On the one hand, Catholic Action's efforts to ameliorate poverty were largely paternalistic in nature—predicated on maintaining the country's social hierarchies—and politically conservative. On the other hand, Catholic Action's efforts to undercut Maya people's reliance on the cofradía system's redistributive economy, also led its agents to support certain progressive political and economic reforms. Catholic Action's missionaries advocated for increasing Maya children's access to education, legally ensuring that employers would pay workers' wages in national currency (rather than in proprietary script, as was the case on many plantations), and in some communities helped Maya *campesinos* purchase land and secure legal titles to their property. Additionally, Acción Católica instituted adult health and literacy programs, and helped introduce modern agricultural technology such as chemical fertilizers and pesticides to help increase farmers' yields.

Acción Católica's ideology asserted the principle that "spiritual membership in the universalistic Catholic Church should supersede ethnic identities;

---

6. Members of the Catholic Foreign Mission Society of America, or Maryknoll, eventually became the backbone of this program beginning in 1943 (Hernández Sandoval 2018, 73).

7. Several governments in Latin America had seen mainline Protestant churches as allies in developing a modern nation and in displacing the Catholic Church's political influence and had thus allowed them to set up missions in both urban and rural areas (Garrard-Burnett 1998). Presbyterians seem to have been particularly successful in ministering to Maya populations.

[singled] out local Ladinos as the major stumbling block for the actualization of economic equivalence for all individuals; and [proposed] ladinoization as a means to achieving social and economic equivalence of Indians and Ladinos in broader society" (Warren 1978, 94). It was thus a fundamentally assimilationist project that sought to subsume Mayas into larger, putatively "universal" and, hence, "neutral" social and soteriological orders, even as it also sought to redress economic inequalities. It also reinforced the idea that the fundamental part of Maya identity was peasant-class status. Thus, "ladinoization" in this context was framed largely in terms of improving material conditions and breaking up traditionalist social structures and modes of production. To do so, the argument went, one had to dismantle the cofradías and thus "free" people from the economic obligations they entailed.[8] Nonetheless, even if a process of ladinoization was part of Catholic Action's project, it was not one that all Mayas wanted or took part in, nor was it something that ended up being practicable in the face of the deeply entrenched structures of racial discrimination and social inequality. Ladinos tended to resist Mayas' attempts to establish more equitable social relations with them despite the discourse of universal Catholicity; and many Mayas resisted the idea that doing away with markers of ethnocultural identity was beneficial in any way. Moreover, Acción Católica's converts' insistence on sacramental orthodoxy and their emphasis on a universalized spirituality clashed with the Costumbristas' well-established practices in which one's spiritual standing depended on making material commitments to veneration of localized santos. Thus, Catholic Action's and Costumbre's framings of how to participate in religious life were generally interpreted and experienced as in direct opposition to each other, and this often led to intra-community conflicts between the new "converts" and the cofradías (see Falla 2001; Murga Armas 2006).

These conflicts within Maya communities tended to be generational ones, since younger Mayas were often chosen to be catechists rather than the older, well-established men who led the cofradías. These young catequistas also made up the pool of candidates from which promoters for education, health, and agricultural projects were selected, which gave these relatively young men and women access to religious influence, material benefits, and

---

8. The conflation of class and indigenous identity has been well documented within the anthropology of Latin America. For example, Judith Friedlander describes how the term "Indian" came to in essence mean the opposite of "modern" and "Mexican mestizo" identity, and became as much a class marker as anything else in Hueyapan, Mexico (Friedlander 2007).

social status usually reserved for people much older than them. Catholic Action thus both intentionally and unintentionally fostered a dual structure of religious authority in the community that effectively eroded the power of the civil-religious gerontocratic hierarchy that had been the guarantor of community solidarity before the mid-twentieth century (Calder 2004). Wherever Catholic Action was active, a new class of educated, socially conscious Maya came to assume leadership over the local church. However, they largely still found themselves categorized as *indios*, and continued to face discrimination from Ladinos and foreigners. An unexpected upshot of this was that in coming into contact with their peers from other *municipios* who had had similar experiences of both conscientization through the Catholic Action and social marginalization through quotidian life, some of these young catechists began to see the possibility of a less geographically circumscribed, but still Maya (pan-Maya, we might say) vision of Catholicism (Wilson 1995; Warren 1998).

The subtext of "development" in Catholic Action also marked an important shift in the way that material poverty was treated in Maya communities. As noted earlier, cofradías leveled wealth by funneling resources into *fiestas*, and thus turned material poverty into a symbol of good moral standing. Action Catholicism, on the other hand, unequivocally framed poverty as a problem that needed to be solved, since it did nothing but create dependency. Converts to Acción Católica criticized the cofradías' fiestas as a waste of scarce resources, and ultimately as an obstacle to people's full spiritual development.[9] Thus, though material poverty remained a feature of everyday life in Maya communities, it no longer conferred any symbolic capital to the person.

Although its architects initially framed Catholic Action as a counter to progressive politics, many of its social programs' practical ends overlapped with the Revolutionary State's (1945–54) agenda for modernization, such as promoting education and development as panaceas to the "backwardness" of life in rural Maya communities. Thus, despite political differences, the state allowed clergy to work in rural areas more than they had in previous decades. Likewise, the concern with modernizing agricultural production, and the fact that a socially conservative orthodox religion was part and parcel of the

---

9. A similar ideological shift was simultaneously occurring among Maya who converted to evangélico Christianity (Annis 1987).

program, made Catholic Action's continued work palatable to the right-wing military governments that ruled after Guatemala's "Ten Years of Spring."

Following Carlos Castillo Armas's CIA-backed overthrow of the Revolutionary State in 1954, the Catholic Church's position was strengthened as more foreign missionaries were allowed to work in the country. North American Maryknoll Missionaries were at the vanguard of this project, promising a "second evangelization" of Mayas, and spread out around the country to train catechists and establish the infrastructure of development programs (Calder 2004; Hernández Sandoval 2018). However, even as the Catholic Church promoted a conservative political program, the Maryknoll missionaries (and others like them) found that what they had learned through their theological training in North America and Europe did not correspond to the social realities they were facing in Latin America, especially in rural indigenous communities. In the face of extreme poverty and massive social inequalities, missionaries began to question their project and the assumptions on which it was founded and started to develop new ideas about the role of the Catholic Church in lay people's lives. This crisis of conscience in turn led them to alter their focus and implement Catholic Action's programs with increased emphasis on addressing material conditions (Early 2012).

By placing the clergy in closer contact with the laity throughout Latin America, the Catholic Church (at least discursively) changed its relationship to poor and indigenous people from being one of paternalism to one of *acompañamiento* (accompaniment), which in this context meant, "the pastoral practice of being with those who were suffering from adversity, thus demonstrating concern and solidarity and providing human support" (Calder 2004, 124 n.67). In principle, if not always in practice, the clergy would now be sensitive to the social and cultural differences they found in the mission field and facilitate (rather than direct or dictate) indigenous people's encounter with God (Cleary and Steigenga 2004; Early 2012).

A Preferential Option for the Poor: The Theology of Liberation

Liberation Theology has been described as an authentically Latin American response to the theological challenges set forth by Vatican II (Levine 1992). Though its origins were rooted in missionary encounters like those described earlier, it also drew inspiration from the political theology that had emerged in Europe following World War II. Whereas Catholic political theology had previously been concerned with justifying the power of states, and thus legitimizing the *status quo*, post–World War II theologians began to posit that faith should be used as an instrument of social critique and public engagement, and that it was incumbent on the Catholic Church to seek to improve material and political conditions wherever it could (Assmann 1976). The priests who would go on to write Liberation Theology's key texts and put its ideals into practice expanded on these principles with specific reference to the social, economic, and political conditions of Latin America during the Cold War.

While individual missionary encounters with marginalized populations set the stage for its development (Berryman 1994), the second general meeting of the Episcopal Conference of Latin America (CELAM, *Consejo Episcopal Latinoamericano*) held in Medellín, Colombia, in 1968, was more so than any other the proximate foundational event of Liberation Theology.[10] The Medellín conference was notable for the Church's adoption of the "preferential option for the poor," which proposed that the Catholic Church had to show compassion for and look after the material and spiritual well-being of its members. This was justified by the idea that the social reality of Latin America was marked by two evils—"external dominance" and "internal colonialism"—which made it impossible to lead a good life, and thus made salvation difficult to achieve (Cleary 1985). CELAM held that the Catholic Church could no longer tolerate the misery of its faithful in the here and now, and instead had to take an active role in helping them improve their material conditions, which would in turn help believers practice their faith with full human dignity. In this way salvation came to be intimately tied to a social project.

In the most well-known exposition of this perspective—*Teología de la liberación (A Theology of Liberation)*—the Peruvian theologian and Dominican priest Gustavo Gutiérrez argued that theology needed to be a "critical reflection on Christian praxis" that could accommodate the Vatican II call for the Catholic Church to be responsive to the "signs of the times" (Gutiérrez 1988, 11). Whereas earlier theologians made a distinction between the trajectories of secular and sacred history that would unite only after the establishment of a Kingdom of God, in Gutiérrez's reading of scripture this world and the next are intimately intertwined in a single movement of sal-

---

10. CELAM had first convened in 1955 in Rio de Janeiro, Brazil to try to organize the various dioceses and establish some basis for a unified institutional identity for the region.

vation history. In his view, sociohistorical conditions make sin materially manifest in the world, and so the Catholic Church's eschatological trajectory must be understood not simply as a spiritual one, but as a social and historical one as well. Furthermore, he framed sin as a form of alienation since it is a "break with God ... a breach of the communion of persons with each other, it is a turning in of individuals on themselves which manifests itself in a multifaceted withdrawal from others ... [and is thus] an obstacle to life's reaching the fullness we call salvation" (Gutiérrez 1988, 85). Economic oppression constitutes a form of sin precisely because it alienates people from each other and from God, and so strips away their social and spiritual agency. Gutiérrez concludes that for salvation to take place, people must be liberated spiritually, psychologically, and politically in this world and that it is thus incumbent on the faithful to work toward social justice since this is a tangible means of fulfilling the promise of salvation.

In practice, Liberation Theology expanded the role of the laity through the widespread adoption of the *comunidad eclesial de base* (CEB) as a concrete institution through which clergy could accompany them in the process of liberation. This organizational model had first been seen in urban Brazil as a means to promote Bible study and was widely adopted following CELAM's Medellín conference as a means of promoting lay engagement. Though CEBs became features of Catholicism throughout the region, the way they took shape and the purposes to which they were put were highly variable (Levine 1992, 45). For example, CEBs in peripheral urban neighborhoods in Brazil focused on Bible study as a platform through which to engage parishioners in political mobilization, albeit not always successfully (Burdick 1993). However, in rural Guatemala, high levels of illiteracy made it difficult for every individual to actively engage in Bible study directly, and instead, CEBs came together as groups to celebrate the liturgy of the Word under the guidance of Acción Católica–trained catechists.

Not surprisingly, this socially and politically engaged form of Catholicism with its attendant critique of dominant structures of power drew criticism from both secular society and sectors of the Catholic Church itself. Pope Paul VI, for example, issued an encyclical in 1975 that cautioned Latin American bishops against allowing their CEBs to become too politicized and the curia generally viewed Liberationists with a degree of suspicion conditioned by European perspectives on Soviet socialism. The arguments presented in Cardinal Joseph Ratzinger's (later Pope Benedict XVI) "Instruction on Certain Aspects of 'Theology of Liberation'" are illustrative of the theological arguments against Liberationist Catholicism (Ratzinger 1984; see also Segundo 1985). Ratzinger argued that Liberationists had neglected the basic Christian doctrine that the locus of salvation is the individual soul and had thus made the mistake of privileging social identity over personal morality. He rejected the idea that systems of economic oppression produced a form of sin and criticized Gutiérrez for erroneously conflating "the 'poor' of scripture and the 'proletariat' of Marx" and uncritically adopting Marxist social theory despite its inherent atheism (IX§10). Ratzinger concluded that in so strongly advocating for the Church to adopt a worldly mission that prioritized building strong horizontal relationships between human beings, liberation theologians risked ignoring the most fundamental task of the Catholic Church's work in the world—fostering communion between humanity and God.

By the time that CELAM held its 1979 meeting in Puebla, Mexico, a conservative wing had coalesced that sought to scale back the extent to which Liberationist Catholicism would be the face of the Catholic Church in Latin America. Part of this shift was due to the Vatican's more conservative social outlook and growing concerns about Liberation Theology's application, and certainly part was the resistance that the movement had met from political elites in the region. Pope John Paul II explicitly expressed his objection to the image of Jesus as a political revolutionary and thus prompted CELAM to curtail discourse of revolution that it had heretofore promoted (Norget 2004). While Puebla's final documents upheld the "preferential option for the poor," these texts were clear to spell out that this was not the Church's only mission and added an option for youth, action among elites, and a broader concern for human rights to its agenda (Bendaña Perdomo 2001, 138). Puebla was also notable for introducing the idea that culture rather than class interest could form the focal point for missionary work, which also diminished the overriding emphasis on social justice as a constitutive part of salvation. Finally, CELAM affirmed the idea that the institutional Church hierarchy had a vested interest in and needed to oversee the actions of the CEBs to ensure that their actions were kept close to the doctrinal principles that the Roman Catholic Church upheld and did not become vehicles for something else.

In Guatemala, Liberation Theology's discourse put it in direct conflict with the state's increasingly reactionary stance against any form of sociopolitical organizing that might have or adopt socialist leanings. Catechists and priests, in their role as community organizers and potential critics of the status quo, became suspected agents of the guerrilla and were placed under surveillance by the military and in many cases became the direct targets of violence (Berryman 1984). In the context of Guatemala's Civil War, Liberationist Catholicism became dangerous to adhere to in principle, and more so to put into practice as the eventual assassinations of Bishop Juan José Gerardi Conedera and over a dozen priests and nuns, not to mention the murder and disappearance of numerous lay people, between the 1960s and 1990s would attest to. The Theology of Inculturation attempted to offer a socially engaged form of pastoral work and evangelization that would not be read as a political threat to the state.

A Preferential Option for Culture: The Theology of Inculturation

The Theology of Inculturation grew out of some of the concerns of Liberation Theology, though it diverged from that tradition by shifting focus from "class" to "culture" in the Church's pastoral work. As Andrew Orta has noted, this theological turn historically mirrored "similar shifts in global politics away from class-based movements and towards identity or ethnic politics" under the broader rubric of multiculturalism (Orta 2004, ix; see also Althoff 2014).

CELAM's Medellín documents had partially set the stage for a Latin American Inculturation in that they referenced the "Latinamericanization" of Catholic practices, and thus highlighted the importance of adapting the Catholic Church's rites to the region's sociocultural realities (Cleary 1985). The Puebla meeting's documents, likewise, did not make culture their central issue but nonetheless proposed that local churches could tailor their evangelization strategies to specific cultural groups as a way of making their missions more effective. Thus, by the time CELAM held its fourth general meeting in Santo Domingo, Dominican Republic, to coincide with the quincentenary of Columbus's arrival in the Americas, it had already critiqued the idea that there was or ought to be a singular universal culture (whether secular or Christian). In Santo Domingo's closing documents, the bishops proposed that the Church's agents should make an inculturated evangelization that respects and valorizes cultural differences central to its mission.

Inculturation sought to make Catholicism anew in each population through a "process of insertion/incarnation of the Gospel in the heart of [all] peoples and culture" (Comisión Nacional de Pastoral Indígena 2003,

5). A touchstone of the Theology of Inculturation was the principle of *logos spermatikos*, which had originally been formulated in the second century as a means of forging continuity between Greek and Christian thought. This theological principle holds that "the seeds of the Word [are] already present in ancient philosophy, subsequently disseminating to refer to all cultures and to a worldwide religious process" (Velho 2007, 277–78). The incarnation of Christ was metaphorically extended here in that as God became particular through Jesus—by being an individual member of a distinct Jewish culture—so should the universal (i.e., Catholic) Church seek to become particular in each community. Inculturationists proposed that missionaries should not seek to convert indigenous people, but rather to accompany and aid them in uncovering the fundamental underlying Christian truth of their culture. As Chilean theologian Diego Irarrázaval put it, "Inculturation is ... not about winning over followers but about giving multicultured [sic] witness to the God who saves humankind" (2000, 9).

Theoretically, the agents of Inculturation would be the "natural leaders" of the communities, and the clergy's job was to "motivate" and "accompany" them in the process (Centro Ak' Kutan 1994). In part, this followed from the Action and Liberationist versions of Catholicism's emphasis on lay participation and leadership; however, Inculturationists diverged from those earlier models by arguing that a community's already established, traditional leadership (including, for example, *cofrades* and potentially the aj iloneleb') should be at the forefront of the process of inculturated evangelization, not a wholly new class of specially trained catechists.

At its core, Inculturation was a rethinking of what it meant to have a "universal" church. Instead of assimilating cultural differences into a putatively neutral universality, Inculturation proposed that it was precisely by highlighting the particularities of local churches that a universal church could be actualized. Culture, understood as what makes a people authentically themselves, was a necessary mediating force for the development of spiritual life and salvation itself. If the aim nonetheless remained one of saving individual souls, the means for salvation would be tailored to the collectively experienced culture of those souls. The relationship of the group to salvation was thus a slightly different one than that proposed by Liberation Theology, for which salvation as a historical reality played out through a narrative of class struggle. Inculturation, on the other hand, built its model of salvation around a narrative of multiculturalism, proposing that there were myriad ways in which the process of salvation could be figured, each according to the partial seeds of truth that exist within the world's many cultures. If the two shared an ideal of uniting this-worldly and salvationist histories, they differed in the way that this conjuncture is meant to come about.

Given the vagaries that the idea of "culture" has had in Western discourse,[11] it is perhaps not surprising that precisely what constitutes "in-culturation" in this theology has also been debated. In its most limited form, it seemed to present a generalized idea for the continued development of participation in the Catholic Church by subaltern groups, who were to be granted greater autonomy to shape the aesthetics involved in practicing the Roman Rite. This might include not just the use of vernacular languages, but also the use of local forms of music and dance in Mass, or even the use of traditional sacred foods in the Eucharist (substituting, for example, cacao and tortillas for wine and bread). More radical forms of Inculturation, however, went on to question some of the deeper elements of the Roman Rite. For example, in one publication the Dominican friars of the Ak' Kutan center in the Diocese of Verapaz asks, "Why is celibacy demanded as a condition for receiving the priestly order in these cultures where God himself is expressed as Father-Mother, and where community religious services must be performed, necessarily, by a human couple?" and "How can we incorporate in our pastoral work the importance that Holy Mother Earth represents for Maya?"(Centro Ak' Kutan 1994, 185–86) These questions haven't been resolved, and the Diocese of Verapaz has not radically altered its rituals to respond to the answers they imply, but the fact that they were asked in a public document produced from within the Catholic Church suggests that some very serious critical reflection has taken place. That document once again illustrates the dialogism of Catholicism and alerts us to the fact that, more so than an institution, what is produced here is a discursive field for arguing the meanings of the religion.

By the time Qawa' Luis and I had our conversation about the aj ilonel's rituals, much of this history of changes in Catholic theology and practice had played out, but more importantly, they had played out as concrete changes in the way that he, his siblings, parents, and grandparents had interacted with the Catholic Church in Cobán. Luis had been a catequista for over a decade and a half at that point and had recently been part of the parish's first cohort of ministers who could give communion. He had received training in

---

11. See, for example, Kroeber and Kluckhon (1952) and Kuper (1999).

the catechism early on from a North American nun who had come to work in Sa'xreb'e in the 1960s. He was now a proponent of Inculturationist ideas but had also once favored Liberationist ones (though he was cautious about sharing that fact). His father, Qawa' Emanuel, had been his village's first catequista and part of Catholic Action, which undoubtedly had set him at odds with the elders of that time; he also now participated in several cofradías and was one of the most vocal proponents of the need to preserve the community's Costumbres. Qawa' Luis attended cofradía festivities, but he was very careful not to be seen consuming alcohol there, since that might be seen as bad behavior for someone in his position in the parish's lay hierarchy. His two brothers each had very different relations to those events. One brother was an enthusiastic participant in the veneration of santos and fully involved in the cofradía's cargo system, but he rarely attended Mass ostensibly due to work commitments that kept him busy on weekends. The other brother was a very devout and active catequista who would help the priest officiate Mass in honor of the santos but would then immediately leave and refused to have anything else to do with the cofradías. Their family alone exemplified the overlapping and complex ways that Costumbre, Action Catholicism, Liberation Theology, and the Theology of Inculturation had shaped Catholic practice in San Felipe. Nonetheless, despite their differences, they all found common cause in opposing La Renovación's growing influence in their village.

A Preferential Option for the Spirit:[12] *The Catholic Charismatic Renewal*

Unlike Catholic Action or the theologies of Liberation and Inculturation, whose geneses lay in the clergy's reflection on the spiritual and social conditions they found in Latin America, the Catholic Charismatic Renewal movement (CCR) was, at its inception, a lay-led movement. The most common telling of its origins begins in a series of ecumenical prayer meetings held at Duquesne University in Pittsburgh, Pennsylvania, where a group of faculty and students were inspired to seek out personal experiences with "gifts of the spirits" or *"charismata"* (which include glossolalia, spontaneous healing, deliverance from demons, and prophecy) after reading a best-selling book about a Pentecostal pastor's ministry with street gangs. The group held a

---

12. I borrow this phrase from Chesnut (2003).

retreat in March 1967, at which several of its members experienced the "Baptism of the Spirit" and otherwise manifested charismata. In the wake of that foundational event, now known as the "Duquesne Weekend," the movement spread rapidly throughout the northeastern and midwestern United States as ad hoc lay-led groups of Catholics likewise sought to have those spiritual experiences.[13]

Although the Duquesne Weekend story is the version of the Catholic Charismatic Renewal movement's origins that is most often recounted in scholarly works and was the one that parishioners in San Felipe knew (they even noted that the reason that some people said that they were evangélicos was because the original retreat in the United States had been ecumenical), Edward L. Cleary has argued that similar events were happening in Bogotá, Colombia in 1967 that were equally important to the movement's genesis (Cleary 2011, 10). The Colombian side of the story centers around a housing cooperative called *Barrio Minuto de Dios*, where its founder—Father Rafael García Herreros—struck up a friendship with a visiting Mexican American Baptist youth minister, who subsequentially facilitated the Catholic priest's baptism in the Holy Spirit. By the early 1970s, Father Rafael was leading Charismatic services at Minuto de Dios that started to attract people from throughout Bogotá and even other cities in Colombia (Cleary 2011, 55). Some of those who experienced charismata with Father Rafael would then go on to lead Catholic Charismatic services elsewhere in the country and spread the movement.

It's no surprise that the Duquesne origin story is clearly the institutionally important one since those early Catholic Charismatics in the United States were white and middle class and, thus, better positioned to argue for the legitimacy of the movement than the brown and *popular* class people who were the early converts in Colombia. However, the story of Minuto de Dios argues for the idea that the Catholic Charismatic Renewal was transnational from its very beginnings and that its membership was more economically

---

13. A national conference in 1968 drew 150 attendees, which more than doubled the membership of the Duquesne group. By 1974, attendance at the US national conference had reached twenty-five thousand (McGuire 1982). At the time of my fieldwork, the International Charismatic Catholic Renewal Services (the CCRM's office in the Vatican) estimated that the worldwide membership of the CCRM is somewhere in the neighborhood of 120 million people, or more than 11 percent of all Catholics, with upwards of seventy-three million of these living in Latin America (International Catholic Charismatic Renewal Services 2005).

and ethnically diverse than is sometimes imagined. Cleary notes that while North Americans undoubtedly influenced how Charismatic Catholicism spread in the Americas, we must also recognize the equally important roles that Latin Americans themselves played in growing and sustaining the movement (Cleary 2011, 11).

Guatemala is a case in point for this. The CCR was first introduced to the country by a wealthy layman who had visited a group in the United States in the early 1970s and converted there. His advocacy led Archbishop Mario Casariego y Acevedo to invite North American representatives of the CCR to hold a retreat for clergy in 1973, making Guatemala the first country in the region where the episcopacy approved the movement (Cleary 2011, 241). The first prayer groups in Guatemala were set up in relatively well-to-do urban parishes and several operated out of upper-class private Catholic schools in the capital city (Thorsen 2015, 31). The Guatemalan CCR thus began as an elite movement that only later gained followers among the popular class. Once that shift started, though, the robust lay-led Catholic organizations that existed in the country for all the reasons discussed above served as an infrastructure through which La Renovación gained converts in poorer urban neighborhoods and among Maya rural communities (Cleary 2011, 243). Though there has been supervision and participation from the upper echelon of the ecclesiastical hierarchy, the Catholic Charismatic Renewal in Guatemala has remained largely lay-led as it has grown, which, as we will see, raised a distinct set of problematics for its place in the larger institutional structure of the Catholic Church.

The Vatican granted the nascent Catholic Charismatic movement official recognition in 1975, yet both in its formative years and up through the present, Charismatic Catholics have encountered varying levels of acceptance from the local institutional bodies of the Church with most offering at best a kind of "critical tolerance" of their presence (Chesnut 2003, 69). In some parishes the CCR was seen as a powerful tool for keeping people in the Catholic fold by providing the same spiritual experiences as Pentecostalism, while in others it was seen as a potential danger that would only entice people to leave Catholicism (72). Leaders of CCR groups have had to constantly navigate that ambivalence to ensure both their place in the Catholic Church's institutional spaces and their commitments to their distinct form of Catholic practice. Though the earliest members of the movement referred to themselves as "Catholic Pentecostals" or "Pentecostal Catholics," the "Pentecostal" label gradually gave way to "Charismatic" as a way for members of that movement to differentiate themselves from existing Protestant Pentecostal churches (McGuire 1982). Along with this strategic shift in name came deliberate attempts to establish ties between the movement's lay leadership and Catholic clergy. In fact, one condition of the movement's Papal recognition in 1975 was that its members submit themselves to sacerdotal supervision through attachment to parishes (Chesnut 2003, 69). The Conference of Guatemalan Bishops followed suit, issuing "Guidelines for Charismatic Renewal" in 1986 that spelled out the benefits that the bishops saw in the movement for lay participation, as well as their fears about the possibility that the movement might develop in unorthodox ways if not kept under tight sacerdotal supervision (Conferencia Episcopal de Guatemala 1997, 416–17).

Unlike Action, Liberationist, or Inculturationist Catholicism, which were formed through theological writings first (albeit ones grounded in the experiences of the clergy) and put into practice second, Charismatic Catholicism first developed through the practices of lay people, which were subsequently justified theologically. The Belgian cardinal Leo Jozef (León Joseph) Suenens (1904–96) was instrumental as an early advocate of the Catholic Charismatic Renewal within the Catholic episcopacy. Suenens, who had played a major role at Vatican II, came to understand Charismatic Catholicism's emphasis on spiritual renewal as an extension of the larger project for *aggiornamento* (bringing up to date) that the Catholic Church had undertaken. In *A New Pentecost?*, published scarcely a year before the CCR gained official recognition from Pope Paul VI, Suenens argued that the new movement fulfilled Vatican II's calls for holiness and mission and that the charisms that people experienced were authentic signs of divine grace constituting a new Pentecost.[14] As such, its practices should be regarded not as deviations from Catholic orthodoxy, but rather as a spirit-filled component of the general institutional renewal that the Catholic Church sought through its recommitment to lay participation (Suenens 1975). Near the end of his life, Suenens stated that, "To interpret the [Catholic Charismatic] Renewal as a 'movement' among other movements is to misunderstand its nature; it is a movement of the Spirit offered to the entire Church and destined to re-

---

14. The original Pentecost is described in Acts 2 as the events that occurred at a feast fifty days after the resurrection of Jesus, at which the Holy Spirit was supposed to have descended on the faithful and through which they experienced glossolalia (Acts 2:4).

juvenate every part of the Church's life" (quoted in Moran 2013, 288). Thus, whatever may be said about the historical circumstance surrounding the CCR's emergence as a lay movement, we must also recognize that clergy have made significant efforts to solidify the movement's place within the Catholic Church on theological grounds.

Unlike the other movements' models of spiritual fulfillment through collective identification and this-worldly action, Charismatic Catholicism promotes "pneumatic" or spirit-filled and highly personalized religious experiences. In one of the earliest scholarly treatments of the CCR, Meredith McGuire characterized its core beliefs as "(1) a belief that the power of God is given directly to ordinary humans (through the 'gifts of the Holy Spirit'), (2) that, as a result, members have the power to see the relevance of religion in their everyday lives, and prayer groups experience a power which serves as the basis for meaning and moral norms, (3) this power has a strong experiential component, and (4) all these beliefs and experiences compel members to seek out a community of fellow believers—a community which both produces and is the product of power" (McGuire 1982, 7–8). Central to the direct experience of power is the manifestation of the "gifts of the spirit" via things like healing, glossolalia and its interpretation, prophecy, and the ability to discern demons and deliver people from their power,[15] which are described as being accompanied by strong emotions and a greater self-understanding (Cordes 1997). These experiences are taken as signs of Baptism in the Holy Spirit,[16] which is categorically different from the sacrament of Baptism (i.e., with water), in that while the latter is a necessary condition for salvation, the former is understood as "overwhelming realization of the loving nearness of God proclaimed in the Church's message and encountered in the individual act of faith" (Cordes 1997, 12). Baptism of the spirit is thus a personally transformative experience that signals God's power in the believer's life.

This version of Catholicism, much more so than Liberationist Catholicism and in contrast to the Inculturationist model, proposes a universalizing view of Catholic practice and identity, in which one's social and cultural identity does not play a significant role in one's spirituality. "[The Catholic Charismatic Renewal] has avoided discussing the tension between the

---

15. Pentecostal and Charismatic Christians cite the Apostle Paul's description of these gifts of the Holy Spirit in 1 Corinthians 12:4–11 as the basis for these beliefs and practices.

16. As the one part of the Trinity that is directly accessible to human beings, the Holy Spirit plays a critical role in Charismatic Catholicism (Suenens 1975).

universal and the local values, and it presents itself as a universal or global discourse.... The movement refers to universal faith rather than a localized, Brazilian, or Latin American Catholicism. It regards universal Catholicism, as well as humanity in general, as the community of all individuals, without mentioning any peoples specifically" (de Theije and Mariz 2008, 41). In this vein, Charismatic Catholicism might be read as a cosmopolitan, albeit politically conservative counter-discourse to the more socially conscious, subaltern-focused Liberationist and Inculturationist theological movements.

Charismatic Catholicism's claims to a sort of cultureless universality needs to be understood as a discursive stance taken on the ideal form of Christianity. David Lehmann has argued that because the CCR has largely been lay-initiated and led and because it has a facility for adapting popular forms of expression to religious worship, Charismatic Catholicism is best understood as part of Catholicism's "repertoire of popular religion [albeit one that is specifically] adapted to a more global context" (Lehmann 2003, 135). De Theije and Mariz have likewise argued that by appropriating certain aesthetic forms of popular mass-mediated culture, Brazilian Charismatics lay claim to a modern, "global" identity that contrasts with a localized, "folkloric" (and Inculturated, I would add) vision of Brazilian popular religiosity (de Theije and Mariz 2008). We can understand this move as signaling the purification (in the sense used by Bruno Latour [1993]) of Christianity, which seeks to make a claim to universal authenticity by excising the particularities of culture. Nonetheless, it is important to recognize that "modernity" and "universality" are themselves culture-bound concepts, and that any attempt to embody these values will be shaped by a person's social and cultural context. Viewed through that lens, the CCR is not all that different practically from what is envisioned by Inculturation except that its cultural referent is mass-mediated popular culture rather than an emplaced ethnic culture (cp. Abreu 2021).

Comparing Catholicisms

I have tried to give a sense of how Catholicism can be understood as a field in which a range of actors have mobilized varied discursive resources around the intersections of religion and ethnocultural identity in response to changing social conditions and ideological movements. The numerous ways that these visions of Catholicism overlap and intersect with one another attests the dynamism of this field. Catholic Action's social work and religious concerns set the stage for Liberationist Catholicism to emerge, but the two diverged in terms of the weight they place on sacramental orthodoxy with the former making it central to its mission and the latter movement offering a critique of its ultimate importance. If the Liberationist and Inculturationist models were in some sense parallel developments that sought to address the specificity of Catholics' social positioning, they diverged from each other in terms of whether it was material conditions or cultural authenticity that formed the central point of their critique. Costumbre offered a fixed point against which Catholic Action's work to promote orthodoxy defined itself, initiating the larger institutional reforms I traced out. However, Inculturationists later sought to rehabilitate precisely the kinds of localized traditions that Catholic Action sought to dismantle as a means of advancing their own project of reimagining what it meant to build a truly universal Catholic Church. Charismatic Catholicism set itself against Inculturation regarding the importance of ethnocultural formations of spirituality, but the two might also be read as socially conservative responses to Liberationist Catholicism's political project. Finally, unlike Inculturation and Costumbre, both of which made local culture a necessary component of religious practice, Liberationist and Charismatic Catholicism both constructed ideally "universalist" versions of salvation that are in principle independent of the cultural identities of its subjects.

Each of these Catholicisms offered a slightly different formulation of the ideal Christian community. Costumbre proposed an all-encompassing order that tied the social, political, economic, and spiritual to the geographically circumscribed ethnocultural unit of the cofradía. The cofrades focused their religious energies on caring for local santos who in turn guaranteed the integrity of their human community. As a riposte to this, Catholic Action and subsequently Liberationist Catholicism promoted a vision of Christianity that located its point of reference outside the boundaries of the local community. These forms of Catholicism asked people to imagine themselves as members of a delocalized "universal" church. Although ethnicity did not play an overt role in these discourses, the specific social location of the Christian subject figured in through the language of class. Inculturation likewise postulated that the human community was a necessary component of salvation, adding the language of "culture" to that of salvation as a way to justify the distinctive and specific ways people ought to experience Christianity. In this formulation, universal Catholicism was composed of particular churches,[17] so that all Christian communities shared a universal ability to access God, but each did so through unique symbols and practices. Though Inculturation maintained that the individual soul is the locus of salvation, it saw the process as necessarily mediated by the person's natal culture. Finally, Charismatic Catholicism minimized the role of the community and placed greater weight on the individual subject in salvation by offering the idea that each person could know God directly through the Holy Spirit. In this model, the Christian subject is first and foremost imagined as part of a global community of "renewed" Catholics for whom the social and cultural differences are set aside in favor of promoting a cosmopolitan spiritual imaginary.

Beyond offering different understandings of spirituality and salvation, these forms of Catholicism implicitly constructed political stances for their adherents, and several have played significant roles in shaping Maya cultural activism. The community organization initiated by the Catholic Action program was a direct contributor to an increased sense of shared ethnicity and laid the foundation for the pan-Maya movement's political organization (Warren 1978; Wilson 1995). More recently, pan-Mayanism and Inculturation have overlapped in their attitude about the autonomy of cultural groups and their right to self-determination. This is especially true in terms of language rights because pan-Mayanism frames language as a central part of Mayan identity, and Inculturation makes use of vernacular languages and the recuperation of indigenous terminology central to its theological project. Likewise, both hold the idea that each culture has a certain "cosmovision" that grants it a particular kind of access to understanding the nature of the world, and which is inalienable from its subjects. Due to its class-based social analysis, Liberationist Catholicism had close ties to the Campesino movements of the 1960s and 1970s and the leftist movements during the Civil War. While the pan-Maya movement diverged from these in its political priorities, it shared the Liberationist language of internal colonialism and oppression to critique the social situation of Mayas in Guatemala (e.g., Cojtí Cuxil 1994). Although the emphases of the two movements were different, they shared a sense that Mayas needed some measure of real social and

---

17. The conference documents of CELAM's fourth general conference in Santo Domingo describe the Catholic parishes as a "community of communities and movements" (Consejo Episcopal Lationoamericano 1992, 105).

material autonomy in order to live their lives in a full and dignified way. It bears mentioning, though, that one of the criticisms that has been leveled at the pan-Maya movement is that in focusing too strongly on cultural rights as a pathway to post-colonial relations, it has neglected taking action on economic injustices and thus may inadvertently perpetuate other social inequalities, especially around gender (Nelson 1999; Warren 1998). Costumbre, due in part to its localism, has a special role in the pan-Mayanist vision of ethnic autonomy both because it is organized around a civil-religious structure with a kind of political authority separate from Ladino domains of influence and because it is seen as reflecting crucial elements of precolonial Maya culture.

Contesting Catholicism in San Felipe

The distinction between Charismatics and Mainstream Catholics was a key issue in the politics of San Felipe in the 2000s, but there were also traces of the division between Costumbristas and post–Catholic Action Mainstream Catholics that occasionally bubbled up. The discourse that Mainstream Catholics marshalled against Charismatics implied that the latter were denying their ethnic identity when they spoke Spanish in church, adopted different expressive styles, and most importantly, separated themselves from established CEBs. However, these very same claims (except with regards to language choice) had been made by Costumbristas against catequistas in the 1960s and 1970s. Charismatics for their part maintained that they were proud of their ethnic identity and, when asked about this directly, firmly maintained that they did not see themselves as in any way rejecting that they were Q'eqchi'-Maya. Rather, they said that because cultural identity was not a necessary part of Charismatic Catholicism, they saw no need to self-consciously or unnecessarily play up Q'eqchi'-Maya identity in church. In their view, Spanish and Q'eqchi' were interchangeable languages in ritual settings because both were adequate means for communicating with each other and God. Hermano Rigo[18] put it this way, "I am Q'eqchi', I never deny that. I am proud of being Q'eqchi' . . . God understands all languages. If someone

---

18. Unlike Mainstream Catholics, who referred to each other as Qawa' or Qana, Charismatics preferred to call each other hermano or hermana, as in Hermano Rigo or Hermana Thelma. I will use that convention when referring to them in recognition that that is how they would have addressed each other. This will also make it easier to track who is a Mainstream Catholic and who is a Charismatic Catholic.

prays in English or in Chinese or in whatever [language], He understands, right? So, if I pray in Spanish or in Q'eqchi', He knows what I'm saying. There are some things that are easier to express in Spanish and others [that are easier] in Q'eqchi', right? So, when I pray, I use both [languages] because God will understand either way."

For Mainstream Catholics, on the other hand, Q'eqchi' language was felt to run deep and be intimately tied to a Q'eqchi' person's ability to express what was in their *ch'ool* (heart), which was the locus of a person's thoughts and feelings. Even if Spanish was an available and appropriate language to use in other contexts, Q'eqchi' was nonetheless the code figured as the ethnic community's true means of expression and thus the best medium through which a person could communicate with God. Qawa' Hugo explained why this was.

> I, as a Q'eqchi' person, always feel better speaking Q'eqchi'. It's true I learned Spanish as a child and I speak Spanish, we can speak in Spanish like we are now and everything is fine. But in Q'eqchi' I feel more, I don't know, more happy/at ease. That's the language of my grandparents and their parents and what the ancestors left to us and that is something sacred to us, something very important. So with Q'eqchi' I can really speak with God using the language of my ancestors. It was the same with Jesus, because when he spoke to our Heavenly Father, he spoke with the language of the place he was born that was the language of his heart as a human, that's how he talked to The Lord.

Each group thus configured the connection between religion, language, and culture in different ways. While Mainstream Catholics' interest in preserving "Q'eqchi'ness" in their religious practice via language and certain key elements borrowed from Costumbre (like using maize in offerings on feast days, and periodically performing mayejak rituals) would seem to be closely in tune with the Mayan cultural activist vision of cultural autonomy and with the stated goals of Inculturation, in practice most of the community leaders in San Felipe did not identify themselves as *"Mayistas,"* and a few even rejected the pan-Maya movement's agenda priorities as irrelevant to their interests and livelihoods. In a population as large as a parish, there are bound to be variations in the political affiliations and leanings, but the overwhelming majority of the parishioners with whom I worked—including both Mainstream and Charismatic Catholics neither self-identified as Maya nationalists nor neatly aligned themselves with the political stances of the pan-Maya movement. For the most part, their social and political concerns were not particularly "cultural" in the sense promoted by the pan-Maya movement but were instead focused on concerns about social and economic instability. This is not to say that they necessarily disagreed with the aims of the movement, nor that Maya cultural activism was wholly irrelevant to their lives; just that pan-Mayanism—either as a political ideology or social movement—was not a particularly salient feature of how they navigated life in Cobán.

This was especially evident on an occasion when two young researchers from Guatemala City visited the parish to conduct a survey on behalf of an initiative that the office of the vice president had set up to address "Maya issues." Padre Agustino asked three senior catechists—Qana' Esperanza, Qawa' Luis, and Qawa' Tomás—to act as a focus group for the parish. Among other things, the survey asked respondents to list four or five issues that they would want the government to take direct action on. Although each person framed his or her concerns slightly differently, they all overlapped in that their main concerns were the rising cost of living and increased feelings of personal insecurity due to violent crime. Culturalist issues promoted by the pan-Maya movement, such as language rights or rights to access pre-Colombian Maya cultural sites were not on their agendas. Qana' Esperanza included education in her list, which has been an important and consistent arena of activism for pan-Maya organizations, but when asked to elaborate, she said she was worried about whether she would be able to afford to send all of her four children to school, not whether once in school the curriculum would provide adequate representation of Maya culture or Q'eqchi'-language courses. Access to land, or more precisely, a guarantee that his right to privately owned land would be protected, was a concern for Qawa' Luis, and he framed it in terms of governmental interventions in land tenure disputes that had received sensationalistic press coverage in previous months after a series of land invasions by squatters in the departments of El Quiché and Petén. While land rights are a concern for pan-Maya organizations, they often advocate for collective land rights and increased access to untended agricultural land, not for ensuring private property rights per se, which was the issue on Qawa' Luis's mind. Similarly, Qawa' Tomás was mostly concerned about the price of consumables. Qawa' Tomás was in his late sixties and made his living growing corn and a few cash crops. As a younger man he would regularly take contract jobs at plantations to earn cash, but due to his age he could no longer do so, and thus, a lack of cash was a recurrent problem for him. He was naturally worried about the decreasing purchasing power his quetzales seemed to have. Thus, even if in other contexts they would readily explain the high value that Q'eqchi' language and culture held for their sense of self, these Q'eqchi'-Maya individuals' ideas about what the government's responsibility toward them should be were framed more in terms of liberal notions of modern, individualized citizenship rather than one of collective ethnocultural citizenship.

These sorts of concerns were common among parishioners, and it was especially true that ensuring material security was a prominent concern for their families and a regular topic of conversation. Several of the catechists had sought or were seeking ways to become small-scale entrepreneurs by, for example, reselling clothes bought in bulk, running small dry goods stores out of their homes, investing in livestock, or buying a car to use as a taxi. Similarly, they wanted their children to go to school and receive professional-level secondary education degrees for secretarial work, primary school teaching, accounting, and other skilled trades that could allow them to earn a living without depending on access to agricultural land. This was true for both Mainstream and Charismatic Catholics, and while certainly these sorts of entrepreneurial activities would not be anathema to the politics of the pan-Maya movement, they show a different focus of attention regarding what was considered to be pressing social goals. It would not be overstating the point to say that parishioners' concerns were more closely in line with the sort of economic development projects advocated by Catholic Action than with Liberationist calls for far-reaching reform of social and economic systems.

Parishioners' experiences with the Guatemalan Civil War were likewise varied and colored individuals' attitudes toward Maya nationalism. Many of the communities that comprise the parish had been seriously affected by the violence of the 1980s and saw people murdered or "disappeared" by the military, including several catequistas who are now remembered as martyrs by their communities. A few parishioners wistfully recalled the much stronger social reform agendas of former parish priests. Those priests, they said, had stood up to the army, spoken out against abuses, and had really looked out for their parishioners. Traces of that form of Catholicism were evident in the boxes of books on Liberation Theology and Marxist social theory that were silently gathering mildew in a corner of the library at San Felipe's clergy house. On the other hand, a few of the catequistas were proud that they had served in the army or had worked at the local military base, not just because of the relative material security this had afforded them but also because they understood it as part of their civic duties. These catechists, unsurprisingly, remembered the former, more socially engaged clergy less favorably, believing that they had not properly focused on their work as spiritual leaders and meddled in politics that brought unwanted reprisals on the parish. Several parishioners, too, had stories about how they had encountered (and, in a few cases, even been temporarily abducted by) the guerrilla, and few people had much positive to say about that side in the armed conflict.

What all of this suggests is simply that none of the religious and political discourses that have shaped San Felipe have been hegemonic. Rather, there seems to have always been an interplay between different ways of approaching the role of Catholicism in Q'eqchi'-Mayas' lives. One of the major upshots of the co-presence and occasional conflict between these discourses has been that in some measure the parish's CEBs have achieved the central goal of the pan-Maya movement—they have forged social spaces that are (or are nearly) autonomously Maya. While the CEBs are still subsumed within the overwhelmingly non-Maya institutional hierarchy of the Catholic Church and supervised by the foreign clergy that minister to the parish, their regular function depends on the actions of Maya laypeople. Although the CEBs were formed as part of the Church's institutional projects, the ways that they developed have given Mayas some autonomy to shape their religious lives. The debate in San Felipe over what sorts of linguistic and other practices were appropriate forms of Q'eqchi'-Maya Catholicism occurred largely within a Maya social sphere and involved few outsiders, as even the foreign-born priests tended to be reticent to do much about them except to try to calm tempers and maintain some semblance of peace between La Renovación and its catequista critics. The issue between Mainstream and Charismatic Catholics in San Felipe was pressing to parishioners precisely because it forced members of the larger Q'eqchi'-Maya Catholic community to discuss the relationship between ethnicity, culture, and religion in their own terms.

If Maya cultural activism did not seem to be a bigger force in San Felipe's parishioner's lives, it was because what was most salient to both Charismatic and Mainstream Catholics' sense of self was their religious identity. While religious identity articulated with ethnic identity, it was as Catholics that parishioners primarily saw themselves and wished to be seen by others. Maya cultural activism has ultimately sought to carve out spaces in Guatemalan society where Mayas can exercise autonomy over their collective future; and perhaps small-scale Catholic groups such as the CEBs, cofradías, and even Charismatic prayer groups, should be understood as fulfilling that goal. The debate in San Felipe was not, after all, one fueled by the clergy and their interests, but was rather a consequence of Q'eqchi'-Maya Catholics engaging with these larger regional and global debates about what it means to be a Catholic Christian on their own terms. In these small groups, Mayas are the protagonists of their history, and given that they understand the work of those groups as participating in the Christian history of salvation, the determinations they make and actions they take were profoundly consequential to them.

Conclusion

Behind Qawa' Luis's hesitant attempt to gauge my reaction to the aj ilonel's ritual on the church grounds lay a lifetime of engagement with the multiple voicings of Catholicism in San Felipe. Although the Inculturationist theology that dominated the parish at the time of our conversation discursively positioned Maya culture as a component part of the Church's mission, it stopped short of being a full-throated endorsement of Maya spiritual agency. My interlocutor (and he was far from alone in this regard) had had enough experiences to make him cautious about, if not outright wary of, how others might want to frame the relationship between Catholic Christianity and Maya cultural identity. It was not just foreign visitors to the parish like me or the missionary priests who might object to the work of the aj ilonel either, since one thing that strongly marked the Charismatics was their rejection of this sort of overt incorporation of Maya spirituality in Catholic life in favor of a less culturally distinct, more cosmopolitan form of Christian worship. At other times, in other settings and conversations, parishioners likewise found themselves negotiating the meaning of Charismatic practices (or the perception of them), reactions to the social and material injustices of postwar Guatemala, and the potentially dangerous political stances that might be attributed to them. All of this could be accommodated into their personal and collective experience of what it meant to be a Q'eqchi'-Maya Catholic, but it both took work to do it and nothing about it was necessarily a given.

The traces of the varied forms of Catholicism that have been practiced in San Felipe since its ascendance to the status of parish could be found in and around the church—in the material, organizational, and biographical artifacts that made up its lived reality at the beginnings of the twenty-first century, which together make up one version of the heteroglot "text" of Catholicism in the parish. Not all the voices that these items represent had the same impact nor were they all equally or easily discernible, but they all contributed to the larger life of the parish. This examination of the multiple strands of Catholic theology that have shaped San Felipe serves as a reminder that centrifugal as much as centripetal forces shape heteroglossic systems (Bakhtin 1981, 272). It should also help us better understand the notion of dialogism, as we can see the complex ways that core principles and ideas (for example, the very idea of lay participation) are reworked and refracted each time they are "voiced" into being (Bakhtin 1984, 202). This discussion has set the stage for us to focus on how differentiation and decentralization can be seen in the debate between catequistas and carismáticos in San Felipe as they each sought to establish the legitimacy of their own voicing of Catholicism.

CHAPTER 3

Catequistas y Predicadores
Constructing Religious Authority

The parish church of San Felipe is one of the most picturesque sites in Cobán. It sits on a pine-covered *cerro* (hill) called *Sa' Retiit*, one of the four that surrounds the historical center of the city. From the front patio of the church one can both appreciate a panoramic view of the city and feel many miles away from it. To reach this vantage point, one must climb 134 stairs counting from the street level, among which are interspersed several inclined pathways. The first flights of stairs seem to go straight up the hill. From here the path turns to the right with a less severe incline, before making a hairpin turn back the other way until one reaches the last two flights of stairs that once again head straight upward to the church courtyard. Along the way one passes four small niches (plus one whose construction has never been finished). Their interiors are perpetually blackened from the smoke of candles and incense burned inside them. Sometimes alongside a burning candle one finds offerings of leaves, branches, ears of corn, tufts of hair or fur, chicken feathers, and small coins stuck to the niche's wall with bits of a fragrant resin called *pom* that is commonly used as incense. These small sacrificial items are left with the hopes that crops, children, domestic animals, and coin purses will grow and prosper. Occasionally one also sees a bottle of cheap rum or *agua florida* cologne next to a black candle, suggesting that not everyone who stops at the niches to transact with the supernatural world does so through strictly Catholic means nor for benevolent ends since these items are commonly used in sorcery. The first of these niches—at the top of the stairs that seem to go straight up the cerro—is decorated with the figures of two jaguars and a flowering branch. These decorative motifs recall the legend of how it was that Sa' Retiit came to have a church built atop it in the first place.

A long time ago, back when this whole area was wooded and was considered far outside the center of town,[1] two men were walking along this hill. Some say that they were out hunting and some that they were collecting firewood, but in any case, near the crest of the hill they were met by a surprising sight. On a flat rock, beneath a tree they did not recognize, lay an image of Jesus Christ. Two jaguars sat next to him as though their task was to guard this miraculous visage of *El Señor en Agonía* (The Lord in Agony), who lay prostrate in the last painful throes of life after having been removed from the cross.

Shocked by the discovery, the two men ran to alert the proper authorities. In one version of the tale, they went to tell don Francisco Pop[2]—the fabulously wealthy Q'eqchi'-Maya man who then owned the land—and in another they went to tell the Dominican friars who lived at the monastery in the center of town. In both versions these authority figures instructed the men to climb up the hill to retrieve the santo. When the men reached the summit of Sa' Retiit again they were relieved to find that the jaguars were no longer there, but that El Señor was still under his tree just as they had last seen him. So, they gently lifted the figure of Christ and bore him down the hill. However, this was no easy task, since the farther away the men got from the place of the miraculous discovery, the heavier their cargo seemed to become. Eventually they managed to reach the image's new home in town—in one version, a room in don Francisco's expansive estate, or, in the other version, a side chapel in the church tended to by the Dominican friars.

By the time the sun rose again, much to everyone's dismay, the image had disappeared. Servants and sacristans were questioned, and every corner of the home and church were scoured for traces of the missing santo, but no

---

1. This telling of the story is an adaptation and synthesis of the legend as it appears in Villacorta, 1977, and Reyes Narciso, 1998, as well as from versions told to me by Qana' Esperanza and Qawa' Hugo in Cobán.

2. Francisco Pop was a real person who lived in Cobán in the nineteenth century. He is famous as one of the wealthiest people that ever lived in the city. Another story has it that he owned such a large herd of cattle that when he would take them to sell in the market in Salamá, approximately 210 kilometers away, the head of the cattle train would arrive before its tail had left Cobán (Villacorta 1977).

clues to its whereabouts could be found. Finally, it dawned on someone that they should examine the place where El Señor first appeared, and so a party headed back up Sa' Retiit to see if the cerro could yield any information about where the image had gone. Lo and behold, El Señor en Agonía was there, laying upon his rock under the *esquisuche* tree,[3] which was now flowering with sweet-smelling white blossoms as if He had never been taken into town at all.

In the first version of the story, don Francisco is wise enough to recognize the meaning of the miraculous dis- and re-apparition of the santo and pledges himself to build a temple on the hill. He goes to speak to the *Tzuultaq'a*—the spirit who is the true owner of the land, and who must be consulted and appeased when building a home, planting crops, or gathering resources—to ask for permission to build on this land and for help in completing the project. The Tzuultaq'a tells don Francisco that he will grant him permission and that he will come into a sum of money with which to construct the temple, but that in exchange his unborn child shall belong to the land. They say that don Francisco Pop became even richer after that supernatural consultation, and that he not only sponsored the construction of the new church but also continued to be its main patron until his death. They say, too, that a few years after the church was completed, don Francisco's wife gave birth to a daughter. The Pops' happiness due to that birth did not last long, however, since the infant girl disappeared one night. Presumably, she was taken by the Tzuultaq'a in compensation for the land on which the church of San Felipe now stands.[4]

---

3. The *esquisuche* tree (*Ehretia guatemalensis*) blooms white, odorous flowers that are believed to have curative properties. This type of tree is closely associated with St. Hermano Pedro de San José Betancur—a seventeenth-century Spanish missionary who was active in Antigua, Guatemala and canonized by Pope John Paul II in 2002. An esquisuche tree that Hermano Pedro is said to have planted still stands in Antigua and people say that its flowers aid in the miraculous cures that saint is known for.

4. Stories like this one, called *leyendas populares*, often feature real historical persons coming into contact with the supernatural. I had a teacher in the first grade in Guatemala City who liked to tell us these tales while we did crafts. She once told us the story of a man named don Julio who had a farm near the town of San José Pinula. While building his farmhouse, the teacher told us, don Julio's workers found a hidden tunnel. Though the workers warned him of potential dangers, don Julio was curious and took a candle to explore the tunnel. Upon entering its mouth, he felt a cold, foul wind blow past him, but he was undeterred and decided to go inside. Deep in the darkness they say that he found a treasure (what exactly it was my teacher didn't say, but in my childhood imagination it was something like a pirate's chest filled with gold

In the second version of the tale, the Dominican friars are much more stubborn and less willing to read miraculous signs. Upon finding the santo once again on the cerro, they ask that the image be brought back to the church in town, and only realize after the wooden figure makes a second and then a third peregrination back up the hill that they should build it a home there. In that version they say that when the townspeople went to Sa' Retiit the fourth and final time, ready to start building the new church, they found the outlines of a foundation already traced out on the ground. Having had to repeatedly insist on where his new home should be, El Señor en Agonía seems to have decided that He should be specific about its size and layout, rather than leave those details to the obtuse priests who had repeatedly failed to correctly interpret his signs.

Whatever may or may not have prompted the construction of the church back in the early nineteenth century,[5] the story of how multiple actors including priests, civic leaders, townsfolk, jaguars, earth spirits, and sacred images negotiated the construction of a church illustrates a fundamental question that continues to drive the practice of Catholicism in San Felipe—namely, how can people know what God wants of them? How do human beings know how to interpret the vague signs that divinities give them and

---

coins and jewels). The treasure seemed a blessing, but strange things started happening around the house after that. Don Julio eventually decided that there were evil forces at work. He sent for the town priest, who came to bless the house and sprinkle holy water in the tunnel before the workers sealed it up again. I remember going home and excitedly telling my mother and grandmother that that day *la maestra* had told us a story about a house in Pinula, where we often spent Sundays at my grandfather's farmhouse. Did they know this story about the secret tunnel and the ghost who guarded it? Of course, they did . . . well, sort of. That wasn't just any don Julio who found a tunnel, they told me; it was my maternal great-grandfather, who I knew as Papa Julio. There was a tunnel, more like a small cave, near where the house was to be built, and yes, people had spread rumors that there had been a secret treasure, but in reality, Papa Julio hadn't found anything there. The haunting, they said, was news to them. When we visited, I often wondered where the tunnel's entrance was supposed to have been exactly, and as a child I always felt a sense of discomfort in the cold, dark downstairs hallway.

5. All historical records indicate that church construction was completed in 1810 (Villacorta 1977; Reyes Narciso 1998). Since then, the building was remodeled and expanded three times—in 1910, 1954, and 1985—so that the church that stands today is considerably larger than the one that was purportedly traced out by the saint in the legend. The image of El Señor en Agonía was restored by the Guatemalan government in 2012. He still lies in a glass coffin mostly hidden behind the altar table and beneath the Black Christ of Esquipulas, who serves as the church's official patron saint and the focal point of the church nave.

transform these into guidelines for ethical living? How do human beings—be they friars or *caciques*—come to be seen as plausible and competent mediators for divine beings? What gives them the authority to read the opaque signs left by sometimes capricious supernatural beings[6] and turn these into collective human action that we might deem religious? The myth of El Señor en Agonía's appearance asks us to consider the complications of answering these questions. It isn't always clear what the best course of action is where divinities are concerned, and human authorities, no matter their qualifications, don't always fare well deciphering their signs. The story shows that no matter how sure they may initially be about knowing how to proceed, just like the Dominicans had been in calling for the santo to be brought to the church, people often err in their interpretations and sometimes have trouble adjusting to new information. Moreover, as don Francisco Pop learned, there are consequential choices to make when entering into devotional labors, and the prices people pay to carry out the will of divine beings can be heavy. Put in more social scientific terms, this myth alerts us to the complications of religious authority and interpretation. How is it that some people (and not others) are taken as authoritative interpreters of the opaque signs that divine beings give? On what grounds do people claim to be able to make those interpretations? How might diverging claims to religious authority be negotiated in the context of religious schism?

In this chapter we examine these issues through the lens of Mainstream and Charismatic Catholic's competing visions of how religious authority is constituted. We will begin with a brief discussion of the importance of au-

---

6. This is in keeping with tales from elsewhere in Mesoamerica in which the major figures of Christianity, including Jesus, can be tricksters (for a Tzotzil example, see Carrasco 2014, 156–57). There is another story about San Felipe's El Señor en Agonía that Qawa' Jorge once told me. Once, when he was very young (this would have been in the late 1930s or early 1940s) there had been a long drought. The crops were failing, and animals and people were getting sick because they didn't have enough water. The *ancianos* (i.e., the community elders) were consulted and they determined that what they needed to do, as their own grandparents had done when there had been a drought decades earlier, was to take the sacred image on a procession through the city's four *barrios*. With all the appropriate pomp and reverence, the figure was taken out to walk through the city. After visiting the four quadrants of town and as soon as He entered His church again, the sky darkened, and the heavens seemed to open up with great torrents of water. It rained like that for weeks, ending the drought but also causing the river to rise and flood the streets. Qawa' Jorge explained that this was a santo with great power, and that for all the good that He could do, people should not take Him lightly.

thority and legitimation of speech and then proceed to descriptions of how the lay leaders of the two congregations became authorized to perform a particular kind of ritual speech—the sermon. In the final section we will examine the ideological underpinnings and consequences of the two models of authorization.

Authority and Legitimacy

One of the main insights of Bakhtin's model of heteroglossia is that all instances of language are always already in conversation with other voices—they are dialogic—and yet we know, too, that in any given social and cultural context, some voices seek to impose themselves as monologic—they appear to speak from a privileged position of truth that places them outside or above the everyday interaction of other voices. When religious elites seek to represent the voice of God or when a state's functionaries seek to represent the voice of the nation, for example, they purport to be voicing a transcendent authority that is above question or reproach and which seemingly admits no critiques or alternatives. Bakhtin's insistence that all instances of language are reflective of some particular perspective prompts us to denaturalize those sorts of claims and interrogate their ideological underpinnings. Monologism, in this view, is a stance that dissimulates dialogism in the service of advancing some partisan interest.

As Talal Asad noted in his classic work *Genealogies of Religion*, in order to fully grasp the way that symbolic systems come to exercise some degree of meaning in people's lives, we must also be aware of the power dynamics that underlie the exercise of those symbolic systems. "Religion requires authorized practice and authorizing doctrine" in order to become meaningful to people (Asad 1993, 39). Religions discursively frame certain practices, ideas, symbols, and narratives as meaningful and truthful, and concomitantly mark others as irrelevant, false, or even heretical. These processes of inclusion and exclusion, of authorization and proscription, themselves depend on social actors' participation in a set of disciplinary practices that make the discursive structures of religious institutions concrete in their adherents' lives (Asad 1993, 125). Moreover, to understand how any given position becomes a matter of orthodoxy for a group, we need to also understand how it marks itself as not an arbitrary choice among many but a singularly necessary one (Bourdieu 1977, 168). Thus, to understand how a voice construes itself as monologic, we need to examine not just its own features but also the social practices through which its speakers adopt and embody that stance as singularly authoritative.

The heteroglossic model of Catholicism that I am proposing in this book, for all its emphasis on the plurality voice and the dialogic construction of religious life, is also one that implies the question of how it is that people take up any given position within the system and why it is that they find those positions (and not others) to be persuasive and worth becoming invested in. As we saw in the previous chapter, the institutional multivocality of Catholic theology has historically engendered multiple ways of practicing Catholicism even as the institution has also made claims to representing a singular "universal" interpretation of Christianity, and so the question of what is authorized and how it has been authorized cannot simply be answered with reference to an institutionally sanctioned orthodoxy disseminated downward from above (or if we prefer, from the metropole outward). Rather, it is necessary to establish ethnographically how each Catholic community constitutes the authority of its lay leaders. Part of what drove the conflict in San Felipe was the fact that the lay leadership of each of the two groups of Catholics claimed the singular authority of their own distinct voicing of the same religion. Catequistas and carismáticos were effectively in dialogue with each other, but the dynamic was one in which each sought to authorize their own positing as monologic, stemming as it did from their own privileged access to God's will. We must therefore ask on what grounds it was that both Mainstream and Charismatic Catholics came to view their own versions of Catholicism as not just legitimate expressions of the religion but also as the authoritative ones that precluded the practices of the other. A critical look at the social processes that each group engaged in to legitimize its own structures of authority will show us the underlying logic of their discursive stances and help us understand why the other group's system was rendered illegitimate in their eyes. How did members of the two congregations come to see their voicing of Catholicism as authoritative? In a context in which contestation was at the forefront, how did they come to see their own position as not just fundamentally correct but as also an inherent refutation of the other's stance? Examining how Mainstream and Charismatic lay leaders claimed the authority to legitimately perform a particular genre of speech— the sermon—helps us understand why the two groups saw each other as in conflict over key questions of what it meant to be a good Catholic.

Sermons are useful to think with here because they highlight key aspects of the debate in San Felipe. They are a speech genre that requires a specific form of institutional authority to perform. Whereas it might be true that Christianity generally makes its central text available in a way that (theoretically) allows all people to engage in the activity of interpreting it, it is also the case that in many, if not most, contexts social conditions exist that mark some people as more legitimate interpreters than others. This may be especially true for Catholicism, in which the massive global institutional structure of the Catholic Church depends on certain classes of people who are positioned as legitimate ritual actors and who are authorized bearers of doctrine and public interpreters of Biblical text. Traditionally this meant that the clergy held a monopoly in interpretation, but as I noted in the previous chapter, following the reforms of the Second Vatican Council in Latin America, that role was opened to at least some of the laity. With the institutionalization of the CEB structure in San Felipe, much of the work of religious instruction was delegated to catequistas, who came to be seen as cultural translators between the Catholic Church as an institution and their home communities and were thus also ideally positioned to deliver sermons at Masses and Celebrations of the Word that would make scripture relevant to Q'eqchi'-Mayas' lives. Likewise, in the Charismatic groups, which acted largely independently of the local clergy, lay preachers (predicadores) took on the important work of religious instruction and "animation," which also included providing Biblical exegesis and moral guidance through sermons. Arguably, the role of these kinds of semiprofessional exegetes has been all the more critical in places like San Felipe, where low levels of literacy have meant that as a matter of course, few people can or do read the Bible independently themselves. Examining how individuals were invested with the authority to act as catequistas and predicadores will help us better understand the two congregations' distinct orientations toward language as a sign of religious and moral authority.

In the next sections, I sketch out the two models of authorization for performing this crucial part of Catholic ritual life. Each model communicated certain ideals about religious knowledge and moral authority at the metadiscursive level. Briefly put, for Mainstream Catholics, a person became a catechist by entering into a particular kind of pedagogical relationship with representatives of the Roman Catholic Church. Catequistas' authority derived from their membership in the Church's institutional hierarchy, through which they received formal (and somewhat circumscribed) models of what counted as proper exegesis of the Bible that could serve as the basis for their sermons. The predicadores who led Charismatic Catholic groups, on the other hand, received no formal training and operated independently of the clergy and each other. Their authority to perform sermons was attributed to the individual person's ability to receive unmediated, divine inspiration during religious rituals. Each group thus determined what constituted a lay religious authority quite differently.

Catechists: Studying to Preach

On the last Sunday of every month, forty or so catequistas met in the church's training center hall for a *cholob'ank* (Q'eqchi' for "explanation"). The cholob'ank was meant to ensure that catechists would all preach a standardized message to their respective CEBs over the course of the following month. Madre Chin—a Filipino nun with the Missionary Sisters of the Immaculate Heart of Mary (*Immaculati Cordis Mariae*, or ICM[7]), who had been working in Guatemala since the mid-1980s—was the person in charge of Q'eqchi' catechist *formación* (training) for San Felipe and several other parishes and the person who thus oversaw these meetings. She was supported in this work by four Q'eqchi'-Maya *instructores* (instructors) who received small stipends from the diocese to aid in the catechist formación project. The instructors (three men and one woman) were all experienced catechists who had been picked for the job by Madre Chin in consultation with Padre Agustino, and who continued to receive extra training to be expert exegetes. The job of instructor was not the sole or even primary source of income for any of them, but holding the title did place them in a position of being semiprofessional lay church workers, and thus distinguished them from other catechists whose participation was strictly voluntary and pro bono. Madre Chin and the instructores worked closely together, meeting with each other weekly over the

---

7. Also known as The Missionary Sisters of the Immaculate Heart of Mary, this is the sister organization of Father Agustino's CICM. Like it, ICM has a fascinating transnational history. The order was founded at the end of the nineteenth century by a Belgian nun working in South India, where it is still a major presence, and later founded houses in the Philippines, the United States, Congo, and China in the early twentieth century. The first sisters of that order came to Guatemala in 1964 (http://carmelchurch.in/mcc/Marie_Louise_De_Meester_and_history_of_ICM_Sisters).

course of the month to prepare for the cholob'ank. Madre Chin's experience and long tenure afforded her the right to operate largely independently in doing this work, but she was nonetheless answerable to the parish priest, her order's national and regional supervisors, and the diocesan-level coordinator for catechist training.

As the catechists arrived for a cholob'ank, they arranged rows of white monobloc plastic chairs in a semicircle around a central area in the room from which the instructors spoke. The instructores' area was furnished with a heavy wooden table and an old dry-erase board, for which there were sometimes, but not always, useable markers. Although the meeting was supposed to start at 8:00 a.m., and Madre Chin asked people to arrive by 7:45, it was usually almost 8:30 before enough people had arrived to begin the meeting. The event opened with the a cappella singing of a hymn and a brief period of prayer, which included the *Pater Noster, Ave Maria*, and an individual prayer for blessings and guidance. After this ritual opening, Madre Chin asked one of the catechists to read the corresponding verses for one of the coming Sundays. Each set of verses included a reading from the Old Testament, one from the Epistles, and one from the Gospels. Psalm readings, which were included in the Mass but not the Celebration of the Word, were not discussed at the cholob'ank. The verses for each week were assigned in a small ecclesiastical calendar or lectionary that each catechist was expected to own and have with them at the cholob'ank. Additionally, every catechist was expected to have a copy of the Bible with them at the meeting.[8]

As the designated lector read the passages, the other catechists sat and listened. It was rare to see someone reading the passage along in his or her Bible. When the catechist was done, one of the instructores would explain the central message of those verses and model how the catequistas should talk about them. The instructores' main task was to explain how the verses fit together for each week around a central message or theme. They also outlined the main points that the catechists were expected to touch upon when preaching to their base communities later in the month. Each instruction

---

8. In 2005, the only complete Bible available would have been the SIL/Wycliffe translation by Francis Eachus and Ruth Carlson. Eachus and Carlson began working on the project in the mid-1950s and published a number of Q'eqchi' literacy texts and religious texts, including the first full edition of the Bible in 1988. Their Bible translation has been reprinted several times and is still the most widely available one. Since then, a translation produced and authorized by the Diocese of Verapaz has become available and catechists are expected to use this one.

FIGURE 4   Catequistas preparing for sermons

took about forty-five minutes, and the same process was then repeated for each set of Sunday verses for the month, with a new lector and a new instructor taking the lead each time. Occasionally, one of the catechists would ask a question about the material, but usually they sat, listened, and, if they were good enough writers themselves, jotted down a few notes in their notebooks.[9] The entire meeting took about four hours, and though there were no formal breaks, people would occasionally wander outside to get some air or buy a snack from the small concession stand that a few women ran for the benefit of the parish.

At the end of the session each catechist paid Madre Chin one quetzal (about USD 0.13, or the price of six corn tortillas) for a set of four or five photocopied pages of typed notes about the readings. The meetings for-

---

9. It is incredibly difficult to find notebooks with plain covers at the stationary stores in Cobán, and so these grown men and women holding important social positions in their communities wrote the notes for their sermons in books featuring garishly colored, wide-eyed, cutesy cartoon characters on the covers. They did not, however, seem to feel embarrassed about it as much as I did when writing my field notes in similar books.

mally closed at about noon with a hymn and the same prayers that had opened them.[10] Cholob'ank meetings had been happening in roughly the same way, twelve times a year since the late 1980s, and a few of the attendees had been coming to them almost since their inception.[11] Because the ecclesiastical calendar cycles around every few years, some of the catechists would have attended multiple cholob'anks for each set of verses during their tenures. However, both the parish and the diocese felt that it was important for them to continue to receive this monthly training to strengthen both their understanding of the Bible and their conviction to continue serving as catechists.

Catechists' preparations for their weekly sermons did not end at the monthly cholob'ank, however. Every week the catechists in each comunidad would meet with each other for an hour or so to discuss their plans for the coming week's Celebration of the Word and the Sunday Mass if it happened to be that community's turn to animate it. They read through the corresponding verses, went over Madre Chin's notes, and discussed their understanding of the verses to map out a general outline of the sermon that one of them would deliver at the upcoming ritual. At these smaller meetings, catequistas sought to form a consensus about what they should say in the sermon. Although a catequista did not need to leave those meetings with an exact plan of what they would say in the sermon, they did use these meetings to check their interpretations and understandings of the key points with their comrades so as not to produce too idiosyncratic an interpretation of the central message. Though Madre Chin's notes and the cholob'ank lectures served as important guidelines for what a catechist should say, the consensus that developed during the smaller meetings was also an important part of the way that catechists set up their sermons. Consensus-building is key to decision-

---

10. While the cholob'ank proceeded, the church bells calling people to Mass would have rung, that service been officiated and concluded, and most people who had come would have left the parish church. There was often a short interruption to the cholob'anks, too, while the CEB tasked with animating Mass that week stored the marimba back in the salon where the catechist met. Padre Agustino would often wander into the cholob'ank to listen for a few minutes after concluding Mass and attending to everyone who wanted a personal blessing or needed to consult with him on some other piece of business.

11. Wilson says that the catechist program was first organized in 1975 (Wilson 1995, 173.) However, as best as I was able to discern, the cholob'ank meetings in their current format did not start until later.

making among Mayas, and so it is not surprising that Madre Chin's teachings were subject to this kind of review and vetting from the community.

In both Masses and Celebrations of the Word sermons were preceded by ritual readings of text. Lectors (usually young men and women) were assigned to each verse (Old Testament, Psalm, Epistle, and, at Celebrations of the Word, Gospels) before the ritual commenced. In Masses, the reading of the most important verse—the one from the Gospels—was done by the priest and marked by the burning of incense, ringing of a bell, and raising of the Bible to display it to the congregation, and the reading was closed with a short hymn. Likewise, during Celebrations of the Word, lectors would perform some of the same ritual actions, albeit in less marked a way than the priest would. In both contexts, after the reading of the Gospel verse, the person in charge would chant *"Raatin li Qaawa'"* (The Word of the Lord) to which the congregation would reply *"Nim laa loq'al, Qaawa' Jesus"* (Glory to Lord Jesus).

After the readings, the designated catequista, who never acted as both lector and sermonist, would take the microphone and deliver the sermon in Q'eqchi' for about ten to fifteen minutes, carefully repeating and elaborating the central message of the day and generally hewing fairly closely to the ideas presented at the monthly meeting. Catechists generally opened their sermons by stating that they wanted to share two or three ideas with the congregation. They would then paraphrase or otherwise retell the narrative presented in the week's Biblical verses and extract the key takeaway message given by Jesus there. The rest of the sermon tended to be an explanation of the importance of that central message for parishioners' lives. It was often a theme of humility, forgiveness, faith, or some other ethical stance that is presented as a key to a proper Christian life, which the catechist would elaborate and then entreat the congregation to take with them after they left the chapel.

Sermons thus followed Biblical readings both temporally and logically. Mainstream Catholic sermons were explicitly figured as explications of the text, and thus in the most technical sense were homilies. The texts to be read on any given Sunday had been determined by the Roman Catholic Church at the global level following the themes of its liturgical calendar, and the cholob'ank was in place to regularize catequistas' interpretations of those texts. Although the sermon was figured as a localized interpretation of the biblical material meant to be applicable to parishioners' quotidian lives, the immediate relevance of the biblical texts was always secondary to its placement within the liturgical cycle. Although catechists occasionally did go "off message" (and, ironically, Padre Agustino was perhaps the person who I observed doing this the most), there was a predetermined structure in place that they were expected to work within, and which limited what any individual could say in a sermon. A catechist's authority depended on a routinized and formalized ritual structure of reading and interpreting the sacred texts, and thus, in a sense, the authority of a sermon preceded the act of verbalizing it.

The catequista's ability to be taken seriously by the congregation, in their function as someone who could correctly explain what the Bible said and how a good Christian should live the text's message, depended on their position as a particular kind of church worker who was authorized to perform this task. Catechists were members of an institutionalized hierarchy of speakers that in principle included the pope and his curia, the local episcopate and clergy, missionary workers like Padre Agustino and Madre Chin, the local instructores, the catequistas themselves, and lay parishioners at large. This structure of authority was unmistakably ranked and though the catechist was ultimately expected to be the point of contact between the parishioners and their clergy, it was also understood that they were to defer to those above them in most matters.[12]

The catechist *formación* program relied on a diffusion of information that stressed the orthodoxy of interpretation across occupational, cultural, and linguistic classes of people within the Roman Catholic Church. Despite the hierarchy implicit in this model and the clear educational and social divisions that existed between clergy and laity, there was an expectation that the message of the text would be reproduced with fidelity. There was a slight paradox here, though, because part of the task of the catechists was to act as a kind of cultural translator who could make particular the universal message of the Gospels. However, catechists' social positions within the parish were contingent on their continued participation in the cholob'ank. Madre Chin took attendance every week, noted absences, and prohibited repeat offenders from officiating their community's Celebrations of the Word until they reestablished regular attendance over several months. Moreover, the parish

---

12. This did not mean that there were not serious disagreements between catechists and the clergy. When these disagreements occurred, however, catechists often found ways to work around the authority of the priests.

required every catechist to reaffirm his or her desire to continue serving every year, and individuals could choose to either cease their work or to take time off. However, because of the investment of resources and the clergy's complaint that it was difficult to find intelligent and committed people to serve as catechists, every effort was made to keep the same people in those positions for as long as possible. Whether it was an expression of faith or the increased social position that came from being a catechist, most people who took up the office worked hard to keep their positions for years and even decades by attending the necessary meetings, studying their texts, and participating in the appropriate weekly rituals with their CEBs.

Charismatics: Inspiration and Preaching

Carismáticos did not participate in Madre Chin's cholob'anks, nor did they have a parallel set of meetings to organize and regularize the sermons La Renovación's members heard each week. Instead, they relied on the idea that each predicador would receive a gift of divine inspiration to help them perform the genre every time they met.

FIGURE 5   Carismáticos praying over a predicador

Before every meeting of La Renovación, while the band was tuning up and people were arriving, the three *hermanos* (both men and women served as catequistas, but all the predicadores I knew of were men) who led the group met for five or ten minutes in a corner of the chapel to prepare for the event. They talked about that meeting's sermon, marked a few verses in their Bibles with pieces of string or scraps of paper, and then went to do other work like setting up the pews, checking the audio equipment, and greeting arriving congregants before starting their services. Sometimes they checked the official lectionary to select the verses for that week, but just as often whoever was tasked with preaching that day would suggest something else. When the time came in the service for the sermon, the hermano who would be preaching knelt before the altar with his Bible in hand. The other two would then stand by him with their hands stretched out above his head and upper back and pray. In the prayer they would entreat God to bless that man (and occasionally the microphone, cable, and speakers, too), to give him knowledge (*naleb'*), to give him strength (*metzew*), to inspire him, and to literally "put Your [God's] word in his mouth" (*pon Tu palabra en su boca*). This prayer was primarily directed to God the Father, but it was also clear that the instrument for the knowledge, inspiration, and strength would be the Holy Spirit (Spanish *Espíritu Santo*, Q'eqchi' *Santil Musiq'e*). As the prayer commenced, other members of the congregation would join in from their seats in the pews to say their own prayers, likewise holding their open palms outstretched toward the preacher. After three or four minutes, the prayer would subside, then the preacher would stand, offer the congregation a ritual greeting, and begin speaking.

The preacher typically began by setting out the general theme of his sermon and explaining its importance to the spiritual lives of the congregants. This was often done with specific reference to why it was important for living as a *católico renovado*—a "renewed" Catholic (i.e., a carismático). These introductions were structured in a highly dialogic manner that called for the participation of the congregation. The preacher would pose questions that required either formulaic answers (such as a simple *"amén"* or a *"gloria a díos"*), or original reasoned responses based on congregants' knowledge of scripture, such as questions about who loves a person most: their parents, children, or spouse (the correct answer was none of those but rather Jesus). After the preacher had properly introduced the topic and hinted at its importance, he would read a relevant Bible verse, which was usually taken from the Gospels, but could also be from other parts of the Bible. The Bible reading served as a platform from which to further expand on the sermon's topic and marked a transition to the main body of the sermon.

Sermons typically lasted twenty to thirty minutes and built on and elaborated a central theme through related topics. As in Mainstream sermons, the themes of Charismatic sermons tended to center around certain ethical or moral stances that congregants should strive to embody as a good Christian; however, carismáticos couched those stances as specifically related to being a católico renovado as opposed to just a católico. Unlike a catequista's sermons in which one or two specific ideas formed the crux of a sermon, a predicador's sermon began with a general trope or topic, which he then built on incrementally, adding new material as needed.

Sometimes the predicador would reread a verse during the course of his performance, and sometimes he would introduce new ones. New verses were incorporated into the main body of sermons in two ways. First, and most commonly, predicadores quoted well-known verses from memory to exemplify basic theological points. The quotes tended to be formulaic and served as sort of conceptual anchors that could be peppered in to elicit an amén from the congregation and to move on to the next major idea. Second, less frequently but still regularly, predicadores would pick up their Bibles to read longer passages. The preacher's Bible usually rested on one of the loudspeakers so that it was within easy reach and the congregation's sight while he spoke. The passages that had been marked before the start of the event, but hadn't been in the opening reading, were typically read at some point during the sermon, though sometimes they were not, and instead the hermano might spend a few seconds leafing through his Bible to find another passage that had come to mind. In these instances, the Bible served as supporting evidence for what the preacher was talking about.

The prayer over the preacher ritually marked the beginning of the sermon, and the Bible readings were not marked as distinct parts of the ritual as they were in Mainstream Catholic services, in which the burning of incense and the chanting of a specific phrase were clear signals that the Gospel reading had ended and that a sermon was about to begin. Rather, the readings were subsumed into the genre of the sermon, with reading of the text and the extemporaneous speech of the sermon intertwined into a single speech event. For carismáticos, a sermon was not figured as a further exploration of a text to be discussed according to a set thematic schedule, but rather as an independent message formulated through the interaction of the preacher and the divine presence that inspired him. The equally divinely inspired but fixed Biblical text was seen as support for the sermon, not its source. Thus, the relationship of relevance was the reverse of catechists' sermons. For predicadores, Bible passages had to be made relevant (through selection, extemporaneous quotes, etc.) to the content of the sermon; for catequistas, the Biblical texts were a given and the content of the sermons had to be authored with them in mind. As a general rule, carismáticos' preaching tended to be more inductive, and catequistas' preaching tended to be more deductive.

Predicadores' sermons featured two other elements that bear further discussion: call-and-response sequences and songs. Carismáticos made frequent use of call-and-response routines between the ritual's leaders and the congregation at large. Predicadores peppered these simple moments of formulaic dialogue through their sermons to request affirmation from the congregation. They also functioned to heighten the sense that their sermons were more conversational than they were in Mainstream Catholic services. Hymns were also sometimes woven into the sermons for a similar effect. When, for example, some point Hermano Rigo made in his sermon reminded him of the lyrics of a hymn, he might sing a line or two a cappella and wait a beat to see if the band picked up his cue. He would then lead the congregation in singing the song before returning to the spoken sermon. If the congregation seemed a little listless or bored, a song could also be used to induce some enthusiasm from them.

A predicador's sermon was thus composed of several different genres of speech including song. The upshot of structuring sermons around an intermingling of readings, songs, and extemporaneous speech, and marking the start of this portion of the ritual with a prayer for inspiration, was that as far as the congregation was concerned, it was by virtue of God's grace that the preacher was able to effectively weave together a moral narrative from Bible verses. Although there were only roughly as many Charismatic preachers per group as there were catechists in a Mainstream CEB, their position was not determined by their training nor by their membership in a class of specialist speakers. In principle, any carismático could become a preacher, they just needed to receive the "don," or spiritual gift, to do so. Once that happened, they could declare themselves eligible to preach. There were no human intermediaries between the predicador and the source of his religious authority, as there were for a catequista; rather, his authority emanated directly from the divine presence invoked by the ritual.

Practices and Ideologies

These two styles of preparing for delivering sermons and, more crucially, acquiring the right to give them, contrasted quite strongly and suggested that each group had quite different ideas about the basis for religious authority. What qualifications a person needs in order to be a lay leader, the ritual structures through which their positions were legitimized, and the very structures of their sermons all converged to distinguish catequistas from predicadores, even if the two categories of ritual specialists performed what functionally constituted the same genre of speech.

Mainstream Catholics' methods stressed social chains of authority that one needed to enter from the bottom, but which one could move up in through a process of careful study and assimilation of information given from people higher up in the hierarchy. The interpretative style catechists were supposed to adhere to was predicated on the idea that information about the biblical texts was disseminated from the top down (with Madre Chin and the instructors working as mouthpieces for the priests, bishop, etc.). A second important principle was that there needed to be community consensus about what the essential message of a scriptural passage was before authoritative speech about it could be disseminated at a Celebration of the Word. The clergy carefully selected who they wanted to be the catechists for each community, ensuring that the person was respected by their home community and capable enough to assimilate the ideas the hierarchy deemed important and reproduce them faithfully. In order to be taken seriously as someone who could deliver sermons, a catechist had to be someone who possessed the necessary practical skills (e.g., literacy, some talent for public speaking, etc.), sufficient social maturity (e.g., be married and the head of a household[13]), and good moral standing within their comunidad. Moreover, they had to be dedicated to the project, since catechists were expected to read their Bibles according to the ecclesiastical calendar and attend meetings regularly to keep their positions. Each CEB kept an eye on the talents, skills, and behavior of its youth so that they could always have a sense of who might be a good choice to be trained as a catequista once they were married.

---

13. Marriage (understood as entering into a long-term, community-sanctioned heterosexual partnership, even if it is not necessarily accompanied by an official Catholic sacrament) is the key event that marks an individual's passage from youth to adult in Q'eqchi'-Maya culture. Q'eqchi'-Maya tend to marry in their mid- to late teens, and it is unusual, but not entirely unknown, for someone in their mid-twenties to remain single.

Because catechists' personal authority was in large part dependent on their ability to access the institutional authority of the Catholic Church, their interpretations of religious texts were authoritative insofar as they originated with and were guaranteed by the clergy.

Charismatics, on the other hand and unsurprisingly, valued charisma in both its secular and religious meanings most of all. The doctrine of the Holy Spirit's charismata or spiritual gifts meant that someone who was a skilled speaker was understood to be so because of God's grace; and since the authority of a sermon also derived from divine inspiration, who became a preacher did not in principle depend on human social relations. Though there was *de facto* consensus about the meaning of Bible verses, that consensus was not ideologically figured as something that derived from a community of interpreters (whether these were integrated vertically or horizontally); rather, they believed, it derived from the singular meaning God intended for the text to carry. Their style of preaching stressed the immediacy (in both senses of the word) of the message, since ideally its explanation was produced in the very moment of inspiration as a more or less direct emanation from God. The Biblical text, in fact, may even have been a secondary concern, since it was really just an artifact through which humans could access God's will. What ultimately guaranteed that people would hear God's word and could come to understand His will was the regularly occurring miracle that the Holy Spirit would inspire a community's *predicadores* to preach the truth.

What, then, should we make of the fact that the people in these two groups, belonging to (at least nominally) the same religion, had such different methods for authorizing preachers as well as for understanding the authoritativeness of their speech? I would argue that these differing practices indexed two distinct language ideological positions that were recursively manifest in several aspects of how they employed speech in their rituals (Irvine and Gal 2000, 38). Analyzing these practices of authorization as part of the larger ideological constructs that underlay them offers us insight into the process of schismatic religious differentiation that was occurring between Mainstream and Charismatic Catholics in San Felipe. The ideological positions of the two groups both derived from and helped to construct their ideas about how one should relate to the divine and, by extension, what it meant to be a morally good person. Their ideas about what made a good preacher and how a person went about acquiring virtuosity in preaching was heavily dependent on what each of the two religious communities valued as proper moral dispositions for efficacious ritual participation. The authorizing practices of Mainstream catequistas and Charismatic predicadores could be respectively characterized according to the basic models of "control, constraint and respect" and "spontaneity, effusiveness and joy" (see Hoenes del Pinal 2009, 2011).

Mainstream Catholics' formal and routinized system of acquiring competence in biblical exegesis evidenced a conservative disposition predicated on the individual person's ability to manage and control their thoughts, words, and actions so that they would be in line with the larger institution's. Catequistas achieved their positions by submitting themselves to a hierarchy of authorized speakers including Madre Chin and Padre Agustino. The organizing idea was that in order for the catechists to serve their ritual function they had to be in a properly humble position vis-à-vis those higher in the Catholic hierarchy. Following the instruction of those above them in that chain and doing their best to assimilate their superiors' knowledge was a way of showing the proper respect for other people and integrating themselves into the institutional body of the Catholic Church. Once a person was identified as a potential catechist and selected to start training, he or she had to be willing to incur the expenses associated with the monthly courses and an annual retreat, as well as the incidental expenses associated with holding the office, which might include visiting infirm members of the comunidad, organizing and leading courses for children ahead of their first communion or for couples who wished to marry, and helping transport people and equipment to the Mass at the parish center. This investment of time and money was strictly voluntary, but it could be a weighty burden on the catequista's household economy, even if in return they gained social standing and earned a measure of presumptive deference and respect from fellow parishioners.

Charismatic Catholics' apparent dependence on inspiration, and the idea that it was a divine gift for preaching that enabled their religious authority, suggested that authority was not cultivated over time but rather spontaneously granted to certain individuals. A preacher could only really discern the text's meaning and relate it to other people's lives by giving up human mediation and coming into direct unmediated contact with the divine. For carismáticos, the only desirable submission was to the divine presence itself since that was the ultimate source of religious knowledge. The sermon's various markers of spontaneity in the performance of sermons (i.e., the prayer, the unplanned readings, moments of call-and-response between the preacher and the congregation, and the general free flow) were signs that the predicador spoke independently of other human speakers and signaled his unmediated access to God.[14] His willingness to skip around topics and introduce other genres of speech, such as more Bible readings or songs, into the sermon created the appearance that little of the performance was preplanned. Charismatic preachers, like catechists, were afforded a measure of respect and deference due to their religious position, too; however, because everyone was theoretically endowed with some spiritual gift or another (or at least expected to receive one once they were ready for it) and because carismáticos placed greater emphasis on the parity of congregants before God, the predicador's social gain was smaller than the catequista's.

The ideologies behind these practices can best be understood when we consider what each model of preparing to give a sermon highlighted and occluded about the act of preaching. Each model involved highlighting certain aspects of what people did as well as the erasure of other aspects (Irvine and Gal 2000, 38), and if we look to the gaps between the ideal forms and what people actually did, we can better understand the ideological underpinnings of the two systems.

For all their preparation, catequistas were essentially improvising when they gave a sermon. I never saw a catechist consult a prepared speech, set of note cards, or even an annotated Bible while delivering a sermon. Catechists told me that they prepared a sort of mental outline of what they were going to say, but that they always spoke extemporaneously. Qana' Esperanza said that it had been very difficult to give a sermon when she first started and that she would worry about getting the message wrong and not remembering what the *madres* (nuns) had taught them at the cholob'ank. Bit by bit, though, she got better at it and more comfortable speaking. The cholob'ank, Madre Chin's notes, and meetings with the other catechists helped her develop a rough set of guidelines and tentpole ideas for a sermon, but ultimately the

---

14. Cheryl Wharry has argued that in evangelical Black churches in the United States, spontaneity is an important value in the production of sermons, since it is considered to be a marker of "spiritual" talk. The use of discourse strategies such as call-and-response phrases and the establishment of particular rhythms mark sermons as properly "spiritual" by configuring them as spontaneous and (co-)constructed on the spot (Wharry 2003). Similarly, Saba Mahmood has shown how "rehearsed spontaneity" in the context of a women's Islamic piety movement, can help cultivate a sense of displaced human agency and, hence, a greater sense of spiritual potency (Mahmood 2001).

composition and performance of a sermon depended on her ability to put those ideas together and into her own words. She said that over time she learned to trust in her own knowledge and to rely on her previous experiences performing this speech genre.

The congregation, for its part, accepted that a catechist's sermon was authoritative because they trusted that the clergy had selected people to hold the office who were trustworthy and had trained them appropriately to perform their duties. The catequistas' training conferred a degree of institutional authority on their speech, which was further reinforced when the priest stepped aside at Sunday Mass to allow these special laypeople to perform the sermon. The catechist came to occupy the physical and ideological spaces normally reserved for the clergy and because of this were marked as legitimate exegetes. The message this conveyed was that a layperson could participate in some of the Church's institutional authority provided that they were in the right kind of relationships of tutelage and submission to the clergy. If during a sermon the congregation was focused on seeing and hearing only the catechist, they also knew that in that moment he or she was acting as the voice of the Catholic Church and had its implicit support.

Mainstream Catholics did recognize that some people were more talented public speakers than others, but they did not necessarily equate eloquence with effective preaching. Ultimately, good preaching for them depended on the quality of the relationship the catequista had to the Catholic hierarchy. For example, Qana' Esperanza and her brother Qawa' Mateo both served as catechists for their community, and although it was widely acknowledged that Mateo was a very talented and eloquent speaker, his sister was seen as the more capable preacher. Even Qana' Esperanza acknowledged that Qawa' Mateo gave more interesting and moving sermons than she could, but she was regarded as a stronger source of religious authority in her community because of the close working relationship she had cultivated with the clergy. She was a regular and diligent attendee at cholob'anks and was further involved in a number of church-sponsored activities and para-church organizations through which she worked closely with Madre Chin and Padre Agustino. Qana' Esperanza had a household to manage, but her husband was often away for days at a time working as a truck driver, two of her children were teenagers, and the eldest (her daughter) was mature enough to help look after the two youngest ones. Her home was on land shared by several members of her kin group, including her mother, who had also been a catechist and encouraged her to pursue this work. As such, Qana' Esperanza had enough support with her home life that she could pursue her work with the parish. To be sure, she was always busy and rarely had time to simply rest, but she was able to balance her work at home and with the church.[15] Qawa' Mateo, on the other hand, ran his own business, one which did not afford him a flexible schedule. He was consequently unable to devote much time to cultivating a close working relationship with the clergy or to be involved in as many church activities as his sister was. No one faulted Qawa' Mateo for prioritizing his economic activities, but the fact that his involvement in church life was limited in comparison to his sister's meant she tended to be regarded as the more important and reliable religious authority figure in their community.

By studying, going to meetings, and transmitting a particular orthodox line of thought, catequistas showed that they were obedient to and respectful of God's manifestation on Earth—namely, the Catholic Church. Their legitimacy came from the idea that they had learned how to adequately "voice" the intentions of the church hierarchy and, to a lesser extent, of the community as a whole. In a Bakhtinian sense, the catechist's authority depends on his or her ability to master the language of the global institutional Church and reproduce its intention in a way that was accessible to Q'eqchi'-Maya parishioners. Ideally, the catechists' duty was to faithfully reproduce the meanings and intentions of the Catholic hierarchy in a language and idiom that was accessible to parishioners with no specialized religious knowledge. Their job was to mediate that message as faithfully as possible. Technically any individual could become a catechist, provided they were literate, had a good moral character, and were able to devote the time to the task. Ultimately, though, being an effective catechist depended above all else on a person's willingness

---

15. Qana' Esperanza was not the only woman working as a catechist, but there were significantly fewer women than men exercising the office. Many women who wanted to be more active in the parish faced resistance from their husbands. Qana' Livia said that she would have liked to be a catequista and had even started the training process for it when she was younger, but her husband had forced her to stop because he didn't like that she left the house so much. She was unhappy about this but relented to his demands because she felt that wives had to obey their husbands. When I returned to Cobán in 2017, Qana' Livia had completed her catechist training and was now very active in the parish. She had enlisted the help of several other catechists and one of the priests to plead her case once her eldest child had entered high school, and her husband had a change of heart. She regretted ever having stopped following the path that God had set out for her but was happy that she could continue that work in the parish now.

and ability to be integrated into the Church's hierarchical structure. Someone who did so was almost by definition understood as a morally mature person who recognized that that their own personal interests and desires were secondary to the service they rendered to the larger Catholic community.

Becoming a predicador in La Renovación did not require formal study and submission to the Catholic Church's hierarchy; rather, it was a status conveyed on the person by miraculous intervention when the Holy Spirit bestowed the appropriate don on someone who God saw fit to serve His will. In this schema, a talent for preaching was one among many gifts, but it was also an important one that bestowed religious authority upon a select few. In principle, then, God directly chose who His preachers would be, and they exercised that office as a function of their relationship to the divinity. However, that relationship had to be made public and dramatized at each of their services through the prayer. The prayer that preceded the sermon recapitulated the idea that preaching was divinely inspired and served as a public (re)affirmation that the hermano being prayed over had received the gift to perform that speech genre before and would do so again that day.

Like catequistas, predicadores were held to high moral standards within their communities. However, their ability to speak convincingly as exegetes depended less on their moral standing before the community than it did on the ethical stance they took during the ritual—namely, the extent to which they could be said to become *voceros* or spokesmen for God. To be a convincing preacher doctrinally, a carismático had to give up his personal agency and turn over his speech to the will of God, and the ritual of praying over the predicador for inspiration was a way of ritually signaling that displacement of agency. To put it in Erving Goffman's (1981, 144) terms, the predicador had to create a context in which he was figured as the animator of the speech event (i.e., the person actively producing an utterance), but where God was clearly the principal (i.e., the agent whose position and wishes were being expressed through the utterance). The mediating role of author in Goffman's tripartite schema (i.e., the person who selects the exact wording and phrasing of the utterance) was left somewhat indeterminate in this context. While it was acknowledged that the predicador was in some ways responsible for the phrasings of the sermon, when I asked Hermano Rigo about it, he said that sometimes it felt as if God was putting words into his mouth. True, a lot of the time it was him speaking, but sometimes that was the feeling he got, as if the words were coming to him from a divine source without him even thinking. It was not fully the case that preaching was thought of as a dissociative state of consciousness in which the ritual specialists claimed to be a direct mouthpiece for physically non-present others (as in, for example, spirit mediumship), or even the way that carismáticos described their understanding of glossolalia as a language that belonged to God and the angels. Nonetheless, they felt that in order for a predicador to adequately convey God's message to the congregation, he needed to (at least partially) disavow his own personal agency and intentions. The hermanos who preached were not simply members of a human community of interpreters with the prerogative to speak but rather the link between a divine authority and its human subjects, and the prayers over the predicadores before a sermon made this idea explicit.

This stance is not an unusual one in religious settings, where the authority of supernatural messages is often predicated on a separation of the animator and the principal behind it (Du Bois 1992). To this I would add that the ways in which interactants co-construct the necessary frame for the speech to be produced likewise alters the location of the agency and authority that the speech conveys. In the Charismatic Catholics' case, the distancing of the animator from the principal was achieved by the initial prayer, asking for inspiration and the various discursive techniques that made the sermon appear to be the product of inspired improvisation rather than preplanning. In the Mainstream Catholic case, by contrast, the reliability of the sermon was largely based on the authority of the larger community of interpreters who came together to support the individual catequista's performance.

None of this is to say, however, that La Renovación's predicadores took their office for granted nor that they were cavalier in exercising its duties. They were well aware that if their preaching was subpar people could become unhappy with them, and that the congregation might move to replace them with someone else who had also received the gift to preach. Since the Holy Spirit could dole out its gifts to anyone at any time, a replacement preacher was always theoretically at hand. Worse yet, bad preaching could lead newer members to stop attending services, and decreasing numbers would have seriously undermined the group's still tenuous position within the parish.[16] Without the benefit of the monthly cholob'ank meetings nor

---

16. The official reason that Sa'xreb'e's carismáticos had left the group in Rub'elchaj was that people wanted to have meetings closer to home, but one person also confided that at the time of the split there were questions about the latter group's leadership.

Madre Chin's notes to use as models, the predicadores had to spend a good deal of time and effort honing their skills as preachers and becoming more sophisticated in their religious knowledge. The predicadores' Bibles all had worn covers and cracked spines from the time they spent studying the text. All reported reading the Bible daily, and Hermano Rigo said that he would study his Q'eqchi'- and Spanish-language copies of the Bible side by side so that he could better understand them. Additionally, he kept a little notebook with his Bibles in which he would write down things that he wanted to talk about in church.

To fill his notebook and otherwise prepare himself for preaching, Hermano Rigo made use of several other resources, too. First, he and his fellow predicadores listened to the radio. Transistor radios were the one piece of communications technology everyone owned (Hoenes del Pinal 2019), and one could easily tune into the diocese's FM radio station as well as the national Catholic Charismatic station broadcasting from Guatemala City through one of its repeaters. Moreover, they would also occasionally tune into evangélico radio stations as well (even if they did not let the other parishioners know that), in hopes of finding some idea or other material that they could adapt to their own sermons. The national office of the Catholic Charismatic Renewal also periodically sponsored a regional conference at which they could hear others speak and pick up new topics for their sermons, as well as buy pamphlets, booklets, and cassette tapes, which were also important sources of inspiration. Finally, like the catequistas, predicadores talked to each other regularly. They could consult with each other about ideas for a sermon and check to see if their understandings of Biblical verses matched those of other community members. In sum, when a predicador took up his microphone to preach, he did not do so as a *tabula rasa*. Ideologically those few hermanos who were authorized to preach might have been accorded the position by divine intervention, and their abilities as orators and exegetes might have been attributed to a spiritual gift, but in truth those skills had to be developed and maintained through hard work and study. If the source of their talents were explicitly attributed to the Holy Spirit's charismata, there was also an implicit understanding that those spiritual gifts had to be cultivated to bear fruit.

It was no coincidence, too, that this first generation of predicadores had all been catequistas before converting to La Renovación. Whether this suggests some of the charisma of office from the Mainstream Catholic institutional structure had carried over into this new religious movement or simply that the Charismatic Catholic congregations recognized that the skills developed in one context are useful in the other is not clear. However, it is unlikely that those men would have been accepted as preachers if other congregants didn't think that they had some mastery over the Bible and access to God's intentions beyond their ability to be divinely inspired. Perhaps it was even the case that divine inspiration would only come to people who had otherwise prepared themselves to receive it by studying their Bibles and living a good Christian life. After all, as Hermano Federico once told me, "God gives those gifts [of the Holy Spirit] to people who are ready [to receive them]."

Conclusion

These two models for becoming authorized practitioners of public exegesis required catequistas and predicadores to figure their relationships to God in particular ways. For the former that relationship was guaranteed through the intermediaries of the local Catholic hierarchy; for the latter it was a relationship that was built around the possibility of an unmediated transaction of ideas between the person and one part of the Triune God. In both cases, however, those relationships and their ideological underpinnings only became evident through the practices through which they came to be seen as legitimate speakers by their communities. The social processes through which Q'eqchi'-Maya Catholic community leaders became authorized as legitimate performers of sermons tell us quite a bit about what each congregation valued in this type of speech. One of the central problematics they seemed to be addressing was the way that the Biblical text's meaning was mediated for the sermon's audience. In both communities, the ultimate responsibility for the meaning of the message lay well outside of the speaker, in an entity to which the sermon-giver only ever had partial and limited access. The sources of the local lay leaders' authority were imagined quite differently, though.

These ritual processes of legitimation derived from the two distinct ideological structures that shaped the communicative practices of Q'eqchi'-Maya Catholics in ritual contexts. These ideologies thus did not just organize who could speak in church but also how they should speak, and the fact that each group had different models for legitimating speakers further separated the two communities. The (limited) legitimation of La Renovación's predicadores within the local Catholic Church had placed into question catequistas' position as de facto community leaders. The new schismatic group, which had forsaken existing structures of authorization and its leaders, claimed a higher source authority for their preaching. In doing so they called into question the catequistas' standing and legitimacy. Ironically enough, as we saw in the previous chapter, catequistas a generation earlier had similarly challenged Costumbre's existing structures of religious authority. At the start of the new millennium, the carismáticos were seeking to gain a measure of legitimacy while somewhat awkwardly standing with one foot inside the institutional structure of the Catholic Church and the other outside of its official hierarchies of authority. In this oppositional context, competing ideas about the source for religious and moral authority engendered two sets of practices that put into question the solidarity of a community of people who nonetheless still shared many of the same social, political, and religious interests.

In the next chapter we examine specific performative uses of language as a means of gaining a fuller understanding of how the two congregations' linguistic choices further contributed to their distinct voicings of how to be good Q'eqchi'-Maya Catholics.

CHAPTER 4

Están listos para cantar en Q'eqchi'? Ma nekeeraj xninqehinkil sa' Q'eqchi'?
Marking Ritual through Code Choice

I had been living in Cobán and attending services in San Felipe for about seven months the first time I came into direct contact with the carismáticos in the village of Sa'xreb'e. By then I was generally familiar with what the catequistas had to say about carismáticos, but I hadn't actually spoken to any member of La Renovación nor been to their services yet. One mid-December morning I happened to be sitting in the parish office chatting with a few people, when a messenger from Sa'xreb'e came looking for Padre Agustino to ask that he perform a Mass for La Renovación's second anniversary on New Year's Day. The priest was off running errands, but gauging from other people's reactions that day, I had just witnessed an extraordinary event. Gabriella, who was the parish secretary, met the request with more than a little skepticism because, as she explained to me after the messenger left, "Carismáticos never go to Mass. Even though Padre Agustino makes the trip to that village every other week, they never come." Qawa' Hernando (the sacristan) concurred, adding that Sa'xreb'e's carismáticos had celebrated their first anniversary without any direct involvement from the parish, and now they wanted a Mass! When Padre Agustino came back to the office just before lunch, Gabriella relayed the request. The priest widened his eyes in a wry sign of surprise and told her to put the event on the calendar for what was shaping up to already be a very busy New Year's Day.

On January 1, 2005, after resting a bit to recover from the many other activities that had already taken place over the previous twenty-four hours (New Year's Eve and Day are ritually important days at San Felipe) and letting our lunch of pan-fried fish, stewed greens, *fufu*,[1] and tortillas settle in our stomachs, we headed to Sa'xreb'e in the parish's red Suzuki Samurai.

As we pulled up to the village chapel, I could see a few people milling about outside and what looked like a full house inside. Several of the men who had been standing near the chapel's door rushed up to meet the car and greet the priest. One of them—who I would later come to know as Hermano Rigo—offered to take Father Agustino's navy blue backpack in which he transported the ritual accoutrements he needed to perform Mass. From the car I could hear music being played on electric keyboard, electric bass, and a four-piece drum kit—it was lively and upbeat. I could hear the congregation singing along in Spanish, too, clapping in unison on the down beats. It sounded a lot like the music I heard when I walked by one of the many Pentecostal churches that dot the street of Cobán, and I immediately started to understand why people in the parish kept saying that *"los carismáticos parecen puros evangélicos"* ("the Charismatics seem just like Pentecostals").

The song was just coming to an end as we were getting out of the car, and I heard the bandleader inside the chapel say something to the effect of *"Amén hermanos. Están listos para cantar en Q'eqchi'? Ma nekeeraj xninqehinkil sa' Q'eqchi'?"* (Amen brothers. Are you ready to sing in Q'eqchi'? Do you want to celebrate in Q'eqchi'?) The congregation responded to the query which had been posed first in Spanish and immediately a second time in Q'eqchi' with an enthusiastic, "Amén!" That "Amén"—a word that plays a wide range of discursive functions in Charismatic Q'eqchi'-Mayas' ritual life and that their critics had latched on to as a stereotypical token in their mocking of the carismático—affirmed that the congregation was ready to pray, sing, and otherwise worship in Q'eqchi' for the rest of the service, or at least as long as the priest was there. We had scarcely stepped foot inside of the chapel when I heard the marimba players strike their mallets against the wooden keys of an instrument that had not made its presence heard until that moment. That wooden timbre marked the beginning of a new hymn, this one sung

---

1. Fufu is a thick dough-like food made from corn and cassava commonly eaten in Central and West Africa (where it sometimes also includes plantains and other starchy plants). Father Agustino always ate fufu and pan-fried fish for lunch and dinner at home, and I get the sense he never really developed a liking for Guatemala's staple food of tortillas and black beans, nor for the *kaq ik'* turkey stew that is Cobán's signature dish. The parish cook, Qana' Alberta, said she still preferred tortillas but also said that she had tried the padre's fufu and liked it, which was a good thing since she had to make it every day he was in residence.

in Q'eqchi' and unaccompanied by percussive clapping. Now, rather than sounding like a Pentecostal service, the space sounded just like the Mass Padre Agustino had celebrated before lunch at San Felipe's main church, or for that matter any of the other Masses and Celebrations of the Word that I had been a part of in the parish over the previous seven months. "*Ahora ya parecen católicos*," I thought: now they really did seem like Catholics. I was struck with how readily the congregation had switched not just the language they were using but also the style in which they practiced their Catholicism.

I can only assume that Padre Agustino had heard the same bit of metalinguistic talk that I had, but it seemed that he didn't quite believe it. As he was putting on his cassock and readying the ritual space of the altar by laying out his chalice, the vessels filled with holy water, wine, and oil, and plates for communion, he asked the two group leaders who had ushered us up to the altar area what language they wanted for the Mass—Spanish or Q'eqchi'? Hermano Rigo said that they wanted it in Q'eqchi'. Padre Agustino's demeanor was often inscrutable, but the face he made to Rigo's response showed more than a hint of surprise and a good measure of suspicion. Just before signaling that he was ready to start the Mass, Agustino leaned around the side of the altar toward the congregation and, in a voice loud enough to be heard by the first couple rows, asked in Spanish what language they *really* wanted to hear the Mass in. They answered, "*sa' Q'eqchi'*." Both the content of their answer and their choice of code in answering a query that had initially been framed in Spanish attested to their desire that the Mass should be celebrated in Q'eqchi'. Padre Agustino did not ask a third time or seek further confirmation. With a small sigh he closed the Spanish language missal that was in front of him, laid it aside, and pulled out the Q'eqchi'-language one from his backpack. He flipped to the pages he would need, pulled the microphone stand a little closer to his face, and in a quick but firm voice intoned, "*Sa' xk'ab'a' li Dios Yuwa'b'ej, li Dios K'ajolb'ej, ut li Dios Santil Musiq'ej*" (In the name of God the Father, God the Son, and God the Holy Spirt). The congregation dutifully replied "*Jo'kan taxaq*" ("let it be so" or amen). The Mass would be in Q'eqchi' after all.

It ultimately made little difference to Padre Agustino which of the two local languages he celebrated the Mass in since he spoke Spanish well and Q'eqchi' better, and neither were his native language. However, he had been prepared to celebrate it in Spanish because he was under the impression that the carismáticos, despite being native speakers of Q'eqchi', always celebrated their rituals in Spanish and in Spanish only. Hermano Rigo's request that Mass be performed in Q'eqchi' contravened the priest's expectations, and while he was able to adjust to the request without much difficulty, he was caught off guard by it. Padre Agustino's annoyance notwithstanding, he celebrated the Mass for La Renovación in Q'eqchi'; or at least mostly in Q'eqchi', because, ironically enough, when it came time to give his homily, Agustino pointedly switched into Spanish several times to emphasize certain points he wanted to make about the need for unity and peaceful relations among Catholics in the village. Nonetheless, the chapel was full, and this was what really interested him. He had spent the previous three years trying to mitigate the tensions between catequistas and carismáticos in this part of the parish and had managed to establish an uneasy peace in this village. The catequistas in Sa'xreb'e were no longer trying to bar the carismáticos from entering the chapel (even if some of them still grumbled about this), and the fact that La Renovación had asked for a Mass seemed to confirm that they were content to stay with the parish and respected his and the Catholic Church's authority over their activities. Plus, all of the carismáticos in Sa'xreb'e had actually turned up to Mass for once, and that was indeed unprecedented, even if many familiar Mainstream Catholic faces were nowhere to be found, including those like Qawa' Emanuel, who could no doubt hear that Mass was happening from their homes.

On the way back to Cobán, still trying to process what had happened and feeling rather confused and excited about the large-scale situational linguistic code-switch (Gumperz 1982) we had just witnessed, I asked Agustino what he thought about the carismáticos wanting the Mass celebrated in Q'eqchi'. He said that it had been strange because carismáticos always wanted Spanish, but he offered no further insight as to why specifically they might have wanted Q'eqchi' on that day. I tried to press him on it a bit more to speculate on a cause. Was it because it was their anniversary? Were they trying to gain favor with him? Had they decided that Q'eqchi' was better? But that long day wasn't over yet, and Padre Agustino was not in the mood to try to figure out what, if anything, had motivated the Charismatics' request. He was a little annoyed that they had surprised him like that to be sure, but otherwise he was willing to chalk it up to yet another instance of what to his mind were the fickle choices that Q'eqchi'-Mayas sometimes made in their religious lives. In his defense, it was now late in the afternoon, and this had been the third Mass he had officiated since sunrise, and the fourth if we count the midnight Mass from the night before, and in between those events he had been busy attending to parishioners who wanted a blessing or to consult him for some other reason. He was tired, and so we rode back to the parish center saying little else and listening to a bootleg *Bee Gees' Greatest Hits* CD that was always on heavy rotation in the car until both were lost three months later to a carjacking in Guatemala City.

I never observed another event quite like this one, where the linguistic differences (not to mention musical ones) between Mainstream and Charismatic ways of being Catholic were so clearly juxtaposed. That night the Charismatics in Sa'xreb'e made a deliberate choice to perform their Catholicism in a way that they were familiar with, but which was also significantly different from how they more habitually worshipped. It was so different in fact that it required explicit coordination and a deliberate framing from one of their leaders. It also flew in the face of what I had until then been told about the linguistic situation in the parish—namely, that carismáticos only spoke Spanish, and that Mainstream Catholics only spoke Q'eqchi' in church. The reality was that carismáticos could and did speak both languages in their services, just as they did in their lives outside of church.

A few months later I also learned that many of my Mainstream Catholic consultants, including those who were the most vocal critics of Charismatics' use of Spanish in church, were also perfectly comfortable participating in a Mass celebrated in Spanish when they needed to. I came to this realization when Qawa' Emanuel, who was one of the most outspoken critics of La Renovación in San Felipe, invited me to his granddaughter's wedding. At that Mass, which was held in the neighboring town of Santa Cruz and officiated by a Ladino priest, I was surprised to find that Qawa' Emanuel and his whole family had no trouble participating in Spanish. That ceremony was celebrated in Spanish in order to accommodate the parties of both a Q'eqchi'-Maya bride and a Poqomchi'-Maya groom.[2] My surprise was soon tempered by my embarrassment that, unlike my hosts, I only knew Mass in Q'eqchi'. A few months later, when Padre Agustino took a few weeks off to

---

2. The couple spoke Spanish with each other, and they planned to raise children primarily in Spanish. Theirs was but one example of the social dynamics that have led to Maya language shift, even as in some respects Maya cultural identity has become stronger in Guatemala.

travel and a priest from another parish was called in to officiate Masses at San Felipe, I heard no complaints about his use of Spanish either. Perhaps none of this should have been as surprising a development as I initially took it to be, though, since most of the parishioners I knew spoke both Spanish and Q'eqchi' in their daily lives. While a sizeable portion of the youngest generation were strongly Spanish-dominant and low-proficiency "semi-speakers" (Dorian 1982) of Q'eqchi', and a slight majority of elders could be characterized as Q'eqchi' monolinguals who had only a minimal passive understanding of Spanish, on the whole people in the central sector of the parish were functionally bilingual.[3] Spanish was not anathema to their sense of being Catholic—they were willing to use it when the context called for it, but they certainly had a stronger preference for Q'eqchi'.

My surprise at both the carismáticos' code-switch to Q'eqchi' for their anniversary Mass as well as at Qawa' Emmanuel's ability to seamlessly transition into Spanish prayers at his granddaughter's wedding attest to the extent to which I had at first uncritically adopted the discourse about language and religion from San Felipe's Mainstream Catholics, who insisted that Q'eqchi'-Maya Catholics should pray in the Q'eqchi' language, and that the problem with the carismáticos was that they refused to do so, instead choosing to "yell in Spanish like evangélicos." If both Mainstream and Charismatic Catholics were bilingual, why did code choice matter so much to them in the context of church? Even if bilingualism was the norm in most of daily life, as the massive code-switch I observed in Sa'xreb'e illustrated, the language one used in church mattered deeply in San Felipe. People talked about the difference between the congregations' code choices in moral terms, and, as we saw in this book's introduction, they sometimes went as far as writing angry letters of complaint to the clergy about the consequences of these differences for their

---

3. Although this was not so in the past, life in twenty-first-century Guatemala all but demands some level of fluency in Spanish, and so Q'eqchi'-Mayas, like so many members of other Maya ethnolinguistic groups, are increasingly using the language on a daily basis and their communities are experiencing some language shift because of this (England 2003; Hawkins 2005). Every parishioner I met, however, reported speaking at least some Q'eqchi' at the home. Among Ladinos in Cobán, Spanish-Q'eqchi' bilingualism was rarer, but not entirely unknown. A few generations ago, when the city had been more isolated from the rest of Guatemala, it was relatively common for Ladinos to learn both languages. My grandfather don Samuel, for example, had learned both languages as a child and retained fluency in Q'eqchi' into old age. Sadly, his children never learned to speak it beyond a few phrases.

communities' well-being. Moreover, as we have just seen, beyond talking about the differences, parishioners also sometimes strategically altered their own individual and collective linguistic behaviors to match expectations, both real and imaginary, about what other parties thought being Catholic should sound like. This all suggests that the language one used in church was not dictated by communicative efficacy alone but was rather the result of deliberate choices that reflected distinct goals and values. Put in Bakhtinian terms, their voicings were, as all voicings are, ideologically laden, and the forms their voicings took reflected distinct interests.

Part of what parishioners were managing through code choice was a sense of cultural identity—marking themselves as members of either an ethnically particular Maya church in the mold of the Inculturationist Catholicism by using Q'eqchi', or as part of a cosmopolitan movement of católicos carismáticos by using Spanish. However, I would add to this that these code choices were not just about identity; they were consequential in that they established the conditions for what counted as Mainstream or Charismatic Catholic ritual space. By exploring how parishioners mobilized language to mark off ritual time and space as distinct from the everyday, we can gain some insight into what they held to be crucial for their religious practice.

At the heart of Mainstream Catholics' discourse about the impropriety of carismáticos' linguistic practices lay the idea that the latter only ever used Spanish in their rituals and that this signaled their separation from the larger Q'eqchi'-Maya Catholic community for whom Q'eqchi' was the preferred code. As Qawa' Emmanuel was wont to put it, "*Solo gritan en Castilla, parecen puros protestantes*" (They only yell in Castillian [Spanish], they seem just like Protestants). Yet the contention that Charismatics only ever spoke Spanish was not literally true. Once I started to actually analyze what language they spoke in their ritual events, and especially once I factored out the singing of hymns (see chapter 5), I realized that Charismatics actually spoke much more Q'eqchi' than Spanish. The presence of Spanish was an important component of carismáticos' ritual practices, but its significance came from the way it was used alongside Q'eqchi', not because it was used to the other code's exclusion. In this chapter I argue that it was the co-presence of the two languages that marked Charismatic ritual rather than the presence of Spanish as such, and that concomitantly, the exclusive and relatively purist use of Q'eqchi' in church was symbolically important for Mainstream Catholics' construction of ritual space. Code consistency in the catequistas' case and code alternation in the carismáticos' were ideologically laden linguistic choices that each represented two distinct voicings of how to be a good Catholic.

Carismático critiques of Mainstream Catholic services focused on the idea that the latter's rituals were *tristes* (sad), and that people there did not feel *júbilo* (joy) in coming together to praise God. In making those characterizations, they emphasized the relative bodily stillness of the congregation (see Hoenes del Pinal [2011] and chapter 6), as well as the verbal restraint of the celebrants in praying and singing. Speaking only one language in church stifled one's faith, they said. As Hermano Rigo put it, "*¿Si Dios entiende todos los idiomas, porque sólo voy a rezar en Q'eqchi'? No, voy a decirlo como está en mi corazón*" (If God understands all languages, why should I only pray in Q'eqchi'? No, I'm going to say it as it is in my heart [i.e., as it comes to my mind]). In framing things this way, he set up the contrast between his current way of being Catholic, in which the aim was to express himself as an authentic individual nimbly using all resources available to him in prayer, and his former way of doing so, in which only the Maya language could adequately be used as an expression of faith. Part of the problem with Mainstream Catholic faith from his perspective was that the expectation that only one language ought to be used imposed unnecessary and indeed potentially harmful restrictions on a person's ability to communicate with God. That form of linguistic hygiene inhibited rather than facilitated religious experience.

Mainstream Catholics, for their part, understood this regimentation of code choice as a means of expressing a culturally rooted and hence authentic form of faith. This followed from the convergence of the legacy of religion as a semiautonomous Maya cultural sphere, the principles of Inculturation Theology that the clergy promoted, their experience as an ethnic minority struggling to maintain distinctive markers of cultural identity in an ostensibly pluricultural nation whose society is nonetheless deeply racist and, perhaps most importantly, their understanding that being controlled in one's linguistic and embodied actions was a way to manifest a properly respectful attitude toward God. For multiple reasons, then, maintaining Q'eqchi' code consistency was a sign of piety.

As Kathryn Woolard has noted, the question of why "people who have multiple 'ways of speaking' would restrict themselves to a subset of them" is just as compelling as the question of why people use multiple codes (2004,

75). Because language is heteroglot and all instances of speech are dialogic, neither code consistency nor code-switching ought to be seen as the "natural" conditions of communication in and of themselves. Rather, both options are potentially meaningful, and each must be subjected to critical analysis to be fully understood. Any actual performance of either code-switching or code consistency is an interactional achievement that is contingent upon a number of factors, including the individual participants' linguistic competencies, motivations, and social positions. Just as important are the cultural values that people attach to specific ways of communicating and the social dynamics that regulate the norms of interaction. When we take this perspective, we see that what differentiated San Felipe's two congregations linguistically was their stance toward the mixing of codes within the context of Catholic ritual, not their linguistic competencies as such. For Charismatics, the co-presence of Spanish and Q'eqchi' signaled something important about what it meant to be a Catholic; for Mainstream Catholics, conversely, it was the consistent use of Q'eqchi' that did so. The rest of this chapter examines how these preferences were enacted at the opening of their respective ritual events. I focus on the linguistic openings of rituals here because those moments neatly illustrate how San Felipe's parishioners mobilized their code choices to mark the time and space of rituals as distinct from the course of everyday life, and in doing so imbued language with religious meaning.

Establishing Code Consistency with Mainstream Catholics

Scarcely a few days after a new year begins, the Hermandad of San Felipe begins preparations for the patron saint's day celebrations, which draw over a thousand people to the parish church from the evening of January 14 to midday on January 15. The festivities include multiple Masses, music, fireworks (including, if there is enough money, a *torito*[4]), the performance of the *Baile del venado* masked dance, and a communal feast of tamales accompanied

---

4. Literally a "little bull," which is a trapezoidal frame made of canes and canvas onto which a sequence of fireworks is rigged. The frame is worn on the shoulders of a brave young man who performs a dance, hopping, spinning, and occasionally charging at the spectators who gather around the church plaza to watch. As the torito dances, the fireworks spark and flare, occasionally shooting off small whistling rockets through the air and dropping small explosives that crack at his feet until eventually the whole man-made beast seems to be ablaze in a glow of red, gold, silver, and green sparks.

with the ancient sacred beverage of the Maya—cacao. Preparing for the event requires coordinating material, human, and spiritual resources. This coordination begins with the celebration of a *novenario* (nine consecutive days of prayers) at the home of the *mertoom* or *mayordomo* (the sponsor of the Hermandad), which serves as the temporary seat for the group. The novenario meetings include important ritual tasks—namely, praying the Rosary for the santo—as well as mundane ones, such as reviewing the group's finances and dividing up the labor that needs to be done in preparation for the main celebration (e.g., who will go out to raise funds or buy materials, who would help carry the santo up to the church, who would be on cleanup duty, etc.).

In January 2005, the seat of the Hermandad was at the home of don Adrián and Qana' Noelia—a couple in the twilight years of their lives who lived within sight of San Felipe's church, but in a part of town that was technically under another parish's jurisdiction. Although don Adrián was neither Q'eqchi' nor a native of Cobán (he was from a town in the western Highlands), he had lived in the city for nearly six decades. His wife, however, was both, and Qana' Noelia had been especially devoted to El Señor de Esquipulas[5]—the santo to whom both the parish and the sodality are dedicated—since her teenage years and well before she ever met don Adrián. The couple had long been active in local Catholic affairs and had a large home and were more than happy to serve as hosts to the santo and the Her-

---

5. *El Señor Crucificado de Esquipulas* (The Crucified Lord of Esquipulas), also commonly known as *El Señor de Esquipulas* and *El Cristo Negro de Esquipulas* (The Black Christ of Esquipulas), is the parish's patron saint. El Señor de Esquipulas is an image of Christ crucified and has dark, ebony skin and resides in a basilica in the town of Esquipulas, Chiquimula, in eastern Guatemala near the border with Honduras. The image was crafted in 1594 by a Portuguese artisan living in Antigua Guatemala and subsequently sent to Esquipulas, where the santo began to develop a following due to a number of miracles attributed to Him. Devotion to Esquipulas seems to have started as an indigenous phenomenon in a part of the country that is now marked as particularly non-indigenous. Spaniards and Ladinos founded a cofradía dedicated to the santo in 1685, parallel to an already existing and active indigenous one (Sullivan-González 2016, 42). Over the course of four centuries, the santo's fame has expanded so that Esquipulas is a major pilgrimage site for Guatemalans, Salvadorans, Hondurans, and Mexicans (Kendall 1991), and devotion to the Black Christ has expanded across international borders southward to Panama and northward to the United States (Horst, Thomas, and Hunter 2010). The Black Christ's distinctive skin color made Him a source of concern for religious elites in the seventeenth century, who worried that it undermined the image of Jesus as ally of European colonialism. However, it later made the santo a symbol of mestizo and hence national, religious identity due to its association with indigenous people's skin tones (Sullivan-Gonzalez 2016).

mandad. Their age and declining health, however, meant that this year would be their last hosting these events.[6]

Eleven people had gathered to begin the work of the novenario—all of them (save myself and Qana' Noelia) active and official members of the confraternity's directorate.[7] Over the course of about half an hour people trickled into an anteroom of the home where a large table with several folding chairs had been set up to accommodate the mundane part of the meeting. As the *qawachineb'* (the men belonging to the Hermandad) came in, they would greet everyone already present by shaking each person's hand in turn with a light, gentle grip and offering a short verbal greeting.[8] Each *qawachin* would then excuse himself to go to the next room where he would pay respect to the santo patrón by kneeling in front of the three-foot-tall crucifix that bore the *Cristo Negro* (or Black Christ, as he is commonly referred to due to His darkly colored skin). The morning of His feast day, this santo would travel to the main church, spend the night there, and return to the Hermandad's house at noon the following day, thus marking a physical connection between the church and the Hermandad's secular seat. In addition to praying the Rosary, the group that was gathering had to sort out the logistics of that sojourn.

After everyone had arrived, there was a brief organizational discussion of plans for the upcoming days in the novenario and a quick check of the group's accounts to make sure that funds would be available for the sundry expenses that would be needed for the santo's fiesta. Two of the qawachineb' broke off from the discussion to clean the santo's case, dusting it both inside and out, and cleaning the glass so no streaks marred people's view of the Cristo. Roughly an hour later, after all these tasks were complete, everyone moved into the santo's room to pray. A number of actions had to be taken to bring about the proper material conditions for the recitation of the Rosary, including lighting candles, filling the censer with embers, and portioning out enough copal pom to cleanse the room with its fragrant smoke. A hymn also had to be chosen, and leaders were designated for each part of the prayer.

---

6. The Hermandad elected to move the santo to the home of a younger Q'eqchi' family who had much stronger and closer ties to the parish the following year.

7. Qana' Noelia no doubt contributed much more labor to the working of the Hermandad than don Adrián and was an active part of the planning process but, as a woman, was not technically counted as a member of the group's *junta directiva*.

8. The exception to this rule would be in greeting Qana' Noelia. Cross-gender greetings were performed not by shaking hands but rather by gently touching one's hand to the other's elbow.

The initial interpersonal greetings had been in Q'eqchi', but most of the business part of the gathering had been conducted in Spanish to accommodate the mertoom's linguistic abilities; it was expected, however, that the praying of the Rosary itself would be in Q'eqchi'. In the following transcript we can see the switch that occurred to mark the start of ritual time. Qawa' Luis, who would be the prayer leader for the day, was nearby getting ready to start the ritual with Qawa' José, and Qawa' Mateo had gone outside with some fireworks. Meanwhile, Qawa' Hugo, Qawa' Francisco, Qana' Noelia, and Qawa' Walter were discussing the logistics of fireworks for the santo's procession to the parish church. This discussion took place entirely in Spanish even though all of the participants were native speakers of Q'eqchi' and there was no other particular need for it to be in Spanish (i.e., Q'eqchi' has all the lexical items needed to talk about the subject). As we can see in the following transcript, however, as soon as the ritual began, Q'eqchi' became the preferred code.

As we can see in the transcript, once Qawa' Luis (L in the transcript) took the floor, he effected a switch to Q'eqchi' (line 33), which everyone else immediately followed. A significant shift occurred in the footing of the participants (i.e., the alignment between them and their relation to the large context of their interaction, Goffman 1981) as they moved from a participant framework in which they were equal partners in a conversation (attested to in part by rapid turn taking, overlaps in speech, and generally free flow of their talk in lines 1–31), to a framework marked by ritual hierarchies in which they had to follow the cues that Qawa' Luis set in his capacity as *aj tijonel* (prayer leader). The change in the roles that they occupied went hand in hand with the linguistic shift into Q'eqchi'. The evidence points to this being a situational code-switch—that is, a change in linguistic codes that "involves clear changes in the participants' definition of each other's rights and obligations," and which "assumes a direct relationship between language and the social situation" (Blom and Gumperz 1986, 424)—since participants moved from being in the mode of an open discussion about logistics to that of a religious ritual. Even though the discussion about fireworks was by no means resolved, and Qana' Noelia was in the middle of making a case for why it was inadvisable to use a cigarette to light the fireworks (line 26, 28), the subject was dropped, and attention shifted to Qawa' Luis as he opened the ritual event. Qawa' Luis's formulaic greeting in Q'eqchi' signaled that the ritual was beginning, as did the "whoosh" and "boom" of the exploding fireworks (lines 29, 32). Together these two auditory signs—one linguistic,

TRANSCRIPT A Mainstream Catholics before a Rosary

Spanish is in *italics*, Q'eqchi' is underlined, bivalent words are in **bold**
Text in brackets [] is descriptive
Participants: F = Qawa' Francisco; H = Qawa' Hugo; L = Qawa' Luis; N = Qana' Noelia; W = Qawa' Walter

1) H: *cuatro entonces*
2) F: *ehhh*
3) H: *cuatro da* . . .
4) F: *tres de inicio::: tres a la mitad*
5) H: *y seis de* . . .
6) N: *seis*
7) F: *ála mucho ah? cuatro, cuatro*
8) H: *pero por eso*
9) W: *cuatro y cuatro*
10) N: *entonces mejor cuatro cuatro*
11) F: *si pues cuatro y cuatro*
12) H: *pero . . . pero y si hay necesidad de quemarlos allá en la iglesia?*
13) N: *pero que no se queme ahh* . . .
14) F: *y quién lo va a llevar?*
15) H: *ah? Cómo allá cuando se lleva se quema*
16) F: *ahh* . . .
17) H: *se . . . se queman dos*
18) F: *se quema en tubo*
19) H: *no, qué? cohetes*
20) W: *sólo cohetes*
21) F: *ah, sólo cohetes*
22) N: *hay tizón?*

1) H: *four* [fireworks] *then*
2) F: *ehhh*
3) H: *four makes* . . .
4) F: *three to start::: three midway*
5) H: *and six of* . . .
6) N: *six*
7) F: *oh that's too many eh? four, four*
8) H: *but that's why*
9) W: *four and four*
10) N: *then better four four*
11) F: *ok then four and four*
12) H: *but . . . but what if we need to burn them there at the church?*
13) N: *but it shouldn't be burnt ahh* . . .
14) F: *and who is going to take them?*
15) H: *huh? When we take it there it's lit/burnt*
16) F: *ahh* . . .
17) H: *two . . . two will be lit/burnt*
18) F: *they're lit in a tube*
19) H: *no, what? rockets*
20) W: *just rockets*[a]
21) F: *oh, just rockets*
22) N: *is there an ember?*

23) H: *ah?*
24) N: *hay tizón allá?*
25) H: *allí no, pero este se lleva aveces allí un cigarro y . . .*
26) N: *dice que es . . . me dijo el cohetero que no*
27) H: *ah . . . entonces digo que se queme aquí*
28) N: *es peligroso dice,* [laugh] *así me dijo el cohetero*
29) [rocket whoosh]
30) H: *ya pues*
31) L: *bueno*
32) [rocket explodes]
33) L: *us b'i ex was wiitzin, ma saa sa' lee ch'ool?*
34) All: *saa*
35) L: *b'antiox li Qaawa Dios anawan taqayib' li qa kanjel rubel roq rubel ruq' li Qaawa' Señor de Esquipulas xban naq* [unintelligible] *xwaklesinkil li xnimal xwankil li xloqb'a re tixqakanab' sa' li naiej* ***novenario*** *aran taawank chi ru li b'eleb' chi:: **bantiox** ut bantiox re li Qaawa' **Dios** naq waeeko ut nawank taqayoo li kanjel toot-ikla sa komonil*
36) [rocket whoosh]
37) [rocket explodes]

23) H: *huh?*
24) N: *is there an ember there?*
25) H: *not there, but erm sometimes we take a cigarette there and . . .*
26) N: *he says that it's . . . the firework maker told me not to*
27) H: *ah . . . then I say that we burn it here better*
28) N: *it is dangerous he says,* [laugh] *that's what the firework maker told me*
29) [rocket whoosh]
30) H: *now then* [i.e., ok, it's time]
31) L: *ok*
32) [rocket explodes]
33) L: *okay then my brothers are your hearts content?*[b]
34) All: *they are content*
35) L: *thanks to Our Lord God now we will make our work under the hands under the feet of the lord Señor de Esquipulas so that* [unintelligible] *to elevate His power, His worth He will be taken to His place at the **church** there we will be during nine during the :: **novena** and thanks to Our Lord **God** who moves us and who will give us life we will begin our work together*
36) [rocket whoosh]
37) [rocket explodes]

---

[a] The clarification was necessary here because fireworks come in two forms: rockets (*cohetes*) and mortars (*morteros*). Rockets are made up of a slightly triangular packet containing both a bomb and a booster attached to a yard-long piece of cane; one lights the booster while lightly holding the cane, so that once it catches, the contraption is propelled high into the sky, where the bomb explodes. Mortars, on the other hand, are balls that contain two explosives—a small one and a much larger one—attached to a long fuse. They are placed inside a metal tube attached to a heavy base, and the fuse is lit. The smaller explosion forces the rest of the package out of the tube into the sky where the larger bomb explodes.

[b] The formula "*Ma saa sa' laa ch'oo l?*" "*Saa*" (lit. "Are you content/good in your heart?" "Content/Good") is a standard greeting formula in Q'eqchi'.

one percussive—cued those present to shift the frame of their interaction. The rocket's initial "whoosh," which came from outside and would have been initiated by Qawa' Mateo's lighting of the rocket, signaled to Qawa' Hugo and Qawa' Luis to begin since they responded to it with short phrases spoken to themselves that marked a break from what came before them (lines 30 and 31; on the importance of percussion in signaling transitions into religious frame spaces more generally, see Needham 1967). All the speech that followed after the ritual event had formally started was in Q'eqchi'. Although Qawa' Luis said "iglesia," "novenario" and "Dios" in line 39, these words, despite originating from the Spanish lexicon, are understood as bivalent terms meaning the same in Q'eqchi' and Spanish.[9]

The change in linguistic code co-occurred with a change in participants' expectations about the nature of their interaction, and thus exemplifies a pattern that I observed frequently in which people who were in the middle of a conversation in Spanish would drop it as soon as it was clear that a religious event was beginning in earnest, and switch to using only Q'eqchi'. The percussive blast of fireworks marked a clear transition point for the members of the Hermandad, but a similar process occurred when the parish church bells rang at the start of Sunday Masses as well as when catechists positioned themselves at the front of their congregations and offered a formal welcome to their CEB's weekly Celebration of the Word. Not only did side conversations, which were just as likely to be in Q'eqchi' as in Spanish, cease, but anyone in a position to speak then also made a concerted effort to maintain code-consistency in the Mayan language. Once the events were over, however, talk in either language or a mix of them resumed.

All of this points to the social importance of using Q'eqchi' in church settings and to the deliberate and motivated changes in linguistic behavior that Mainstream Catholics observed when they entered into a religious frame of action.

---

9. Sometimes Dios is rendered as *Tiox* in written Q'eqchi', but in my experience people, and especially bilinguals like Luis, tended to pronounce it more as /diːos/ with Spanish phonology rather than the more Q'eqchi' phonology /tiːoʃ/. Similarly, the Q'eqchi' and Spanish terms for church—*iklees* and *iglesia*— were used pretty interchangeably, and people would regularly use the more Spanish-sounding phonology of the noun alongside the Q'eqchi' article *li*, like Qawa' Luis does here, making the word effectively bivalent. Novenario could be rendered in Q'eqchi', but like many neologisms, it presented a complicated and far too literal formulation along the lines of "nine-day prayer," which was not frequently used.

Establishing Code-Switching with Charismatic Catholics

If Mainstream Catholic services called for the establishment of Q'eqchi' code-consistency, those held by La Renovación did the opposite, requiring that the co-presence of and active alternation between Spanish and Q'eqchi' be established as normative for the interaction.

Carismáticos held prayer meetings twice a week in the village chapel at Sa'xreb'e on Wednesday evenings from roughly seven to nine o'clock and Sunday mornings from about eight to eleven o'clock (though sometimes these would stretch past noon.) Hermano Rigo was typically the first person to arrive since he lived just down the road from the chapel and had been entrusted with a key to the door (but only after a lengthy negotiation with Padre Agustino as well as with Qawa' Emanuel, who lived directly across the lane and had previously been the property's sole caretaker since his family had donated the land for it). Setting up the choir band was a first priority at these events, and the other musicians typically arrived soon after Rigo and quickly set themselves to running cables to the speaker system, tuning their instruments, and otherwise readying themselves to play music. As other members of the congregation started to arrive, they would also pitch in by sweeping the floor and moving the benches that served as pews from their storage position along the lateral walls into two neat rows facing the altar. There was no need for specific directions to be issued for these tasks; everyone just knew what needed to be done and most seemed pleased to be able to contribute in these small ways (though some people also avoided participating in these tasks by lingering outside the chapel to chat with friends until it was time to start).

Once the space had been set up and the core of the congregation's leadership had arrived, Hermano Rigo and Hermano Felipe would parse out some of the ritual duties that these services called for, including who would lead specific prayers or hymns. These lists were actually generated before the event itself, so people came to church knowing that they would have a part to play in celebration; but Hermanos Rigo and Felipe nonetheless felt it was good form to repeat the assignments to ensure that everyone who was supposed to be there was there and that they remembered what they were supposed to do. Just about five minutes before the service was set to begin, Hermano Rigo would read this list out over the speaker system so that everyone present could hear it and know their role.[10] The following transcript is an example of how Charismatics typically distributed ritual roles before a service and illustrates the extent to which Spanish and Q'eqchi' were both used.

In this example, Spanish is used largely in matters of nomenclature having to do with the various functions that members carry out in the ritual (e.g., *alabanza* [paise song], *oración sobre el mensaje* [prayer over the Gospel], etc.). From a purely semantic point of view, it should have been possible for Charismatics to name these duties in Q'eqchi', since most of them have direct analogues in Mainstream Catholic rituals that people would have known (e.g., *oración de ofrenda* is analogous to the *tijok sa' xb'een li mayej*). As with Qawa' Luis's use of "novenario" when he opened the Rosary at the Hermandad house, the use of these technical terms is not necessarily evidence of situational code-switching because it isn't clear that a shift has occurred in the rights and responsibilities of interactants to each other. What it does suggest, however, is that carismáticos adopted a much larger set of Spanish-language terms for parts of their religious services. As this brief example illustrates, these terms, which were pronounced with Spanish phonology, were used in mixed code performances alongside Q'eqchi' words and grammatical structures. This usage, I would argue, played a key role in marking Charismatic services as distinct from Mainstream Catholic ones. Evidence for this can be found in the contrasting ways Hermano Rigo mobilized Spanish in lines 1–4 and lines 5–8. In the first half of the transcript the utterances follow a simple formula of pairing a person's name with that of the ritual task. We might note that he consistently used the formula [task name] + [gendered honorific] + [personal name] to construct his utterances, which established a straightforward cadence both semantically and poetically consistent with a sort of task-oriented Spanish. Note, though, that he initially used the Q'eqchi' article "li," which suggests that there was another Q'eqchi' language frame that encompassed the list. In fact, we could say that his recitation of the list has a noticeably different set of linguistic characteristics than the utterances that follow it. After listing four tasks, Hermano Rigo changed the poetic forms of his utterances to make increasingly more explicit the distribution of tasks (lines 4–7). In line 5 he used the formula

---

10. Analogous duties at Mainstream services were always assigned offstage well before the event started. The very different formal structures of the events accounted for this, as did the Charismatics' ideological emphasis on more egalitarian and distributed participation from their smaller congregations.

TRANSCRIPT B Charismatic Catholics Listing of Tasks

Spanish in *italics*; Q'eqchi' underlined; bivalent words in **bold**
Text in brackets [] is descriptive

Hermano Rigo	Hermano Rigo
1) <u>li</u> *alabanza Hermana Jacinta*	1) <u>the</u> *praise hymn Sister Jacinta*
2) *invocación del Espíritu Santo Hermano Alberto*	2) *invocation of the Holy Spirit Brother Alberto*
3) *oración sobre el mensaje Hermano Uriel*	3) *prayer over the message* [Gospel] *Brother Uriel*
4) *oración de ofrenda Hermana Telma*	4) *prayer over the offering Sister Telma*
5) <u>li oksiink aatin a'an li</u> *Hermana Magdalena* <u>ut</u>	5) <u>The intercession that is</u> *Sister Magdalena* <u>and</u>
6) <u>ehh</u> *oración fina: final* <u>a'an naru naxb'anu li</u> *Hermano Raymundo*	6) <u>ehh</u> *prayer of close: closing* <u>that can be done by</u> *Brother Raymundo*
7) <u>ut nintzamach eeru</u> *hermanos* <u>naru neekexnume chaq taqapatz li</u> *oración* <u>re li Qaawa'</u> **Dios** <u>re naq a'an taatenqank teexbantioxink li xkanjel</u>	7) <u>and I ask you</u> *brothers* <u>that we pass to ask in the</u> *prayer* <u>to Our Lord</u> **God** <u>so that we can assist Him, so that we thank him for his work</u>

[task name] + [determiner] + [gendered honorific] + [personal name], to make the coupling of task and performer more explicit (i.e., the intercessory prayer belongs now to Hermana Magdalena). That framing was even more distinct in line 6, in which the phrase "a'an naru naxb'anu" (that can be done by) makes it a clearer directive that Hermano Raymundo is the responsible party. With that change in the utterance's construction, Hermano Rigo also shifted (or shifted back) to using Q'eqchi' as the dominant language of his speech. This shift was seemingly prompted by his use of a Q'eqchi' term for a ritual duty (for a prayer of intercession in line 5). While that was a term that had a Spanish-language equivalent, and I can't know exactly why he rendered it in Q'eqchi' on this occasion when on others he did not, the effect was to prompt a shift to a mixed-code performance in which both languages were used. By the time he concluded his speech (line 7), he had shifted mostly into Q'eqchi'. Thus, what was at stake here wasn't necessarily the semantic value of the Spanish terms being used, but rather the metaphorical value of that language as part of how the ritual event was being set up. That this was a Charismatic Catholic event was signaled in part by the preference for Spanish language terminology for specific ritual genres; and in part because the use of Q'eqchi' for expository talk alongside those Spanish terms meant that both codes were legitimated. This listing of duties, which was talk that was neither fully "onstage" nor "offstage," introduced an expectation that the co-presence of both languages and, in fact, active switching between them was normative for the event. This will be clearer if we examine what happened next in the ritual.

After Hermano Rigo finished reading the list, the congregants who had been named did as he asked, approaching the altar to offer short prayers asking God for guidance. Once these prayers had been said and it was clear that the choir band was ready to begin, Hermano Rigo took up the microphone once again and formally addressed the congregation. The next transcript shows how he welcomed them that day and introduced the first official part of the ritual (i.e., the opening hymn sung by Hermana Jacinta.) His opening spiel was relatively short, moving quickly from conventional call-and-response routines that served as a greeting (lines 1–4), to a statement about the gathering (line 5), and finally to an introduction of the next speaker/singer.

While no two openings to the prayer meetings were ever exactly the same, at each service the hermano in charge of animating the event improvised a greeting similar to this, drawing on certain conventionalized call-and-response formulas and also adding his own talk to establish the frame of the ritual. The following example recorded at a prayer meeting in the same place a few months later illustrates some of this variability.

Though these two examples of openings are different, together they illustrate how Spanish and Q'eqchi' were set side by side as soon as the Charismatic prayer meetings began, establishing the expectation that both codes would be used alongside each other. Charismatic group leaders had a fair

TRANSCRIPT C Charismatic Catholics Introduction to Prayer Meeting: Example 1

Spanish is in *italics*, Q'eqchi' is underlined, bivalent words are in **bold**
Participants: R = Hermano Rigo; C = Congregation in unison

1) R: <u>Jarub naxye junaj</u> *"Gloria Dios" hermanos?*	1) R: <u>How many say a</u> *"Glory to God" brothers?*
2) C: *Gloria a Dios*	2) C: *Glory to God*
3) R: *A su nombre*	3) R: *To His name?*
4) C: *Gloria*	4) C: *Glory*
5) R: *Gloria Dios*	5) R: *Glory to God*
6) <u>jo'kan</u> *hermanos* <u>sa' li hoonal a'in</u>	6) <u>so then</u> *brothers* <u>at this time</u>
7) <u>naru na nume chaq li</u> *Hermana Jacinta*	7) <u>let (her) to come up here the</u> *Sister Jacinta*

Están listos para cantar en Q'eqchi'? Ma nekeeraj xninqehinkil sa' Q'eqchi'?

TRANSCRIPT D Charismatic Catholics Introduction to Prayer Meeting: Example 2

Spanish is in *italics*, Q'eqchi' is underlined, bivalent words are in **bold**
Participants: R = Hermano Rigo; C = Congregation in unison

1) R: *Bien hermanos y hermanas ¿quién vive hermanos y hermanas?*	1) R: *OK brothers and sisters, who lives, brothers and sisters?*
2) C: *¡Cristo!*	2) C: *Christ!*
3) R: *¿Cuánto dicen gloria Dios?*	3) R: *How many say glory to God?*
4) C: *Gloria Dios*	4) C: *Glory to God*
5) R: *¿Cuánto dicen un amén?*	5) R: *How many say amen?*
6) C: *Amén*	6) C: *Amen*
7) R: *Hermanos, levántense, hermanos,* aj-aj-ajsi leeru, *hermanos*	7) R: *Brothers get yourselves up, brothers,* wa-wa-wake up your faces, *brothers*
8) R: li **Jesús** kixye *estén despiertos,* chan	8) R: the **Jesus** said *be awake,* he said
9) C: *Gloria::* a Dios	9) C: *Glory::* to God
10) R: *Amén::: Y firmes en la fe,* chan	10) R: *Amen::: And strong in the faith,* he said
11) C: *Amén*	11) C: *Amen*
12) R: Jokan naq naxye *hermano* se'eb'al li qach'ool aj aj qu *hermanos* ut jokan sa' li hoonal a'in, b'e yaal, okex li xloqoninkil li **Dios**	12) R: So then it says *brother* let's quicken our hearts/minds [i.e. let's be awake] let's be alert *brothers* and so that in this hour, right, we begin the worship of **God**

degree of flexibility in exactly what they would say and how they would say it. However, my analysis of the corpus of recordings of ritual openings I collected, and of which these two examples are illustrative, shows that there were recurring features of their talk and that, thus, Spanish served a few identifiable discursive functions. Specifically, Spanish was used in three ways: (1) as part of a specialized terminology that was understood to mark participants as members of the Catholic Charismatic community as distinct from the general Mainstream Q'eqchi'-Maya community, (2) to perform conventional call-and-response routines that established a mode of participating in Catholic Charismatic religiosity (Thorsen 2015, 91), and (3) for voicing quotations and pseudo-quotations (cp. Gumperz 1982, 75–76). Each of these is worth exploring further for what they teach us about how *carismáticos*' religious sensibilities were constituted through language use.

I noted earlier that naming specific parts of the ritual (e.g., prayers over the offering, etc.) in Spanish was one way in which Charismatics established the distinctiveness of their form of Catholicism from that of Mainstream Catholics. What I did not discuss earlier, but that also stood out in the assignment of tasks, was the use of *"hermano/a"* (Spanish for brother and sister) coupled with the individual's first name as a form of personal reference. That conventional form of address was a key marker of carismático identity since they used "hermano/a" constantly and consistently throughout their rituals as well as in normal conversation as a sort of title or honorific. Just in the two previous examples we see variants of the terms used twelve times and that would have continued throughout the rest of the service. At a semantic level, hermano/a reinforces the idea that co-religionists are equal members in the family of God. That in and of itself is not extraordinary since Christian communities around the world use similar formulas, including San Felipe's Mainstream Catholics who used *"as"* and *"iitzin"* (older male sibling and younger sibling, respectively) when addressing the congregation to denote inclusive membership. In fact, we saw Qawa' Luis do so in his opening to the Rosary prayer above (Transcript A, line 35) when he said, "us b'i, ex was wiitzin" (ok then, my elder/younger brothers).[11] It is important to note, though, that meaningfulness comes not from the terms' semantic meaning, but rather from the fact that it contrasts with more common forms of address in Q'eqchi'. While *"hermanos y hermanas"* was sometimes used as part of a larger Spanish phrase (Transcript B, line 1), it was also frequently embedded within utterances that were primarily in Q'eqchi', such as "naru na nume chak li *hermana*" (Transcript C, line 7), and "so then, it says, brother, let's quicken our hearts/minds" (Transcript D, line 2). Used as a generalized pronoun—as in *"levántense hermanos"* (Transcript D, line 7)—the word's use contrasted with Mainstream Catholics' conventional use of "ex was wiitzin." When used as titles—as in Hermana Telma or Hermano Rigo—they likewise contrasted with the gendered Q'eqchi' honorifics Mainstream Catholics used, as in Qana' Noelia or Qawa' Luis. Thus, at the most basic level, by using

---

11. Mainstream Catholics' most used form for addressing a group is "ex was wiitzin," which would translate as "you [pl.] my older brothers [and] younger brothers" and would be inclusive of everyone present, regardless of gender. In Q'eqchi', possession is shown by adding a prefix to the root word to determine the case and number, so that the roots "-*as*" (older brother) is modified as "*was*" (my older brother), "*aawas*" (your older brother), "*ras*" (his/her older brother), "*qas*" (our older brother), "*eeqas*" (your [pl.] older brother), and "*eeras*" (their older brother). The term -*as* by itself presumes a male's older brother, but it can be used in conventional phrases without necessarily making a gendered distinction. Q'eqchi' makes a series of gendered and age-graded distinctions in sibling kin terms. *Iitzin* can refer to either a man's or woman's younger sibling of either gender, although *iitzin ixq* can also be used to specify a woman's younger sister. A girl's older female sibling is properly her *chaq'na'*, and a boy's older sister is his *anab'ej*.

these terms of address, carismáticos were drawing a distinction between "we Charismatic Catholics who refer to each other as hermano/as," and the implicit non-present others who do not (i.e., Mainstream Catholics).

In making that implicit distinction, though, Charismatics were also perhaps inadvertently confirming their critics' sense that they were something other than católicos, since "hermano/a," beyond its kinship meanings, was widely associated in Guatemala with evangélico Christian identity even among monolingual Spanish speakers. In fact, Catholics often euphemistically referred to Protestants as *los hermanos separados* (the separated brothers). That valence was not lost in San Felipe,[12] and it was not unusual for Mainstream Catholics to point to that feature of carismáticos' speech as evidence that they were really evangélicos and not católicos.

The second way that Spanish was conventionally used in La Renovación's religious services was through conventional call-and-response routines. Transcript C, lines 1–4, and Transcript D, lines 1–6, offer examples of a few of the conventional sequences that carismáticos performed frequently throughout their services. Some variation of them was performed each time a new speaker came to the microphone, and predicadores would pepper them into their sermons, too. As our examples illustrate, at least two call-and-response pairs were performed each time, and I regularly observed people performing as many as four as a prelude to some other speech event such as a prayer, song, sermon, or even the community's announcements. These pairings were all composed of a stock question or request and its corresponding response, and they were always in Spanish.[13] If a speaker began an utterance in Q'eqchi' (as in Transcript C, line 1), they would always switch to Spanish to perform the call-and-response routine, and the congregation could be relied upon to take up the new code and produce their response in Spanish. In my experience with La Renovación in San Felipe, no speaker ever initiated a call-and-response routine in Q'eqchi', to the point where my field recordings don't contain even a single instance of the most conventional Q'eqchi'-language

---

12. Mainstream Catholics attending services in Spanish-language parishes could use the terms without implying allegiance to evangélico Christianity, provided that they knew to switch to the proper Q'eqchi' forms when participating in a Q'eqchi'-language Mass. So, for example, Qawa' Emanuel had no problem offering "*la paz, hermano*" (peace, brother) to the attendees during the sign of the peace at his granddaughter's wedding.

13. There is a sole quasi-exception for a formula in which the caller asks for a "*grito de júbilo*" (shout of joy), that is appropriately responded to with a high-pitched "Ooo!"

greeting *"ma saa sa' lee ch'ool? / saa."* We can note, too, that the Spanish used did not always conform to standard Guatemalan Spanish. In Transcript D lines 3 and 5, the preacher says *"cuánto dice"* ("how many say") which would in standard Spanish be rendered as *"cuántos dicen."* Variations in verb conjugation and grammatical number marking like this were a common feature of Q'eqchi'-dominant parishioners' Spanish, which some of their critics cited as evidence that despite the fact that Charismatics wanted to speak Spanish, many of them did so imperfectly and would thus presumably be better served by sticking with their native tongue.[14]

The very form of these conventional verbal routines is also indicative of Charismatics' ideals about how rituals should be structured. By performing them, La Renovación's leaders produced a moment of back-and-forth talk between them and their audience, which potentially served two functions. As conventional greetings with fixed answers, performing these routines micro-interactionally established a speaker's turn at talk. Formulated as adjacency pairs, these routines ratified the person at the microphone and recruited the congregations' collective verbal participation to turn their attention to the person initiating them.[15] However, the call-and-response routines also played another function—namely, they gave the ritual the appearance of cooperation and co-authorship (Wharry 2003). These formulaic back-and-forth verbal exchanges were discursively framed as a means for congregants to be actively involved in the ritual activity and—as Transcript D, line 8 suggests—to "keep them awake." This is especially meaningful if we recall that one of Charismatics' main criticisms of Mainstream Catholics was that the latter often look disinterested, sad, or bored in church, which they said one could see from how quiet and inactive congregants were, leaving only the priest and the catequistas to do the work of a religious service. Carismáticos valued a feeling of joyousness and spontaneity in church and these routines,

---

14. These sorts of criticism reproduced a larger metalinguistic discourse with strongly racist overtones about indigenous Guatemalans' (in)ability to master Spanish grammar due to an inherent lack of intelligence or skill. I want to be clear that I reject that discourse and do not interpret phrasings like this to be errors in speaking. Rather, I think that they are signs of a distinct variety or dialect of Spanish that has to the best of my knowledge not been adequately described.

15. An adjacency pair is a sequence of verbal utterances between two parties in which the utterance of the first person practically demands a conventional response from the second. These formulations are especially common in opening and closing interactions, so greetings and leave-takings often follow this form (Schegloff and Sacks 1973).

though fully conventionalized, gave the sense of active participation that fed into those feelings.[16] By eliciting these responses through a set of adjacency pair routines, the Charismatics' leaders figured their congregants as co-constructors of the event, and by shouting back phrases like "glory to God," congregants got to perform a joyous and active form of religiosity.

We can see the third use of Spanish in Transcript D, line 8, where a code-switch from Q'eqchi' is performed to animate a pseudo-quotation. Hermano Rigo first gave his congregation a directive to be awake and alert (Transcript D, line 7), and in the next line justified his command by attributing it to Jesus. When he said, "li Jesús kixye 'estén despiertos' chan" ("Jesus once said 'be awake' he said"), he animated Jesus' voice in Spanish, but bracketed the quotation in Q'eqchi'. His formulation of the utterance framed the Spanish phrase as reported speech that occurred long ago (the tense marked "ki-" places the action in the distant past) and the use of the evidential "chan" (roughly "he said" or "it is said") also signaled that the phrase is something that is known to have been said. The congregation responded to this pseudo-quotation with a "*Gloria a Dios*" (Transcript D, line 9), effectively affirming its veracity and authority through acclamation. Hermano Rigo in turn affirmed the congregation's response with an "Amén" and then added another phrase in Spanish, which he again framed as a quotation with the evidential "chan" (Transcript D, line 10). Hermano Rigo was not, to the best of my knowledge, invoking specific parts of scripture in either of his utterances, but he nonetheless framed them as reported speech. What is interesting for our purpose here is that Jesus was voiced in Spanish. It may have been the case that Hermano Rigo's setting off the pseudo-quotations in Spanish allowed him to distance himself from the words and thus imbue them with a bit of Jesus's authority (Gumperz 1982, 75–76), or that he was drawing on the cosmopolitan value of Spanish and thus linking a foreign-but-familiar language with the foreign-but-familiar deity. In either case, this switch followed a consistent pattern in which code-switches from Q'eqchi' into Spanish helped

---

16. Of course, Mainstream Catholics did also perform some call-and-response sequences in which the officiant (usually the priest) said a conventionalized phrase that the congregation responded to in an equally conventional way. However, they were less frequent over the course of a ritual, and, with the exception of greetings (as in Transcript A line 33–34), their usage was more attached to specific parts of a ritual than they were in Charismatic Catholics' events. As with so much that distinguished the two congregations, this difference was a contrastive one, rather than a categorical one.

frame the authoritativeness of these pseudo-quotations from a sacred figure. Arguably the effect of the pseudo-quotations was heightened by the way that "foreign" words were supported by Q'eqchi' discourse markers, since the evidential (i.e., "chan") gave the reported speech an aura of facticity. In these formulations, then, it was the co-presence of the two languages that made the speech vibrant and convincing.

To summarize, Spanish played several discursive functions in La Renovación's religious services, but it was arguably its use alongside Q'eqchi', not in isolation from it, that mattered. By making the two languages co-present from the outset of the ritual event itself, as well as by reestablishing that expectation every time a new speaker took up the floor, Sa'xreb'e's carismáticos constituted their services as distinct from those of Mainstream Catholics. Although Q'eqchi' was actually the primary code used when predicadores preached, when individuals prayed, and when the group leadership did any talk ancillary to the ritual event (such as during the community announcements), Spanish was utilized in these conventional ways. These uses did the important symbolic work of marking the event as a whole, in which code-switching and mixing were normative. The meaning of that mixed-code preference was only apparent, though, when viewed in light of the larger sociolinguistic world of the parish in which Mainstream Catholics insisted on code consistency as a way of performing the community's distinct ethnoreligious identity through linguistic constraint.

Conclusion

Examining in detail how Mainstream and Charismatic Catholics mobilized language at the opening of ritual events shows us two things. First, that we need to understand that both Mainstream Catholics' code consistency and Charismatic Catholics' code alternation were deliberate and meaningful choices. Although code-switching and code restriction would at first blush appear to be opposites of each other, neither is necessarily the inevitable outcome of people's linguistic competencies. Bilingual people regularly perform monolingualism in response to social and cultural pressures and doing so can be just as meaningful as a deliberate performance of skillful multilingualism. Catequistas who spoke Spanish fluently and frequently in other contexts nonetheless adjusted their linguistic behaviors when entering into ritual spaces, using Q'eqchi' not only dominantly but exclusively. Conversely, carismáticos who might navigate daily life largely in Q'eqchi' eagerly employed at least a limited range of Spanish terms and phrases when participating in La Renovación's ritual events. What ultimately differentiated the two congregations linguistically was their stance toward the mixing of codes—for Charismatics the co-presence of Spanish and Q'eqchi' was a positive sign of religious engagement, and for Mainstream Catholics it signaled that something was amiss.

Considering both code consistency and code-switching as interactional achievements brings us to a second insight—namely, that if these patterns of language use held in religious contexts, but not other parts of daily life, then they must have not only been ideologically motivated, but also in some way understood as consequential for religious practice. The very presence of Spanish in spaces marked as both religious and Q'eqchi'-Maya was a fundamental touchstone for the larger conflict between the two groups. Mainstream Catholics' insistence on Q'eqchi' code consistency led them to read the presence of any Spanish in Charismatic rituals as its predominance, and hence a betrayal of their distinctive indigenous form of Catholic practice. Catequistas' critical statements about carismáticos' use of Spanish were less a reflection of how the latter actually spoke than categorical judgments about this problematic cultural other based on a generalization of variable practices (cp. Labov 1969). Similarly, that Charismatics marked their rituals by using Spanish alongside Q'eqchi' should alert us to the importance that producing a mixed code ritual had for constituting Charismatic Catholicism as a sort of modern or cosmopolitan vision of the religion (cp. MacKenzie 2016; Althoff 2014). With that as their position, we can better understand why Charismatics read Mainstream Catholics' code consistency as a sign of a "cold" or "sad" faith, by which they ultimately meant that it was disengaged from contemporary realities. Underlying that criticism was an implicit statement that their own form of religiosity evinced values that were diametrically opposed to those of their antagonists.

When the Sa'xreb'e carismáticos opted to have Mass celebrated in Q'eqchi' for their anniversary in 2005 and signaled that intention internally by asking the congregation in Spanish if they were ready to sing and pray in Q'eqchi, they were managing several distinct formulations of what it meant to be Catholic in San Felipe. They seemingly acknowledged that the practices which they had enthusiastically been engaged in just minutes before would seem heterodox to the priest. They furthermore showed that they were willing to adjust to meet his expectations by reverting to the linguistic norms to which they had adhered just a few years earlier before La Renovación had arrived in the parish. The code-switch was meant to please the priest (although it did not) and was performed in recognition of his special status as someone who could celebrate the special rite of the Eucharist. As católicos, the carismáticos still valued the Eucharist, even if the communion with God via the Holy Spirit they cultivated in their prayer meetings was more the focus of their religious lives.

The Bakhtinian model of heteroglossia is predicated on the idea not only that different uses of language signal different positions but also that different positions are constituted in relation to each other. Understanding this helps us better see the dialogic construction of Catholicism in San Felipe and why the language one sang and prayed in was so consequential to being a good católico.

CHAPTER 5

The Politics of Audibility
Language, Music, and Pious Noise

As the story goes, every one of the conquistadors' attempts at a military incursion into Tezulutlán (the "Land of War" in Nahuatl) had met with failure. Impassable mountains and fierce local opposition had thwarted the Spanish troops who had otherwise been effective in subduing resistance throughout New Spain. In an act of desperation or perhaps showing a keen sense of strategic innovation, the acting governor of Guatemala—Alonso de Maldonado—took the advice of Bishop Francisco Marroquín and wrote a letter to the bishop of Chiapas—Fray Bartolomé de las Casas. Maldonado's letter asked de las Casas to help him solve the intractable problem of Tezulutlán by sending some Dominican friars to try their hand at a *"conquista pacífica"* (peaceful conquest) of the region. In this context, "peaceful conquest" meant the annexation of the region via evangelization—a project stemming from de las Casas's famous pleas to the Spanish Crown to use religion as the basis for incorporating indigenous peoples into Christendom and the Empire, rather than force of arms to annihilate or enslave them.

The popular version of the story tells that the two friars who were sent approached the fearsome Mayas' settlements barefoot, armed only with a catechism, simple musical instruments, and their faith. To the friars' good fortune, the heretofore-hostile Maya liked their songs and invited the Dominicans to stay for a time so that they could enjoy the music and, at least from the perspective of the friars, so that they could be taught the catechism. Thus began the capitulation of Tezulutlán, which by 1547 had not only been incorporated into the Spanish Empire but also been renamed La Verapaz, or "The True Peace," at the behest of Bartolomé de las Casas himself.

What exactly happened on the ground in Tezulutlán a half-millennium ago was no doubt a much more complicated affair than what this just-so story suggests about how the "Land of War," which had resisted conquest by force of arms, was transformed into "The True Peace" by faith and song.[1] Of course, anyone familiar with the abuses that the European invaders and their *Criollo* descendants perpetrated against the indigenous peoples of the Americas, as well as the cataclysmic impact of European disease on native populations, should naturally be skeptical of the tale. One is tempted to say that the story proves even more suspect in the context of post–Civil War Guatemala in which all claims to multiculturalism and pluri-ethnic nationhood must be read in light of a long history of state-sponsored violence disproportionately targeting Mayas and culminating in the genocidal policies adopted by the state in the 1980s.

This story is nonetheless interesting for a few reasons. First, it is widely known and retold by both Ladinos and Mayas in Alta Verapaz today, suggesting that in one way or another its mythic character holds some explanatory power for people living in the region. And second, the story's trope about the purported power of song as an instrument of religious conversion and sociopolitical change, resonates with the roles that music and song play in the

---

1. Historical accounts suggest that the intersection of music and religion in Colonial Latin America was complex and multifaceted. Some European missionaries, like our Dominican friars, believed songs to be an effective tool for evangelizing because they imagined indigenous people as having a natural affinity for music. Other religious and political authorities, however, viewed these evangelization strategies as problematic, fearing that instead of propagating faith, music would be responsible for further morally corrupting people (Van Oss 1986, 20). For example, a decree issued in Guatemala in 1565 ordered that the "great excess and superfluity of music in the churches" be halted due to the moral danger pleasurable music posed for spiritual life in the colony (20).While the agents in charge of religious institutions debated the relative merits and dangers of evangelizing through song, it is also clear that playing music facilitated indigenous people's participating in religious life. Geoffrey Baker argues that music helped to shape indigenous parishes as semiautonomous spaces in colonial Cuzco, and that rather than church music being an imposition that contributed to the 'musical conquest' of the continent (*pace* Turrent 1993), it provided indigenous people with the "means to manage unequal, changing relationships with the outside world" (Baker 2008, 247). Musicianship, Baker claims, was one of the few avenues through which individuals could construct identities as "decent" Christians, which could in turn afford them a modicum of social mobility and respect.

evangelizing practices of contemporary Maya Catholics, and thus in subtle ways continues to shape religious life in the Verapaz.

The myth of Tezulutlán's peaceful conquest is worth pausing to reflect on because of the way its plot turns on a song's ability to accomplish two tasks. The first, to draw potential converts nearer by dint of its aesthetic qualities. The second, to be an adequate vehicle for conveying crucial parts of the religion. We might well imagine that the Dominican friars singing their way through the dangerous mountains would have failed in their task had either their songs not been sufficiently beautiful to arouse people's interest or, if found pleasing, the songs had not also been able to adequately serve as a medium for transmitting some element of Christian doctrine that could act as the basis for Mayas' eventual conversion to the religion. To put it another way, the songs needed to meet both expressive and rhetorical criteria in order to be successful instruments of conversion (Bauman 1983, 60).

That religious songs or hymns are thought to serve this dual function seems to be confirmed by the practices of the myriad congregations whose churches dot the streets of Cobán. The urban soundscape one encounters on a Sunday morning in Cobán is peppered with sounds including those of acoustic guitars and tambourines accompanying Spanish-language hymns at La Catedral in the center of town, familiar tunes like "When the Saints Go Marching In" played on marimbas with new lyrics at San Felipe's Q'eqchi'-language services, and a polyphony of speaking, singing and weeping in both Spanish and Q'eqchi' over synthesizers and electric guitars from a Pentecostal church located in a small, open-air lot near the bus terminal. *Librerías cristianas* (Christian bookstores typically owned by and catering to evangélicos), stands run by parachurch groups just outside the doors of parish centers, and market stalls sell hymnals, cassette tapes, and CDs of popular Christian music. Radios in homes and businesses are often tuned to stations whose programming includes hymns alongside preaching and other religious programming. Religious music, in short, can be heard or otherwise consumed in many places through a variety of media, and its sounds are an inextricable part of the larger sensorium of Cobán.

As Martijn Oosterbaan has noted, music played publicly and semipublicly in social spaces can embody "an assertive identity politics" (2009, 81) through which people "communicate group identity and reproduce boundaries" (85) as well as make claims on space. The stylistic and linguistic differences we can observe in the musical soundscape of Cobán are thus not just incidental to congregational difference but may in fact be a key way through which Catholics and evangélicos (as well as Seventh Day Adventists, Mormons, Jehovah's Witnesses, and others) differentiate themselves from each other and lay claim to a position for themselves in Guatemala's larger religious marketplace (Chesnut 2007). Heard in the context of our dialogic model of religious changes and contestation, hymns can be said to act both as tools for circulating doctrine within church walls and as beckoning calls that carry outward into public spaces in search of potential converts. Converts who, depending on one's affiliations, commitments, and perspectives, might include the destitute in search of solace, young people in need of moral guidance in an increasingly dangerous society, drunks and addicts in need of healing, joyless católicos in need of the immanent power of the Holy Spirit, or prodigal hermanos separados who should return to the Catholic fold. In this dual movement—moving centripetally to cohere congregations and centrifugally to reach others in the hopes of extending them—hymns become sites for the production of congregational differences and the grounds for religious identity. When one listens for hymns the heteroglossia of Cobán's religious landscape becomes not just a theoretical construct but a lived, sonic reality.

Both Mainstream and Charismatic Catholics in San Felipe hold hymns to be a particularly important part of their respective practices of Catholicism. Qana' Esperanza once remarked that she thought that hymn singing was an especially vital part of her participation in Mass because hymns are doubly pleasing to God. "Singing is like praying twice," she said, "God likes to hear people singing because the words are like prayers, and what's more the music helps us show Him what we feel for Him."[2] In her estimation, music facilitated a deeper affective connection with God and thus made her petitions during prayer more efficacious. Interestingly, her statement seems to echo Pope John Paul II's theological vision that "praying through music raises prayer to a more beautiful and dignified level" because of the connection it fosters between the human and the divine (Pavlick 2010, 18). Qana' Esperanza's reflections on songs as a kind of prayer suggests that she saw a close relationship between the aesthetic dimensions of language use and their ritual importance, so that it isn't simply what was said but also how it was said that marked certain kinds of speech as sacred. This was, of course,

---

2. In mainstream Catholic celebrations prayers such as the *Pater Noster* are sometimes accompanied by music, further blurring the lines between prayers and hymns as genres.

part of the rationale that she and other Mainstream Catholics employed to argue for the necessity of praying in Q'eqchi'.

That parishioners made significant material investments to put together and maintain choirs for their CEBs also suggests that music held important value for their religious lives. While the parish owned a marimba that could be played during Mass, individual comunidades also purchased and maintained the instruments that they used for their Celebrations of the Word, and in fact, some preferred to haul their own marimbas to San Felipe's church when it was their turn to animate a Mass. The marimbas that Mainstream Catholics used could cost upward of GTQ 15,000 or USD 2,000, and Charismatics' electronic keyboards, drum kits, and amplification systems likewise represented investments of tens of thousands of quetzales. Communities also had to recruit and train musicians (usually young men), and periodically pay to send some of them to regional conferences to learn new hymns. Those musicians, furthermore, had to give their time and energy to rehearse each week so that their performances were pleasing enough to match the importance of their ritual function.

Given the ideological, human, and material investment that San Felipe's parishioners made into musical production as part of their devotional lives, it is not surprising that hymns emerged as a flashpoint in the conflict between Mainstream and Charismatic Catholics. This should remind us that heteroglossic systems are predicated not just on multivocality, but on the tensions that exist between the various positions that make up the larger system since it is precisely those tensions and contradictions that help maintain the vitality of the larger socioreligious whole. So, I must add that hymns did one other important thing in Cobán—they disturbed the sometimes-uneasy détente that existed between congregations. In San Felipe the voices of Charismatic Catholics carried outward from their meetings as both a by-product of the aesthetic choices they made in performing worship music and as an intentional tactic for drawing potential converts to their twice-weekly prayer meetings. This was a problem for Mainstream Catholics who lived within earshot of the prayer meetings. Qawa' Emanuel described the situation like this: "They don't let us sleep. 'Aleluya, aleluya, amén, amén,' they yell, and then they start singing and jumping around. They really don't let us sleep. They keep us awake until late, very late with their yelling. The way they sing, they seem just like Protestants. And they are doing it in our chapel, and the priest doesn't say anything about it." He found it suspicious that those sounds were coming from his community's Catholic chapel since they sounded so much like the music associated with evangélicos. However, Qawa' Emanuel's complaints weren't primarily about the sharp notes of the electric keyboards, the thumping *"púm-ba púm-ba"* of bass guitars, the snap of the snare drums, clatter of cymbals, nor the clapping of hands; rather, it was the human voices that seemed to irritate him the most (though, to be sure, those other sounds were part of the problem as well). As I suggest in this chapter, attending to the material, discursive, and embodied dimensions of music in San Felipe's religious life further illuminates the process of religious contestation I observed there.

Let Us Turn to Our Hymnals

Although it was ultimately the sonic qualities of hymns that mattered most in San Felipe, examining the material and semiotic forms of the two congregations' primary "musical media" (Brennan 2018, 21) — namely, their hymnals — will give us some insight into the distinct ways that Mainstream and Charismatic Catholics' oriented themselves to music in religious contexts. In this section I briefly discuss how the composition of the two congregations' hymnals reflected their general ideological orientation toward the circulation of religious music.

The hymnal that Mainstream Catholics used was a small pocket-sized book (6.5" × 4") that was professionally typeset and bound with a glossy paperback cover. It was originally compiled in the 1960s by Belgian-born CICM missionary Padre Esteban Haeserijn, who served in the Diocese of Verapaz over the course of three decades.[3] Working in the years immediately following Vatican II, Haeserijn believed that songs were a good way to promote spiritual engagement among Q'eqchi'-Maya lay people and set out to produce the book with that goal in mind. Titled *Qanimaaq xloq'al li Qaawa': Eb'li b'ich jo'wi' li tij sa' Q'eqchi'* (*We Praise/Venerate the Lord: The songs as well as the prayers in Q'eqchi'*), the book is now published by Salesian priests

---

3. A CICM missionary like those serving San Felipe, Haeserijn worked in San Juan Chamelco (a town southeast of Cobán) from the 1960s to 1980s. Haeserijn was one of the people most involved in the creation of the Q'eqchi'-Maya catechist training program and, in addition to his work on the hymnal, also published a Spanish–Q'eqchi' bilingual dictionary which, despite following an outdated orthography, remains an excellent resource on the language (Wilson 1995, 171; Stewart 1980, xxi). For a detailed discussion of an analogous case of a Catholic priest composing music for a Maya congregation, see MacKenzie (2016, 189–94 *passim*).

based in San Pedro Carchá (a town about 10 kilometers east of Cobán) and is sold relatively cheaply for fifteen quetzales or about two dollars. The hymnal is written entirely in Q'eqchi', and most Mainstream Catholic parishioners with basic literacy skills owned a copy of the hymnal, even if it wasn't the most recent edition. The book's wide circulation, accessibility, and the fact that the printed words can be matched to catchy tunes also seem to have turned it into an important didactic tool for Q'eqchi' language literacy.[4]

Though the book's origins lie with Padre Esteban, new songs have since been composed and added to it. The Salesians publish pamphlets with eight to ten new compositions semiannually in summer and winter, and every few years an updated edition of the full hymnal incorporating the new songs is printed.[5] This has meant that the repertoire of songs is constantly expanding. The 2004 edition of the hymnal was just over 320 pages long and included the texts of 307 different hymns and prayers, and by the time the 2014 edition was published, nearly one hundred pages of songs had been added to the text.

The hymns in *Qanimaaq xloq'al li Qaawa'* are organized according to their theme or purpose so that, for example, songs of thanksgiving, songs about the Holy Spirit or the Virgin Mary, and songs appropriate for the Christmas season are each grouped together. The hymnal also includes an abridged catechism that sets out the basic structure of the Mass and includes congregants' responses to the officiant, as well as the approved texts of the *Pater Noster, Ave Maria*, the Rosary, and other important conventional prayers. The text also includes two forewords. The first is an explanation of the book's purpose, laying out an argument for the sacredness of the songs contained in the book and which bears the bishop's signature. The second

---

4. In the preface to his grammar of Q'eqchi', linguist Stephen Stewart mentions the story of a boy from the town of Santa Maria Cahabón who claimed to have taught himself how to read using the hymnal as his sole textbook (Stewart 1980, xxi). Though none of my consultants went so far as to say that they learned to read using the hymnal alone, several did mention it as a positive factor in helping young people develop Q'eqchi' language literacy. I can attest that the hymnal was an invaluable resource helping me get better at reading Q'eqchi', making sense of the structure of the Mass, and learning the texts of prayers. In that regard, I felt a sense of kinship with that possibly apocryphal boy from Cahabón.

5. There is also another hymnal that is produced by the parish of Santa Catalina La Tinta, in the southeastern corner of Alta Verapaz, and although it is available for purchase in Cobán, it is used only infrequently in San Felipe. There were two songs that seemed to be hits from that song book that a few comunidades' bands liked to perform occasionally, but generally they preferred to stick to the songs in *Qanimaaq xloq'al li Qaawa'*.

foreword is by the hymnal's unnamed editor and is a brief explanation of music theory geared toward teaching people the basics of musical scales and rhythm to help them sing. Finally, at the very back of the book, there is an index listing all of the hymns alphabetically by title.

Most hymns take up one full page of the book, although there are a few that spill over from one page to the next. At the top of each page is the title of the song, which almost without exception is the first line of its lyrics. Beneath the title in parentheses there is a minimal description of the music that includes the key and genre of the song. So that, for example, the translation of "Silent Night" has the notation "(La M -vals- seeb')" indicating that it should be played in A major as a waltz[6] and softly. The hymnal, for reasons I explain in more detail later, does not include musical notations beyond this, much less any transcriptions of melodies to accompany the lyrics.

Interspersed in the text are several illustrations in various graphical styles that include a cropped reproduction of Warner Sallman's famous *Head of Christ* painting, a close-up picture of Robert Powell from Franco Zeffirelli's 1977 film *Jesus of Nazareth*, a relatively sophisticated illustration of Mary holding an infant Jesus with Joseph and a donkey by her side, a rudimentary pixelated image of people standing in front of a cross, and seemingly secular 8-bit computer clip-art images such as a group of children singing and what appears to be a tropical sunset complete with two flamingos in the foreground and palm trees in the midground. Qana' Esperanza, who had never seen a flamingo in person but knew them from television and photographs, thought that that last image was meant to remind people of all the pretty things that God had made in the world. Her explanation made some sense since the song that accompanies the image refers to God's involvement in all aspects of life, though the song refers more specifically to God's involvement in work, rest, and love. Even if the meaning and relevance of the images are not always easy to discern, the presence of the pictures nonetheless does make those pages more visually interesting and helps to fill out spaces that

---

6. Other genres include *balada* (ballad), *bolero* (in the sense of a slow-tempo Latin American song), and *son*. The *son*, or more properly, *Son Chapín*, is a distinctly Guatemalan genre of folk music (as well as an accompanying dance) typically played on the marimba. While the genre clearly derives from the intercultural mixtures stemming from Spanish colonialism, it is closely linked to the spiritual culture of the country's indigenous people (Gandarias 2014, 2015). The ritual dimensions of this genre of music could be appreciated more fully at cofradía festivities, where the son was danced by the meertom and the ranking qawachines of the sodality in honor of the santo.

would otherwise be blank, suggesting that care was put into the typesetting and production of the text.

This is all to say that the material object of the hymnal illustrates the significant amount of institutional effort and resources that the Diocese of Verapaz invests in creating and curating a repertoire of officially sanctioned sacred music for its Q'eqchi'-Maya congregations. By collecting the texts of Q'eqchi' language hymns in this professionally typeset and glossy bound book, delegating its production to a religious order, organizing the content in strict ways, and including other markers of institutional authority (such as the bishop's signature in the front matter), the Diocese of Verapaz projected a certain vision of ordered and official Catholicism through *Qanimaaq xloq'al li Qaawa'*.

In contrast, La Renovación had no fixed hymnal in Q'eqchi', which was not surprising since there were no Q'eqchi' language Charismatic hymns to sing. Then again, the carismáticos in San Felipe did not use the Catholic Church's official Spanish-language hymnal either, nor was there as far as I knew any official songbook endorsed by the Diocese of Verapaz for La Renovación. Instead, several ad hoc collections of songs circulated as photocopied booklets. At a regional Catholic Charismatic Renewal event, I purchased a copy of one such book—*Unidos en un mismo espiritu* [sic]: *Oremos cantando* (*United in one same spirit: Let us pray singing*)—that had been put together by the *ministerio de alabanza* (praise ministry) of a Charismatic community in San Pedro Carchá. The booklet is composed of about twenty sheets of 8.5" × 11" white office paper folded in half, stapled twice along the spine with a single pink sheet of paper of the same weight and texture acting as a cover. Rather than being professionally printed, these pages had been photocopied and appeared to have been typeset on several different word processors and perhaps even typewriters over an extended period of time since several different fonts and conventions for laying out the text are used. The text on pages is not uniformly justified, and though most pages are numbered, not all are. The quality of the print also varies from page to page, with some pages showing the noticeable decay of visual fidelity that is the inevitable result of multiple generations of photocopying photocopied photocopies. Although the hymnal includes the name and address of the group that produced it, the editor's name, and a telephone number one could call to order more copies, its layout and composition suggest a distributed authorship (rather than a single authoritative source) and as a whole the text appears to be designed for easy expansion, ad hoc duplication, and wide distribution.

Unidos en un mismo espiritu includes more than 120 songs,⁷ which are arranged more or less alphabetically, with songs whose titles begin with "A" (e.g., *"Aleluya Abba Padre"* ["Hallelujah Abba Father"], *"Alegres los católicos"* ["Happy are the Catholics"]) toward the front and those beginning with "Y" (*"Yo soy testigo del poder de Dios"* ["I am witness of God's power"], *"Yo canto amor"* ["I sing love"]) toward the back. However, because the lyrics of some songs take up a whole page and others half of one or less, the order of titles does not strictly follow alphabetical order and sometimes titles even seem to be randomly placed so that, for example, on three subsequent pages we find in order *"Pon aceite"* ("Put oil"), *"María nuestra madre"* ("Mary our mother"), and *"No puede estar triste"* ("Can't be sad"). Besides noting where a chorus should be repeated within a hymn itself, there are no musical notations or other clues as to how they should be performed anywhere in the text. And indeed, besides an index that reproduces the exact order in which the hymns appear in the booklet, there is no other text or even image inside the booklet except the hymns themselves.

That the hymnal has this ad hoc quality is not surprising since carismáticos did not rely on written texts for singing their songs anywhere near as much as Mainstream Catholics did. At Mainstream services typically less than half, but nonetheless a significant number of the attendees, arrived with their hymnals in hand and opened them during the service to read along. At Charismatic events, on the other hand, I never saw anyone with a songbook in their hands. Members of Sa'xreb'e's choir band all said that they owned copies of *Unidos en un mismo espiritu*, but they never brought them to church.

These differences in the composition of the supporting musical media of hymnals suggest differing constructions of the congregations' respective musical repertoires and relationships to religious music more generally. The Mainstream Catholic hymnal's official status and relationship to institutional structures of authority echoed the themes of hierarchical authority we discussed in chapter 3, as well the general ideological tendency toward consistency in language use discussed in chapter 4. The ad hoc quality of the Charismatic Catholics' songbook, on the other hand, reproduced that

---

7. At least two songs appear in different places in the booklet with the same lyrics, but typeset slightly differently. This would again speak to the way in which the object itself evidences its ad hoc editorship.

congregation's ideals of distributed human authority, and the lack of musical notation might be read as another move toward fomenting an openness to inspiration as the key to religious knowledge. The next sections will explore some of the social and performative conventions that contributed to the two congregations' diverging relationships to song and help us further connect music to their distinct religious sensibilities.

Music and Lyrics

Although the lyrics of the songs that Mainstream Catholics sang were transmitted via the written texts of the hymnal, the music circulated "by ear." Music literacy was exceedingly rare among parishioners and at no point did I observe or hear about anyone using sheet music to learn the songs. Instead, once a year San Felipe hosted a two-day conference for community choir leaders. Each comunidad sent a few *jóvenes* (unmarried young men and women) from their choir band as representatives to the conference to learn the new hymns. At the conference employees of the Salesian Center that publishes the hymnal would teach the jóvenes to sing the melodies that accompanied the lyrics of new hymns printed in the semiannual pamphlets. The instructors first modeled singing the whole song for their students along with a prerecorded instrumental track, and then taught it to the students by parts. Beginning with the chorus, the instructors would sing each line of the song a cappella and have the students repeat it. Once they had learned all the lines, they would put them together to sing the whole chorus in unison. They would then repeat the chorus several times to make sure everyone remembered it. Once the chorus had been mastered, they would use the same process to learn each individual verse in the song. Once the instructors felt that the students had adequately learned to sing each of the verses as well as the chorus a cappella, they would have the group sing the whole song along with a prerecorded instrumental accompaniment. The next song would then be introduced, and the process would repeat. By the end of the day, the jóvenes would have learned how to sing five or six new songs from the expanding repertoire of published Q'eqchi' language hymns that they could take back to their comunidades.

Back home, these choir leaders first taught the new hymns to their community's marimba players, who were responsible for working out exactly how they wanted to play instrumental accompaniment to the sung melodies. This involved first working out the principal melodic phrases, and then building around them depending on their inclinations and skills. Because each group did this independently, each community had some creative freedom to interpret the music in their own way by, for example, adjusting the tempo, introducing key changes, playing sections with different stylistic conventions such as syncopation, or adding flourishes like arpeggio runs during instrumental breaks. Once the marimba players (and drummer and bassist if the choir band had them) settled on a version of the music they liked, they rehearsed it with a full complement of singers (who, in the meantime, would have been learning the new songs' lyrics with their choir leader) before publicly performing the song for their comunidad. New songs were typically introduced by playing them before the formal start of a Celebration of the Word so that the band and choir could feel confident in the performance and also to familiarize their audience with the tune. Once that had been done a few times and if they liked the song, the choir band would decide whether or not to add it to their repertoire for Celebrations of the Word. Only after they were very comfortable performing a new song for their home CEB would they attempt to play the hymn as part of a full-fledged Mass. From learning a new song to working it into the band's repertoire to gradually performing it for larger audiences, the dissemination of music among Mainstream Catholics followed a gradual process of scaffolding that was tied to the nested hierarchies of the institutional Catholic Church.

The repertoire of music represented by the Mainstream hymnal included both original compositions and translations or reinterpretations of religious and secular songs from abroad. Among the melodies I recognized played by the marimba choir were the African American spirituals "Michael Row Your Boat Ashore" and "When the Saints Go Marching In," several Christmas carols, including "Jingle Bells" and "Silent Night," and Bob Dylan's protest song "Blowin' in the Wind." This hints at the historical process through which the Q'eqchi' hymn repertoire was created, although my informants did not necessarily know these songs through any other context that would have tied it to other musical traditions—for them, they were simply their own repertoire of hymns.[8]

---

8. The sole exception to this rule that I found was "Jingle Bells," which they knew via the Spanish language version ("*Navidad, dulce Navidad*"). Like the Q'eqchi' version, the Spanish translation rewrites the lyrics of the song to make the focus Christmas itself rather than brumal sleighing. Like the English language earworm, "Navidad, dulce Navidad" could be heard in shops, school pageants, and a wide range of public and semipublic spaces from late November

Charismatics' hymns or *alabanzas* circulated less formally than those of their Mainstream counterparts. There was no local tradition of Catholic Charismatic hymn composition, nor was there an office of the Diocese of Verapaz that specifically looked after carismáticos' musical needs, as there was for Mainstream Catholics.' Instead, La Renovación drew its musical inspiration from larger transnational networks of Hispanic Pentecostal/Charismatic Christian mass media. The alabanzas that San Felipe's carismáticos preferred could be heard on Radio Estrella (a Catholic Charismatic FM radio station that broadcast from Guatemala City) and the myriad commercial and bootleg cassettes and CDs available for purchase at market stalls in Cobán. Like Mainstream Catholics, Charismatics relied on the aural/oral circulation of the melodies. Unlike Mainstream Catholics, however, Charismatics also largely depended on hearing in order to learn the lyrics that accompanied those melodies, rather than learning them as written texts. Several factors contributed to their success in doing so. First, although the members of the choir band were competent and occasionally quite accomplished musicians, they performed a much smaller repertoire of hymns than their Mainstream Catholic counterparts. Sa'xreb'e's choir band regularly performed pieces from a repertoire of just over a dozen hymns, whereas each of the villages' CEB bands could draw from a list of hymns three times that size due to their access to the standardized hymnal. Second, the carismáticos' hymns were relatively structurally simple, featuring a lot of repetition and minimal variation in their lyrics. Following is an example of a very popular hymn that the band played at practically every service I attended:

Vamos a alabar al Rey	Let's go praise the King
Vamos a alabar al Rey	Let's go praise the King
Vamos a alabar al Rey	Let's go praise the King
Vamos todos a alabar al Rey	Let's all go praise the King
Toda rodilla se doblará	Every knee will bend
Toda lengua lo besará	Every tongue will kiss him
Toda rodilla se doblará	Every knee will bend
Toda lengua lo besará	Every tongue will kiss him

---

through early January. In December 2005 it could also occasionally be heard inside the church as faint electronic beeping coming from a set of musical Christmas lights that the parish had purchased to decorate its traditional crèche, and which also played "Frosty the Snowman," "Silent Night," and other familiar tunes.

Que Jesucristo es el Señor	That Jesus Christ is the Lord
Que Jesucristo es el salvador	That Jesus Christ is the savior
Que Jesucristo es el Señor	That Jesus Christ is the Lord
Que Jesucristo es el salvador	That Jesus Christ is the savior

This alabanza's lyrics are highly repetitive, featuring just six distinct phrases across the chorus (the first four lines) and two verses that follow. The lyrics repeat the same three grammatical constructions and contain just nineteen different words. Moreover, the entirety of the hymn consists of singing these two verses twice and the chorus four times. While this song is an extreme example of the extent to which Charismatic hymns rely on repetition, it exemplifies the general pattern of syntactic and semantic parallelism. Additionally, all their songs featured predictable rhyme schemes based on conventional pairings of terms. For example, *Señor* and *salvador*, or Lord and savior, are two commonly invoked descriptors for Jesus Christ that also happened to rhyme and hence seemed to be a perennial favorite for these songs' composers. All of the hymns included in *Unidos en un mismo espiritu* as well as others I heard carismáticos perform regularly exhibited a similar repetitive structure, which made learning the lyrics very easy. Moreover, although congregants were expected to sing along with the choir band for the whole song, in practice the emphasis was on adding their voices during the chorus. The band often sang the verses by itself and cued the congregation to join in during the chorus by pointing a hand-held microphone toward them in a gesture recognized worldwide as inviting the audience to sing along with the performers on stage.

By contrast the Mainstream Catholic hymn lyrics were much more structurally complex. The following are the first verse and chorus of a representative hymn:[9]

Li Jesukriist, hulajaq li xkamik	Jesus Christ, his death has come
K'ajo' naq xraheb' chaq li apost	How much he loved the apostles
Kixtaqlaheb' xk'uuba'ankil li na'ajej,	He sent (them) to prepare the place
B'ar wi' tninq'ehi chaq li xPasw	Where one will celebrate his Pasch
Rik'in kaxlan wa ut viin re li uuv	With bread and wine from the grape
Taqak'uub' li xmayej li Jesus	We will prepare this offering for Jesus
Taqaninq'ehi xkamik li Qaawa',	We will celebrate the death of the Lord
Jo'wi xwaklijik chi yo'yo	As well as his arising alive

---

9. This is the hymn sung to the tune of Bob Dylan's "Blowin' in the Wind." The line "*Li Jesukriist, hulajaq li xkamik*" would correspond to "How many roads must a man travel down."

We can see that other than articles ("*li*"), no words are repeated, and the text's author seems to take pains to refer to Jesus in at least three different ways ("*Jesukriist*," "*Jesus*," and "*Qaawa*'" [i.e., Lord]). The only grammatical construction that is repeated is in the second and third lines of the chorus and even there we see different verbs and nouns used. There is no explicit rhyme scheme to the song, either. The other four verses of the song are similarly complex, and each has its own formal grammatical construction. While parallelism, repetition, and rhyme are not absent from the Mainstream Catholic's repertoire of hymns,[10] this example illustrates the relative paucity of those poetic conventions when compared to Charismatic hymns.

Beyond differences in the composition of lyrics, there were also significant differences in their discursive forms. The content of Mainstream Catholic hymns tended to be narrative or expository, whereas Charismatic hymns tended to be expressive and commissive. Mainstream hymns, as the previous example illustrates, were much more likely to lay out some piece of Church doctrine, retell a Bible story, or overtly describe the community engaging in pious action. In the earlier example, the first verse lays out doctrinal statements about Jesus, his death, resurrection, and the importance of the apostles, while the chorus narrates the preparation of the Eucharist and its purpose. Another hymn went:

At Qaawa', b'antiox aawe,	Our Lord, thanks to you,
Katk'ulun chi qakolb'al;	Who came to save us;
Xab'oeqb' laa tenamit;	Called your people [lit. town]
Naab'aleb' li xe'paab'an	We many who believe
Tootioxinq chawu, Qaawa',	We will give our thanks to you, Lord
Naq xk'ulun laawesilal	that your message reached

---

10. As a counter example we could cite the chorus to hymn "*Ralankil, Ralankil,*" which is sung to the tune of "Jingle Bells":

Ralankil, Ralankil, a'in Ralankil.	Christmas, Christmas, this is Christmas
Anaqwan li xkutankil li sahil ch'oolejil	Now is the day of joy
Ralankil, Ralankil, a'in Ralankil.	Christmas, Christmas, this is Christmas
Anaqwan li xkutankil li sahil ch'oolejil	Now is the day of joy

Nonetheless, the verse of this song is more complex:

Q'axal sununk li xb'ook	The fragrant smoke/smell
Xb'anneb' li utz'u'uj:	from the candles/flowers
Naxk'e xsahil qach'ool	Give us joy
Sa' Ralankil wanko	That we are in Christmas time

Sa' xteepal eb' laj Q'eqchi'	To the land of the Q'eqchi'
Xkolb'aleb'lil kok', li ninq.	Savior of the small, of the big.

Here the lyrics thank God, lay out doctrinal statements about salvation, and use a third-person voice to describe a course of action for the community. This example is also interesting because it localizes itself by thanking God for sending his message to Q'eqchi'-Mayas specifically in the penultimate line of the second quoted verse.

The first-person singular voice was rarely used in Mainstream Catholic hymns. Instead, lyrics were written either from a neutral third-person voice when the aim was to describe something, and in those few instances when the first-person voice was used, such as when thanking God, it was conjugated in the plural. The only time that a singular first-person voice was used in song was when the *Nicene Creed* and *Confiteor* were accompanied with music, but this is not a surprising exception since those texts are structured as personal creedal statements and were direct translations of existing foreign texts. Otherwise, the lyrics of their hymns reflected that ideological position that Mainstream Catholics sang as members of a collectivity.

The lyrics of Charismatic hymns, on the other hand, tended to revolve around the singer expressing some desired affective state or describing the effects of having a pneumatic religious experience. One song, for example, said:

Estoy enamorado de Jesús (x4)	I'm in love with Jesus,
Amaré, amaré, estoy enamorado de Jesús (x2)	I'll love, I'll love, I'm in love with Jesus
Estoy enamorado de Jesús (x4)	I'm in love with Jesus,
Reiré, reiré, estoy enamorado de Jesús (x2)	I'll laugh, I'll laugh, I'm in love with Jesus
Estoy enamorado de Jesús (x4)	I'm in love with Jesus,
Bailaré, bailaré, estoy enamorado de Jesús (x2)	I'll dance, I'll dance, I'm in love with Jesus

The lyrics combine an affective stance toward Jesus in the first line, which is repeated four times, with a commissive utterance for a future action (love, laughter, dance) taken in response to being in love with Jesus. The song continues for eleven verses with the only variation being a change in the verb used. Subsequent verses use *gozar* (to enjoy), *orar* (to pray), *saltar* (to jump), *saludar* (to greet), *cantar* (to sing), *caminar* (to walk), and *alabar* (to praise), before concluding with a repetition of the first verse built around *amar* (to love). These verbs are not random but rather are taken from key affective and embodied ideals of Charismatic Catholicism (with the possible exception of *caminar*), in which feelings of profound love, enthusiastic singing and praying, and effusive actions like jumping, dancing, and "holy laughter" are interpreted as signs of the Holy Spirit's immanent presence. The song therefore models what it is supposed to be like to be a carismático, as well as another recurrent theme in the repertoire—bodily movement. I discuss that theme in greater detail in chapter 6, but for now it suffices to say that carismáticos linked physical body and the metaphysical body—the soul—and interpreted effusive physical movements as signs that one was in the appropriate emotional and moral state to receive the Holy Spirit's gifts (see also Hoenes del Pinal 2011). It was not surprising then to find that these themes were present in both the lyrics and the embodied performances of popular hymns.

Choral Variations

The choir band was pragmatically the focal point of La Renovación's rituals. Its members, and especially its leader, were tasked with "animating" the congregation's prayer meetings, and thus had an explicit responsibility to direct the flow of the ritual and perform in some manner throughout it. This was also a matter of convenience since in practice much of the group's leadership were also members of the band. Hermano Rigo, for example, was the band's sole keyboardist and often its lead singer, and Hermana Irma, although not a permanent member of the all-male band, always had a tambourine with her and was often featured as either a singer or prayer leader. From his position at the front of the chapel, Hermano Rigo could easily shift from his role behind the Yamaha electric keyboard to his role as preacher and back again, and in fact, he would occasionally break up his sermons with musical interludes by simply walking over to his instrument and cueing the band to follow his lead.[11] Although the carismáticos' prayer meetings were struc-

---

11. The practice of having a "worship leader" who both directs the musical ensemble and performs other tasks meant to "facilitate an experience of divine presence through music as well as other extramusical worship practices" seems to be widely spread among Pentecostal/Charismatic Christians worldwide (Ingalls and Young 2015).

FIGURE 6 Carismáticos singing an alabanza

tured and followed a predictable sequence of events, with the band at the center, its members serving multiple roles directing both song and prayer, and vibrant music suffusing almost every part of the meeting, the impression one got was that these were dynamic and free-flowing happenings rather than deliberately planned or strictly ordered rituals.

The choir band also featured prominently at Mainstream Catholic services, but it was figured more as playing a supporting role to what other ritual actors did. In Mass the Eucharist was clearly the focus of the event, the priest was the ritual specialist in charge, and the structure of the event was much more explicitly established and formally replicated than it was among Charismatics. Similarly, at Celebrations of the Word the focus was on the Bible readings and the catequista's sermon. Thus, although music was important, it was ideologically figured as secondary to the main business of the ritual. The band and choir were positioned at the front of the nave, but outside of the altar section and against a lateral wall, and thus were near where the important ritual action happened but physically separated from it. Likewise, although the language of "animation" was used to talk about what the band

FIGURE 7   Marimba choir band

did, and although the choir and band were integral parts of the larger performance, there was a much stricter separation of roles between them and the people performing other ritual duties (e.g., lectors, prayer leaders, catechists, and priests). Finally, music was played only at certain specified times, and it did not suffuse the ritual to the same extent as it did in carismáticos' prayer meetings. Participation in the band and choir, though seen as a valuable contribution to the larger spiritual life of the community, tended to be thought of as an early step in a parishioner's spiritual career, and the expectation was that as a person matured into adulthood and began to take on greater responsibilities both in the home and in the CEB, they would leave the choir band behind as a province of youths.

There were also important differences in the musical aesthetics that Mainstream and Charismatic Catholics adopted. Carismáticos favored modern, up-tempo, popular Latin American musical styles such as *cumbias* and *merengues* (cp. Thorsen 2015, 103). These stylistic choices reflected something of the way that carismáticos configured their religious subjectivities in relation to both Mainstream Catholics in San Felipe as well as a larger transnational Christian public. Played on electric instruments to contemporary Latin rhythms and sung in Spanish, Charismatic hymns musically resembled popular music heard on both secular and religious radio (even if they also differed from them in terms of lyrical content), and thus connoted a kind of cosmopolitan Christian subjectivity that was marked in contradistinction to Mainstream Catholic hymns, which by being sung in Q'eqchi' and played on marimbas as "traditional" genres of music, were marked as more "folkloric" (cp. MacKenzie 2016, 189).[12] As I noted earlier, some of the melodies of Mainstream hymns came from abroad and could thus be read as indexing a kind of cosmopolitanism as well, but parishioners did not know them from other contexts. Moreover, by performing them on the marimba and in genres associated with specifically Guatemalan musical traditions, they were domesticated and marked as part of a more localized cultural sphere. I don't want to suggest that the meaning of these markers of identity were absolute or unchanging, but rather that in this context the kinds of music each congregation played signaled two distinct stances with regard to what it meant to be a Q'eqchi'-Maya Catholic. The musical styles of Mainstream Catholics indexed a distinct ethnonational position, while the stylings of Charismatic Catholics pointed toward membership in a larger hemispheric Christian public.[13] Nonetheless, both of their meanings derived from the way the members of the two congregations placed music into dialogue with each other as alternative constructions of how to be Catholic in Alta Verapaz.

Careers and Conversions

These aesthetic and organizational choices San Felipe's Catholics made were deliberate, and they are also seemingly effective since parishioners consistently highlighted the importance of music in their religious lives. This was especially true for people who had reached leadership positions in their respective congregations. Parents would note with a sense of pride when their children started singing along in church as this was taken to be a good sign that they were paying attention to what was happening and that they might need to start thinking about moving them along toward the sacrament of

---

12. The dynamics of signaling local versus cosmopolitan identities through church music recur in many societies (e.g., de Theije and Mariz 2008; Lange 2003; Rommen 2007).

13. One might also read this distinction in terms of the divisions that local bodies of the Catholic Church make between the "*pueblos*" (peoples) they serve. In policy documents the Diocese of Verapaz clearly distinguishes between its "Urban" (that is, Ladino) and "Q'eqchi'" missions (see Hoenes del Pinal 2016a).

First Communion. Moreover, just about every catequista I knew began his or her involvement in the Mainstream Catholic hierarchy either as a marimba player or choir singer for their CEB. Though it is likely that they would have also helped with the collection, sweeping their community's chapel, or other tasks before they became singers or musicians, in interviews they tended to name those roles as their first real involvement in the CEB's activities.

Qawa' Hugo was a longtime catechist, generally involved in parish activities and the Hermandad and, shortly after I left the field, he even started to travel with the priests on their village rounds when he could. His story is a case in point:

> When I was a little, I would go with my mother to church. She liked to go to the Mass, so she would take me. . . . When I got a bit older, I would get bored and I didn't like it any more, so I stopped going. I had had my First Communion, but I would get bored [at church] and I wanted to go wander in the streets or to play. . . . What changed [things] was that I got interested in the marimba. I always liked marimba music, because that's our autochthonous instrument here. For our people it's very special. And my mother saw that I was interested in marimba, so she said, "OK, go play with them" [i.e., the CEB's choir band.] I had a cousin of mine who played with them, and he started to teach me. I was ten, eleven years old maybe. And little by little I learned how to play. . . . We would play at the Celebrations and Mass. I always helped with the band. Well, at church I started to pay more attention and I realized that [church] was good/beautiful. . . . One day they asked me "Why don't you do one of the [Bible] readings?" "OK, I will do that," I said. So, I did a reading, and they saw that I did alright, not so good, but alright. Well, then the next week I did that again and then again. So, then I was more involved in the comunidad. . . . Then when I was nineteen one of the nuns came [to my house] and invited me to some workshops. And I liked that nun, so I went, and those were workshops where they were also trying to see who could be a good catequista. So that's how I started. . . . My son did the same, he also started by playing the marimba. He doesn't want to be a catequista, but he helps the comunidad and it is because of the marimba that he is there. He even plays with a *marimba orquesta* (a professional secular band) now, but that's how he started.

Though *jóvenes* were widely encouraged to be a part of the choir band and though most of those who did become members never took up another office within the CEB system, as Qawa' Hugo's story illustrates, the comunidades first looked to the young men and women already involved in the choir band to find lectors for Celebrations of the Word. Those lectors who showed a special aptitude or talent for that task were then encouraged to pursue becoming catechists. Involvement in the CEB's music could thus be said to be an important part of a Mainstream Catholic's spiritual maturation.

Among carismáticos, the process was a little bit different given the relative newness of its organizations, but people often cited music as one of the things that initially attracted them to La Renovación in the first place as well as a key contributing factor to their continued participation with the group. Among them was Hermano Rigo who was a founding member of the Sa'xreb'e group and was central to its continued existence and day-to-day workings as its preacher, band leader, keyboardist, and de facto liaison with the parish clergy. Hermano Rigo said that he had first attended a Charismatic prayer meeting at the invitation of a friend, and that, though at the time he was very committed to his Mainstream group, he kept going back to the Charismatic meetings because of the music.

> In 2000 one of my neighbors invited me to go to Rub'elchaj to see La Renovación, and I accepted. I wasn't sure because I had heard some rumors, but I said, "OK, let's go see what this is. Let's see if it's like what they say." We went and at first I thought it was a bit strange because I wasn't used to people being like that, moving like we do. But I liked the music, so I went another time, and then another. Because I liked the music I entered the dynamic of La Renovación. The music interested me. It was *alegre* [joyful] and the music attracted me to go back, so I went to listen [to the music]. And then I started praying with them too and it was during a song maybe the fourth or fifth time that I went, I felt something. [It was] like heat and lightness in my body, and I thought maybe that's the Holy Spirit. The hermanos prayed over me, and then I was sure it was the Holy Spirit, and so I decided "I'm staying here [with La Renovación]." . . . They knew I was a catequista and they welcomed me. One of them said, "Why don't you help with the music?" I had played marimba and I learned the melodica[14] a bit in school, so with that I learned

---

14. The melodica is a windblown reed instrument composed of a two-octave keyboard like one would find in a small electronic piano but with a mouthpiece attached that resembles the one found on a recorder. Sometimes there is also a plastic tube that connects the two pieces allowing the player to see the keyboard more easily.

to play the keyboard a bit. I had a *don* (spiritual gift) for music, so I played keyboard. It wasn't until later, maybe another eight [or] nine months that I also received the don to preach, so now you see I do both, thanks to God I have those blessings.

In Hermano Rigo's telling, the initial conversion was not due to a deep personal crisis that drove him to seek out a new religious home, or a feeling of awe at the presence of the power of the Holy Spirit at the prayer meeting, but rather it was spurred by the pleasure he derived from the music (on the importance of pleasure in music, see Samuels 2004, 100; Stokes 1994). It was only later, after weeks of continued attendance at prayer meetings that he felt the Holy Spirit touch him and decided to commit himself to Charismatic Catholicism fully. His ability to pick up the electronic keyboard as an instrument and play with the choir band facilitated his place in the Rub'elchaj community, and now served him in his role as the group leader in Sa'xreb'e.

Though a recurrent theme in Christian conversion narratives is the converts' experience of the brokenness or "the dark night of the soul" followed by a turn toward a new faith, anthropological studies have consistently shown that conversion is processual and continuing, so that far from being instantaneous or absolute, it depends on social practices (Austin-Broos, Buckser, and Glazier 2003; see also Gooren 2010). These practices are as much discursive as anything else, and, as Peter Stromberg has shown, the experience of conversion, with all of its deep affective, ideological, and social implications, tends to be supported by the narrative framings that new converts build for themselves in the process of telling and retelling their stories of self-transformation (Stromberg 1993). Conversion, whatever its actual experiential dimensions might be, can thus also be examined in terms of how people narratively frame their transition from one soteriological status to another, and attending to what is included in conversion narratives offers us insight into what elements of social and cultural life converts view as important to that change. It is telling that Hermano Rigo chose to highlight his aesthetic appreciation of music and its role in convincing him to become an active member of the Charismatic group in Rub'elchaj, even if he also stressed that this was but the first step in his new spiritual life and that the ultimate determining factor was an embodied experience of the Holy Spirit's presence. Several other congregants also told similar stories about how they had become involved in the Charismatic group. The idea that exposure to music and song could be a preliminary step toward gaining a new convert was evident in the ways that adolescent members of the congregation evangelized their peers, too. It was common to invite a neighbor or acquaintance from school to come along to a La Renovación's prayer meeting by emphasizing the music, with the hope, of course, being that a musical hook would keep them coming back until they were fully open to experiencing the Holy Spirit.[15] Thus, whatever else might have factored into La Renovación's growth in San Felipe, as these examples illustrate and as other scholars have noted, music certainly played an important role in drawing potential converts to this form of Catholicism (cp. Chesnut 2003 139–40; Thorsen 2015, 104). Why, though, should music and song be especially powerful factors in evangelization and conversion?

Musical performance is an activity that is fundamentally cooperative and that requires a high degree of coordination among individuals to achieve a shared goal. Its rhythmic elements help focus individuals' actions and synchronize them with each other and in doing so create a sense of social bonding (Tarr 2017). This effect potentially extends beyond simply the performers of music and can also work at large scales because the music itself acts as a sort of reference point for others to join in on the process. Christopher Small has proposed the verb "to music" and its gerund form "musicking"—which he defines as "[taking] part, in any capacity, in a musical performance, whether by performing, by listening, by rehearsing, or practicing, by providing material for performance (what is called composing), or by dancing"—as a way for musicologists to foreground the social aspects of music (Small 1998, 9). Small's project is to develop a theory of the social life of music focused on processes of participation, and his neologism is a way to shift the frame of reference from a dialectic that figures producers of music as active and the consumers as essentially passive, to one in which a whole range of people are active agents mutually implicated in music's existence in the world. While

---

15. Mainstream Catholic parents were not always happy to see their children take up with the carismáticos, but forbidding them from going to an event at the village's Catholic chapel was a difficult thing to do since a prohibition like that could be interpreted as a more general proscription against involvement in Catholic life. Invitations to an evangélico church were easier to decline. Faced with the prospect of having to tell their children *not* to go to a Catholic event, most preferred to let them go than to be seen as standing in the way of their children's desire to participate in Catholic religious life more fully, even if the specific form that participation took was suspect.

Small approaches the issue from the perspective of a musicologist largely interested in the social life of art music, his intellectual project is well suited for thinking about music anthropologically, since attention to social and cultural context of musical performance is precisely what one would want to glean from examining music ethnographically. Adopting the perspective of musicking allows us to think about the social processes which underlie any given manifestation of music and account for the affective power that music has on people in context. There is ample evidence to suggest that musical performances are especially effective at recruiting participation in a shared activity, and that moreover, shared experiences of musicking may work to "homogenize participants' emotional states" (Koelsch 2014, cited by Tarr 2017, 155). To take but one example, in his ethnography of Navajo rock musicians, David Samuel vividly describes how audience members, who "desire to add onto the textural grain of a song, to expand and thicken the participatory experience," do so at concerts by performing their own auxiliary percussive acts (clapping, foot tapping, etc.), dancing or just bobbing their heads along to the music, or by simply gathering around the band to produce a kind of surplus of affect (Samuels 2004, 197). Fully understanding the effect that music has on collectivities of people thus almost requires us to bracket the rhythmic, harmonic, and melodic aspects of music—the materiality of its sounds—and instead focus on the way that the performance produces a surplus of affect and sociality out of the coordinated actions of co-present others (and perhaps also absent but nonetheless implicated ones like the Holy Spirit, Jesus, or a potential convert walking within earshot of the chapel). As Samuel's example suggests, much of this affective surplus has to do with music's ability to recruit bodies into the larger process of musicking.

Beyond these embodied and affective dimensions, though, we might also consider the pragmatics of hymn singing from a linguistic perspective. As Robin Shoaps found in her study of North American Pentecostal song, there are discursive features in hymn lyrics that make the individual performance of a fixed text artifact seem like a deeply personal experience (Shoaps 2002). When Mainstream Catholics sing the Nicene Creed (*"Ninpaab' li Dios Yuwa'b'ej,"* "I believe in God the Father") this is evident, but the process is heightened among Charismatics whose songs consistently feature this kind of creedal statement formulated from the first person. Carismáticos' lyrics, as I showed earlier, tend to be deictically grounded in the first person enjoining the singer to animate the authorial voice of its lyricist, and thus occupying, however tentatively, his stance (Goffman 1981, 144; cp. Bakhtin 1981). The personae of the singer and author are thus performatively merged. The lyricist's voice consistently makes representative or expressive statements about affective states and/or beliefs, inviting the singer to inhabit its subjective position. So that when the lyrics say, "I feel the Holy Spirit" or "Jesus is here," the singer temporarily commits to those things being the relevant stances (and indeed someone who has already converted or otherwise committed to Charismatic Catholicism would want to hold those points to be true). Of course, the effect isn't always lasting, but the experience of collectively singing these stances lends them a further degree of authority by embedding the individual singer within a collectivity that holds these things to be true.

Among Charismatics there is a further recruitment of bodies into the musicking collective. Choir band leaders in Sa'xreb'e enjoined everyone to clap along with the music, and everyone present did so. Furthermore, in a number of the Charismatics' favorite hymns the performances went beyond the vocalization of the lyrics and asked congregants to perform little bits of choreographed dancing to iconize the lyrical content of the hymn. For example, when "*Vamos a alabar*" (see the earlier discussion) was performed, congregants were asked to bend their knees in a sort of curtsey to the line "*Toda rodilla se doblará*" (Every knee will bend), and to place their hand to their mouth and then extend it outward and upward to the line "*Toda lengua lo besará*" (Every tongue will kiss him) to imitate blowing a kiss to someone above. This was a relatively new way of behaving in public for Q'eqchi'-Mayas and it was markedly different from the way that they would have sung hymns as Mainstream Catholics, where the norm was that one should stand still and sing somewhat softly. It is possible that the pleasure Charismatics derive from these songs had a lot to do with this new orientation toward bodily behavior. Those dances also served as a technique of self-formation that created the embodied grounds for feeling like a católico carismático renovado. The communal performance of these songs linked certain kinds of bodily movements to specific beliefs about the immanence of sacred beings in congregants' lives (Hoenes del Pinal 2011). Thus, the structure of participation of singing in church reinforced the new kind of Christian subjectivity upon which La Renovación's claims of orthodoxy were predicated. As Tanya Luhrmann has noted, mutually reinforcing linguistic and kinesthetic practices do significant work in laying the experiential groundwork of religious conversion by making its affective and ideational constructs manifest in bodily sensation (Luhrmann 2004; see also Mahmood 2005). Thus, hymn singing may be understood as a constitutive part of "doing being" a Catholic (Sacks 1984). In singing these songs participants took a stance that positioned their selves dialogically in relation to both the object of devotion as well as to their coparticipants and hence made being a member of that particular kind of Catholic Christian community real.

When viewed in terms of Small's concept of musicking the importance of hymn singing in San Felipe can be seen for all its social complexity, and the story of how the sixteenth-century Dominican missionaries evangelized the "land of war" through song starts to make more sense. In La Renovación's services the choir band was undoubtedly at the center of the performance, but the grain of the performance was also a product of the collective singing, clapping, and dancing of the rest of the congregation. The anonymous authors of the music and lyrics as well as the national and international networks that produced and circulated the makeshift hymnals were as necessary to Charismatic Catholic musicking as was the triune God that the songs qua ritual performances invoked. To a lesser extent, material objects were also a part of this process, especially when pre-performance prayers explicitly asked that the electronic equipment used for amplification be blessed and imbued by the power of the Holy Spirit. Implicated as well were the non-Charismatic neighbors, both actual individuals like Qawa' Emanuel who regularly complained about the noises coming from the chapel on Wednesday nights and presumptive ones—converts-to-be—who were targeted by the music as it seeped out the doorway and echoed down the hill and across the village. Likewise, on the Mainstream Catholic side of things each act of singing implicitly invoked the parochial and diocesan structures of the Catholic Church that helped support a repertoire of doctrinally orthodox hymns. Though their songs did not explicitly call for an extraordinary spiritual experience, the collective voice of its singers helped to recapitulate the idea that God could and should be praised from within Q'eqchi'-Maya culture using the language and instruments of its heart and soul.

Dissonance and Harmony

By way of concluding, I return to a query posed near the beginning of this chapter—why was the human voice singled out as the most irritating part of the others' music? Philosopher Mladen Dolar has argued that the human voice occupies an indeterminate space between communication (or perhaps signification more generally) and aesthetics, and that as such, it points to a tension in people's experience of the social (Dolar 2006). Though one can try to understand the voice starting by either viewing it as an instrument of communication or as an object of aesthetic appreciation, giving precedence to either has the effect of causing one to lose sight of the other, and ultimately the real power and complexity of the oral/aural dimensions of human sociality. Regarded in terms of its communicative function, the human voice is a vanishing mediator that must get out of the way for meaning to be conveyed. Even taking into consideration the ways in which prosodic features of speech (timber, intonation, etc.) might play into the meaning-making, the voice disappears in the act of speech; it is in some sense epiphenomenal to language when we understand the latter primarily in terms of semiosis. At best what is left of a voice after the act of speaking is a trace, a vague resonance of its sonic quality that is subsumed in the signifying act of speaking in which the conveyance of meaning takes precedence. Conversely, taken as an object of aesthetic appreciation, signification tends to be suppressed in favor of the voice's expressive qualities. When the whole point of attention to the human voice revolves around its sonic, material quality (as, for example, operatic arias do), what is being said matters much less than how it is vocalized. One could also make such a claim regarding uses of the voice that are neither necessarily "artistic" nor only understood as aesthetic, such as in religious chanting or ritual wailing (see, for example, Urban 1988; Briggs 1993). I do not mean here to reify the difference between the sonic and the signifying, but only to say that to some extent Dolar's distinction, though certainly subject to complication by ethnographic fact, is useful insofar as it allows us to identify an ambiguity inherent of the human voice's work as a medium of social interaction and an object in and of itself.[16]

---

16. A growing literature on the anthropology of voice suggests that it might be an error to radically separate these dimensions and that instead we need to find ways to understand them as mutually constitutive. Nicholas Harkness in his ethnography of Evangelical Christian song in Korea proposes that we need to think of anthropological research on voice as investigating the "phonosonic nexus" at which "the phonic production, shaping, and organization of sound . . . [and] the sonic uptake and categorization of sound in the world" meet (Harkness 2014, 12). Building on this insight, Patrick Eisenlohr's study of Muslim devotional poetry in Mauritius emphasizes the role of the human voice in generating the "sonic atmosphere" of religion by dint of its ability to affect bodily sensations (Eisenlohr 2018).

Of course, these two perspectives on the human voice aren't mutually exclusive, and, in fact, what Dolar wants to suggest by drawing this distinction between the voice as medium of signification and the voice as object of aesthetic appreciation in the first place is that when viewed together, they point to a third position that exists in the gap between the two modalities. That gap is meaningful because hearing a voice also implies that there is a space in which it resonates, a void that it fills, if only fleetingly (Dolar 2006, 41). Sometimes this can be comforting, as it suggests that there is an "other" out there to communicate with or to appreciate aesthetically, but apprehending that there is a void to be filled can also be an uncanny experience in the Freudian sense. The voice echoing down the dirt lane from the chapel and across the hills in Sa'xreb'e points to a gap—a void asking to be filled—and it is here that Dolar's insights help us explain why the singing voices of religious "others" can be unsettling.

To amend Dolar's argument a bit, we might say that the carismáticos' singing voices indexed the social distance that had been created between the two congregations as its members sought to fulfill different paths to piety. Though the two congregations' paths had diverged, and parishioners saw their modes of spirituality as incompatible or even antagonistic, they also recognized that they were socially and historically implicated in some of the same spaces of Alta Verapaz. As Rupert Stasch has argued, both solidarity and alterity are critical components of identity formation and thus both are the basis for creating a sense of community (Stasch 2009). Insofar as people create a sense of self through the feelings of solidarity with some set of individuals, creating a sense of difference from another set of people is also a constitutive part of the process of identification (Barth 1998). Inventing difference, however, is not without its problems; its by-products may include a sense of unease, of the uncanny—something both recognizable but also undeniably other and unsettling. The voices singing out from the chapel in Sa'xreb'e signaled a presence that Mainstream Catholics regard with a high degree of ambiguity since it seemed to simultaneously claim identification and alterity. Mainstream Catholics were skeptical of Charismatics' claims to Catholicism, and the latter's hymns provide evidence that "they" are not like "us." Code choice, instrumentation, tempo, loudness, and so on all pointed toward this being the case. And yet, these were one's neighbors, maybe even one's kin. They were the people with whom one had sat in the pews not so long ago, and perhaps they were even the people once tasked with leading one's own congregation's prayers and songs. Because of these shared personal histories, regarding them as wholly other would have implied that a tear existed in the social fabric of not just the church but also of the village and the family that would not be easy to reconcile. Moreover, La Renovación's alabanzas were seductive. They beckoned you nearer to the chapel, their rhythm asked you to join the community in a sung display of faith—this was precisely the point of their hymns. Should the skeptic enter the chapel and find him- or herself singing along with the congregation, clapping to the beat, and vocalizing texts laden with statements of faith, they may find themselves abandoning a subjective position as an uncommitted observer and contending, however briefly, with the possibility that the transcendence promised by the hymn is real. Adding one's voice to the chorus, "*Ya llegó, ya llegó, el Espíritu Santo ya llegó*" (He's arrived, he's arrived, the Holy Spirit has arrived), one could easily find oneself wondering whether there was truth in the song and, critically, whether one wasn't just swaying to the music but had already been swayed by it.

CHAPTER 6

Lo siento en mis manos, lo siento en mis pies
Embodying Piety

Three times per year the carismáticos in Sa'xreb'e gathered en masse to hold all-night events called *vigilias* (lit. "vigils," although "revival" might better capture the spirit of these gatherings). These vigilias marked important moments in the liturgical calendar, and members of La Renovación gathered from dusk until dawn in numbers significantly greater than those of their semiweekly prayer meetings. The night was spent doing both things that were a standard part of their ritual repertoire, such as preaching, singing, and praying, as well as things that were less common, such as performing skits, healing prayers dedicated to specific populations within the community, and feasting. The length of the event and the amount of activity that was packed into a vigilia meant that they were both energizing and exhausting. Between the recitation of the opening prayer as the sun set and the final "Amén" that came well after the cocks had crowed, ten or eleven hours would have passed. By the end of the vigilia congregants were simultaneously bleary-eyed from a lack of sleep (the Mainstream catequistas within ear-reach of the amplification equipment might well have felt the same way), hoarse from singing and praying, aching from standing and dancing, grateful for the chance to come together in fellowship, and enthusiastic about the blessing that the Holy Spirit had undoubtedly bestowed upon them.

Sa'xreb'e's carismáticos' New Year's Eve vigilia in 2005 was to be their largest to date. Rather than holding it at the village chapel as they had the year before when I first met the congregation (see chapter 4), or at Hermano Rigo's home as they had for All Souls' Day a couple of months earlier, La Renovación's leadership chose to use a semi-open storage space at Hermano Lalo's home. That space normally sheltered his cargo truck and stores of grain and wood that he helped transport, but for this night it would become a religious space. Several large blue tarps were hung along one edge of the space to make a wall, in front of which a stage was built to accommodate the events' animators. A motley collection of low wooden benches and plastic chairs that had been collected from different households were set up in arcing rows around the stage. Balloons and twisted lengths of crêpe paper were hung on the walls as well as from the metal rafters, and pine needles were strewn on the hard-packed dirt floor to give the space a festive feel.[1] Just off to the right of the stage and around a concrete block wall, fires were burning to keep large pots of tamales, black beans, coffee, and cacao warm for a late-night meal, and there were also baskets filled with stacks of warm handmade tortillas and bags filled with *pan dulce*.

The size of the event was thanks in part to the steady growth the community had experienced since its founding four years prior and in part due to the importance New Year's Eve and Day have for Cobán's Catholics regardless of affiliation.[2] The community's third anniversary celebration would be memorable, too, because special guests had been invited to animate the event. Those guests were the musical group Renacer en Cristo, who were a polished and regionally well-known group of Q'eqchi'-Maya musicians based in San Pedro Carchá. Renacer en Cristo was closely affiliated with the carismático communities who had first brought La Renovación to Alta Verapaz and had recently produced a cassette tape of their music, which was for sale throughout the country and had gotten some airplay on Guatemala's national Catholic Charismatic FM radio station. The band's founder and lead singer was also well-known as an engaging preacher and efficacious prayer leader.

---

1. Guatemalans traditionally decorate with pine needles for big parties. Branches may be hung on walls or the backs of chairs or woven together into garlands, and for especially big events the needles are scattered on the floor. In addition to covering up whatever flooring may be under them and creating a lush green carpet, this has the effect of filling the space with a pleasant verdant scent, which is only amplified as the party goes on and people walk or dance on them.

2. While many people attend midnight Mass on December 31, many more make it a habit to visit church on January 1. Churches that sit atop hills, like San Felipe, are especially popular destinations since it is propitious to offer prayers and light candles to their santos for prosperity in the coming year. Although not everyone makes this explicit, the connection of these places to the *Tz'uultaq'a* suggests that this tradition, which is also widely adopted by Ladinos in the region, has Maya roots.

Having Renacer en Cristo at the event was thus a cause for excitement and about 350 people came out that night—a number that far exceeded the normal attendance at regular prayer meetings and surpassed attendance for the previous vigilia by about a third.

Renacer en Cristo's music was of course a big attraction, and it came with the added boon that they would be teaching the congregation some of the songs from their album. One of the songs they taught the congregation also included a small bit of choreography that dramatized the lyrics. The song says:

Ay esta mano que no me da,	Oh this hand that doesn't work,
la tengo tiesa como un compás.	I have it stiff like a metronome.
Al espíritu santo voy a aclamar	I am going to praise the Holy Spirit
para moverla de aquí pa' allá (x4)	so I can move it from here to there (x4)

As we saw in the previous chapter, songs with lyrics about bodily movement were a regular part of the carismático musical repertoire, and like many of those, this song was constructed around repeating this basic verse with only the named body part changing in each new iteration. Subsequent verses replaced "hand" with other body parts that were first stiff and then moved, including one's "other hand," each foot, head, waist, body, and finally and most dramatically, one's soul. When Renacer en Cristo performed the song at the vigilia, they prompted congregants to move the named body part in a broad side-to-side motion along to the beat so that by the time body and soul were called out, people would ideally be swaying in big, broad movements.

Sa'xreb'e's carismáticos were enthusiastic about Renacer en Cristo's performance and eager to learn the new song (though in truth many of them probably already knew it from the radio, since this was not an original composition but rather part of an existing repertoire of Pentecostal/Charismatic hymns that circulate internationally), and yet, that night as well as upon subsequent viewings of my videorecording of the event, I was struck by how stiffly, abruptly, and mostly off-beat the congregants moved while mimicking the lyrics' spiritual metronome. If on the one hand the disjuncture between the ideal actions the lyrics evoke and the actual embodied performances I observed neatly dovetails with the song's description of a person experiencing an intervention of the Holy Spirit, whereby rigid and unresponsive limbs take on new life, then, on the other hand, that apparent disconnect also clearly illustrates how much effort carismáticos seemed to put into becoming Catholics of the sort for whom ecstatic bodily experience was not just desirable but normative. San Felipe's carismáticos very clearly valued the affective states and bodily effects their theology attributed to close interaction with the Holy Spirit, but many of them struggled to embody those ideals. Speaking in tongues and being "slain in the spirit" (i.e., a condition in which a person begins to shake and then falls down) were exceedingly rare occurrences among the parish's Charismatics, even if discursively they formed a core part of what they thought set them apart from Mainstream Catholics and gave them the status of truly being católicos renovados.

As we have seen in previous chapters, becoming a carismático entailed much more than just a nominal change in one's group affiliation; it also required recognizing new structures and sources of religious authority, adopting new linguistic practices, and cultivating new aesthetic sensibilities. Moreover, as I shall argue here, converts to La Renovación needed to develop a new set of bodily dispositions that were significantly different from those they had grown up with as Mainstream Catholics. These bodily dispositions were especially important because, as the song quoted above illustrates, they were thought to facilitate the kinds of ecstatic experiences that were the central driving force of the religion's spiritual renewal. This linking of the physical body with the metaphysical body points to the argument I want to make in this chapter and the next—that bodily practices, performed both individually and collectively, are critical loci for cultivating religious sensibilities. This was as true for Mainstream Catholics as it was for Charismatic Catholics even though they each cultivated distinct, almost diametrically opposed, sets of bodily practices, which they each justified according to their own ethos. Nonetheless, the two groups shared an understanding that bodily behaviors were critical for piety. In the next section I give an overview of how anthropologists have approached the relationship between gesture and the embodiment of culture, before returning to a description of San Felipe's parishioner's characteristic bodily practices in ritual settings.

Gesture, Language, and Culture

It is perhaps banal to note that human communication at some level always implies the presence of human bodies, yet it is also true that the embodied dimensions of communication have historically received much less sustained attention from researchers than other aspects of language (Kendon and Müller 2001).³ This is in part because modern language ideologies, predicated as they are on a Cartesian mind-body dichotomy, tend to frame language as primarily situated in disembodied mental processes that are only secondarily embodied, even though it is fairly obvious that bodies are implicated in communicative processes in myriad ways—including the way our vocal apparatuses produce the soundwaves of speech, how our auditory systems receive those soundwaves, how our manual and ocular organs produce and decipher various forms of writing, how gesture and posture help us to manage communication, not to mention the fact that all of this is dependent on the larger workings of neuromotor systems. That ideological erasure has been compounded by technological and methodological issues that have further tended to "dis-embody" the study of language.

First, the technology available for recording high-fidelity analyzable audio in the field has been available for much longer than it has for comparable video recording. It is only in the last two decades that high-definition video has become cheap enough and portable enough to be part of the anthropologist's toolkit and allowed researchers to adequately examine manual communication in field conditions. When I went to do fieldwork in 2004, I was able to take a handheld camcorder that used small digital video cassettes capable of recording sixty minutes of video at a resolution of 480p, which was higher than that of VHS tape but far lower than what midrange smartphones could produce a decade later. Low-resolution video hampers researchers' ability to closely examine the quick and complex movements of gesture, and this can further be compounded by the poor lighting conditions of many field settings. As such, much of the study of gesture until very recently has occurred in laboratory settings where lighting and subject placement can be controlled to produce video data with higher visual fidelity. This tendency has led to gesture studies being more common among cognitive scientists and formal linguists whose works lends itself to those settings than among linguistic anthropologists and sociolinguists whose work tends to be based on the collection of more naturalistic data in "the field," where lighting conditions and camera shots are less easy to control.

---

3. Although there is certainly a case to be made for treating gesture and body language as something distinct from verbal language or as the "Other of language" (Ruthrof 2000; see also Csordas 2008), my approach here is based on seeing body movement as an integral part of language and communication (Kendon 2004; Birdwhistell 1970).

A second problem facing scholars of embodied communication is that the notational system we use to represent spoken language (i.e., alphabetic writing) for all its deficiencies is far more conventionalized and advanced than what we have for representing gesture. While there is an established technical language for describing the underlying mechanics of gestures (see, for example, Kendon 1997, 2004; Goodwin 2000; McNeill 2000), there is no widely adopted standardized system for transcribing hand gestures comparable to alphabetic writing (much less is there anything for postures, facial expressions, etc.), and so, researchers are faced with devising their own schemes for translating raw field recordings into analyzable data. These issues have limited how much linguistic anthropologists and sociolinguists have been able to adequately examine gesture as an important part of communication.

This is not to say that the role of the body in language has been wholly ignored, however. For example, Erving Goffman's interactionist sociology with its emphasis on the microprocesses of human sociality presumed the importance of bodies and embodied practices in regulating interaction, and the ethnography of communication as developed by John Gumperz and Dell Hymes likewise highlighted the necessity of a thorough description of the cultural systems that accompanied linguistic practices. In addition to this, and even if we grant that speech is a privileged channel for human interaction, there is a long-standing literature that alerts us to the importance of other embodied ways that people communicate with each other, including gesture (Goodwin 2000; Kendon 2004), gaze (Kendon 1990; Goodwin 1980), kinesics or body movement (Birdwhistell 1970), the spatial arrangement of bodies or proxemics (Hall 1969), not to mention the myriad ways in which bodily adornment can communicate status or identity (Turner 2012).

More recently Mary Bucholtz and Kira Hall have called for linguistic anthropologists and sociolinguists to make a concerted effort to develop an "embodied sociocultural linguistics" that more fully examines how human bodies function in linguistic interaction and meaning-making (Bucholtz and Hall 2016). When we focus on communication as an embodied practice it is easy to see that people tend to use two or more forms of communication simultaneously and complementarily (e.g., gesturing as they speak, manipulating their facial expressions to add meaning to a posture, relying on sartorial codes to establish the right to speak and be heard, etc.). It thus seems necessary to theorize human communication as a fundamentally multimodal process that encompasses a range of embodied semiotic practices, each of which merits examination on its own, but perhaps more critically as they relate to each other (see Kendon 2004; McNeill 1992; Goldin-Meadow 2003; Norris 2004). Following from this core insight, a steadily growing anthropological literature[4] has developed around examining how bodily movement contributes to the production of meaning in a wide range of settings with defined cultural norms including childhood language socialization (Baquedano-López 2008; Moore 2008), disputation and debate (Goodwin, Goodwin, and Yaeger-Dror 2002; Lempert 2005), storytelling (Farnell 2002; Soulaimani 2017), the performing arts (Elisha 2018; Haviland 2011), nation building and politics (Covington-Ward 2016; Ayobade 2015), and healing (Hanks 2006; Perrino 2002).[5] Nonetheless, as Michael Lempert has argued, what remains to be developed in earnest is a more "integrative anthropology of gesture" that explores the multiple sociocultural entanglements of bodily movement, including people's critical reflections on what it means to gesture (Lempert 2019).

My aim in this chapter is to advance that goal by discussing how gesture and bodily movement contributed to the production of the Mainstream and Charismatic Catholics' distinctive forms of religious practice in San Felipe. I

---

4. There has also been growing interest in the cultural importance of gesture from historians (Braddick 2009). For example, it seems clear that gesture systems were highly elaborated and gestural practices were deliberately cultivated in several cultural domains in the Classical Mediterranean world including religion, medicine, politics, and oratory (Corbeill 2004; see also Jorio [1832] 2000). There is strong evidence too that gesture has historically played an important role in establishing and maintaining social and political orders (Allert 2008; Brubaker 2009), as well as in subverting and critiquing them (Arnold 2009; Rothschild 2017). Moreover, as Céline Carayon has persuasively argued in her account of cross-cultural encounters in early colonial North America, gesture may offer a sufficient channel for mediating intercultural communication and exchange in the absence of shared linguistic codes (Carayon 2019). The historical literature prompts us to consider the social work that the codification of bodily movement has done at various moments and should lead us to ask why gesture has more often than not been rendered relatively invisible in Western modernity.

5. There is also a cultural anthropology literature that has focused on body movement that is an important antecedent to the growing interest in gesture. In 1934 Marcel Mauss, for example, wrote about the *techniques du corps* through which cultures shape individuals' actions (Mauss 1979). In the 1960s Alan Lomax proposed establishing "choreometrics" as a methodology for a positivistic cross-cultural study of dance (see Lomax and Paulay 2008). Gregory Bateson both singly (1936) and with Margaret Mead (Mead and Bateson 1942) explored the meanings of bodily postures and practices in Balinese culture. Although those projects did not necessarily spark major fields of research, some scholars did follow in their footsteps. Corinne Kratz's examination of the body in women's initiation rituals in Kenya (1994), Sally Ann Ness's work on dance in the Philippines (1992), and Brenda Farnell's work on Plains Sign Talk (2009), with their sharp focus on intersection of cultural symbolism and body movement, are worth noting as more recent examples of this literature.

do so by examining how parishioners mobilized their bodies alongside three speech genres in their rituals, each of which presupposed different participant structures and norms of behavior—preaching, singing, and praying. In preaching, as we have seen in previous chapters, the participant structure was built around a single person speaking from a position of authority to an audience who was meant to be focused on what was being said. The extent to which hand and arm gestures accompanied that form of oratory offers us insight into how each community construed authoritative discourse as something that was embodied as much as it was verbal, and thus sheds light on how religious speech ideally should look. Praying, on the other hand, is structured as a moment when all people, regardless of their position in the Church's hierarchy, individually address speech to God. Examining how people used their body as a communicative resource when speaking to a presumably present but non-visible divine interlocutor allows us to discern something of the broader ethos that governed their understanding of how one should behave oneself in the presence of the sacred. Finally, hymn singing is a genre of collective speech with a fixed text that emphasizes affect. As this chapter's opening vignette illustrates, the extent to which collective singing was performatively conventionalized helps us uncover some of the ideological underpinnings of people's preferred forms of religiosity. Taken together, these exemplary genres allow us to identify the distinct patterns that characterized each congregations' style of ritual participation and to better understand why bodily movements as much as language choice became subject to cross-congregational critique.

Preaching: The Ethos of Performance

As discussed in chapter 3, even though catequistas and predicadores approached the task of preaching in different ways, both congregations held this genre of speaking to be a crucial component of their ritual lives. Examining how these two categories of lay leaders enacted their authority through the full embodied performance of preaching offers us insight into how their congregations' ideals about bodily comportment differed.[6]

---

6. Because priests had markedly different racial, ethnic, and national identities, and because they did not marry, they were not taken as role models of Q'eqchi'-Maya moral personhood in the same way as catequistas and predicadores were.

When Mainstream Catholic catequistas gave a sermon, they tended to do so while standing relatively still. This was especially true when sermons were delivered as part of Mass at San Felipe's church where a pulpit was a permanent part of the church's furnishings. Catequistas as well as lectors and other lay people authorized to speak during services there invariably spoke from the pulpit. The pulpit had a microphone stand attached to it and the structure effectively anchored speakers to that place. The pulpit was also tall relative to the average Q'eqchi'-Maya person, which further inhibited their movements and occluded their body from view of the congregation. From the vantage point of the church nave, one rarely saw the catequistas' hands move, and when they did it was for marked effect. Even when preaching during a Celebration of the Word in small, simple chapels where the altar might just be a wooden table covered with a cloth and where there was no pulpit or lectern to stand behind, though, catequistas tended to remain relatively still while speaking, holding their microphones close to their chests with both hands and standing in a single spot. On one occasion I even observed a catechist with no microphone deliver his sermon while clasping both hands together near his solar plexus; he released them from that position only twice briefly to shake out his wrists before returning to that posture over the course of the six or so minutes he spoke. None of this, however, is to say that their preaching was boring. Although of course some people were more skilled and charismatic than others, catequistas all aimed to be engaging through their verbal performance by modulating the cadence of their speech and their vocal tone to emphasize key ideas, animate different voices, and otherwise add dramatic structure and rhetorical power to their sermons.

When carismáticos preached, on the other hand, they were as active visibly as they were aurally, so their bodies moved as much as their voices did. Predicadores would shift their weight from one foot to another, pace around the space, and move their arms in broad sweeping gestures to further animate their speech. This was facilitated by the fact that carismáticos' meeting spaces did not feature pulpits or lecterns (although the top of a loudspeaker was often a convenient place on which they placed their Bibles), and so the only limiting factor to the predicadores' movements were the cables that connected their handheld microphones to the sound-amplification system. Even with mic cords acting as tethers, however, La Renovación's preachers moved relatively freely across a space of several meters, pacing from one side of the chapel to another, or moving nearer and farther away from the pews for dramatic effect. Although one of the preacher's hands was always holding the microphone, the tendency was to use the other free hand and arm to gesture broadly by, for example, pointing for emphasis, illustrating alternatives by gesturing to one side of their body first and then the other, pantomiming both good and bad behaviors, and otherwise augmenting the content of their speech through bodily movement. Consequently, carismáticos' preaching was a much more physically animated performance than that of their catequista counterparts.

At a very basic level, then, we might characterize the catequistas' and predicadores' performances of preaching as being respectively marked by bodily stillness and animacy. However, that contrast needs some unpacking and interpretation both because it is a broad generalization and because my contention here is that these modes of behavior were cultivated and meaningful.

The first thing to note is that despite the general ethos of stillness that characterized Mainstream Catholic sermons, catequistas' hands did in fact move. Based on a simple quantitative analysis, some catequistas actually gestured more frequently than their carismático counterparts (see Hoenes del Pinal 2011, 609). The real difference between the two congregations' religious authorities, however, lay in the performative quality of their respective gesturing and can be better understood with reference to the length and kind of movements they made as well as the space they employed when in motion, rather than the frequency with which they moved their hands and arms. Catequistas gestured plenty, but their gestures were confined to a relatively restricted space close to their bodies and/or the wooden surface of the pulpit and were not easily visible to their audience. To understand why this was meaningful, we need to briefly discuss how and why human beings gesture in the first place.

Unlike spoken language, which relies heavily on shared grammatical structures and lexicons with generally fixed meanings, most gesturing does not follow conventionalized forms or follow a regular syntactic order.[7] It is

---

7. Scholars of gesture tend to categorize communicative hand and arm movements into four typological categories ("Kendon's continuum" per McNeill [1992]) that range from the highly improvisational to the highly conventionalized. While conventional gestures ("emblems") and sign languages may seem to non-specialists as the exemplary forms of gesture, it is in fact more improvisatory ones ("gesticulations" and "pantomimes") that predominate in interaction. These kinds of gestures tend to co-occur with spoken language rather than replace it, and so

true that every culture does have certain hand shapes and movements with conventional meanings that are "quotable" (Brookes 2004), but most gesturing tends to be idiosyncratic and improvisational.[8] That makes it somewhat harder to analyze and compare cross-culturally, but one way that we can

---

their meaning depends on the total multimodal interactional performance rather than the hand shape and movement by itself. The issue of how gestures become conventionalized remains an open question, but studies of home-sign and village-sign languages offer evidence for how ad hoc hand movements and shapes can become "lexicalized" as well as how their combination can lead to the development of syntactic structures when verbal language is not a readily available channel of communication to support that process (Haviland, 2013; Padden et al. 2013). The study of Native American sign languages that developed independently of European language ideologies likewise offers tantalizing hints about how manual-visual communicative systems can shape social relations. Erich Fox Tree (2009) has argued that a largely unrecognized Mayan sign language exists that has allowed members of different ethnolinguistic communities to communicate with each other nonverbally. Similarly, Brenda Farnell (2009) has written about Plains Sign Talk as an indigenous North American lingua franca that continues to play an important cultural role despite centuries of neglect and misrecognition by outsiders. Both Fox Tree and Farnell argue that the iconicity of gestures undergirds these systems and is part of what has allowed them to endure; this is contra European assumptions about the primacy of indexicality as the foundation of verbal language. Likewise, Céline Carayon's historical study of nonverbal communication between indigenous and French people suggests that human interactions can be rich and satisfying in the absence of conventionalized codes (Carayon 2019).

8. There are certain ways in which it makes sense to adapt some of the vocabulary of linguistics to analyze gesturing. Gestures, or more precisely "gesture phrases," have three components: (1) preparation, (2) stroke, and (3) withdrawal (Kendon 2004, 112). Although it is the stroke (i.e., the moment when a recognizable hand shape is displayed, as when one's thumb points straight up and the other fingers curl tightly into the palm to indicate approval) that is typically thought of as the meaningful part of the gesture, preparation and withdrawal also play important roles in conveying meaning insofar as gestures come into being as part of dynamic flow of movement. More to the point, like linguistic or musical phrases, gesture phrases may be combined into larger "gesture units," which encompass the entire range of actions in the movement of the articulator's body between periods of rest in a neutral position (Calbris 1990, 113). We can think of gesture units as rough equivalents to verbal utterances in that both are complex acts of meaning-making composed of smaller parts. Additionally, just as the meaning of spoken phrases can be shifted in both subtle and overt ways by the loudness, pitch, or speed with which they are vocalized, so too the meaning of gestures can be adjusted through the velocity, intensity, or relative space used in their articulation. Understanding the performance of gesture in these quasi-linguistic terms allows us to scale our analysis down to specific phrases and their immediate meaning or up to larger performances encompassing several gestural phrases, gesture units, or interactional turns, and attunes us to the dynamic interactional work they do, offering a rich picture of gesturing as something that unfolds from a flow of bodily movement alongside speech (Hoenes del Pinal 2011).

begin to do so is by assessing differences in how much physical space a person makes use of when they gesture. Gesture's ability to communicate relies on visibility, and the space in which one articulates a gesture can function to amplify or minimize its communicative potential, and can also be exploited for dramatic effect (think, for example, of the difference it makes to wave at someone by raising a hand to chest level and lightly shaking it once as opposed to throwing a hand up above your head and tracing multiple large arcs by bending the elbow). This being said, people also seem to gesture when they are alone. If you have ever talked to yourself or tried to work through some idea silently, you have more than likely done some gesturing in the process, even though there is no one there to see you do so. Whether we want to attribute this to cognition being a fundamentally embodied process in which bodily motility plays a key part or to human beings being fundamentally social animals who engage in conversation-like interactions even when they are alone, the fact remains that gesturing happens even when there is no one there to see it.

Catequistas did move their hands when they spoke, but their gestures were small and confined to a tight space close to the body, making them practically invisible to people sitting in the nave of the church. Based on my analysis of my own video recordings of sermons, catequistas' most common form of gesturing were small beats performed with a finger or two; after that were hand movements (such as pointing, turning a palm upward or downward, moving a loosely grasped fist from one side to another), all performed close to the surface of the pulpit. It was relatively rare for the stroke of a gesture to be above chest level where it could be seen by most congregants, and in those rare instances that they did so they tended to be short "gesture phrases" that were deployed for deliberate dramatic effect as a supplement to spoken language. Typically, here a single hand might be raised to either perform a single emblematic gesture (i.e., an easily recognizable hand shape with a more or less fixed meaning) or a bit of deixis (e.g., pointing toward heaven or to one of the saints' images along the walls of the church). The more common kind of gesturing remained close to the body, tended to be out of sight of the congregation, and was part of longer sequences of gesticulation that flowed along with speech. Other than the fact that they occurred in a tightly restricted space and were barely if at all visible to the audience, these hand and arm movements resembled in length and complexity the kind of gesturing that Q'eqchi'-Mayas routinely did in casual conversations and other non-ritual settings. In sum, the two kinds of gesturing that catequistas did while preaching seemed to serve two distinct functions: (1) the rare kind of highly visible, short gesture phrases that had a clear interactional function of communication between the speaker and their audience and (2) the more common kind of almost wholly invisible but longer phrases of gesticulation that seems to have primarily served to help the speaker regulate the logical and poetic forms of their talk.

Predicadores habitually performed much longer and more complex units of hand and arm movement between periods of rest than the catequistas did, and they utilized a much larger physical space to do so, making their gesturing highly visible to their audience. While one of the predicador's hands was constrained by the need to hold a microphone, his free arm was often in motion. That arm might shoot straight up with a flat palm extending heavenward to proclaim God's power, or extend at shoulder height to the right, then move in a flat arc that crested at about eye level until it reached the opposite side of his body to visually illustrate the contrast between two opposing moral positions, or be raised while the middle and index fingers rubbed lightly against the thumb to perform a conventional emblem for "money" while noting that the community's leadership spent a significant amount of it to bring Renacer en Cristo to perform for their congregants that night (implying that the latter should contribute generously during the collection; see Hoenes del Pinal 2011, 616–617). These hand motions would also be accompanied by other bodily movements that added further contextual meaning to what was being said, such as a bold step forward with a straightening of the spine and puffing of the chest to indicate valor in the face of the world's sins, or a twist at the waist to augment the great distance between the morality of two alternative actions, or a widening of the eyes and raising of the eyebrows to convey awe at the Holy Spirit's miracles. In sum, all of the predicadores' gesturing was clearly intended to be seen by their audiences; and thus, clearly held interactional communicative value.

There was thus an evident contrast between predicadores' and catequistas' gesturing while preaching. However, predicadores' gesturing while preaching also diverged from the kind of gesturing that they did outside of church. Predicadores did not make these larger gestures when speaking conversationally with each other or when I interviewed them. In fact, in conversational contexts there was no discernable difference between the amount or quality of my interlocutors' gesturing regardless of their congregational affiliation. Of course, preaching was not just an everyday speech event, but rather a ritual one for which there were clear expectations about the oratorical skills and moral standing of the performer. This would suggest that there was a deliberate performative quality to the bodily movements of catequistas and predicadores tied to each congregation's expectations of what good preaching should not just sound like but also look like.[9] Both were mindful of how they were perceived while preaching and because of this, they enacted differing ideals in their performances.

As we saw in chapter 4, Mainstream Catholics also expected strict code consistency from ratified speakers in ritual contexts. Thus, it was bodily stillness alongside code consistency that marked good oratory in their religious services. Catequistas' religious authority was projected through performances that evidenced a clear and conscientious control of their bodily and verbal communicative faculties, which, again, was not necessarily expected in other contexts.[10] Minimizing visible bodily motions like carefully monitoring speech to avoid switching into Spanish evidenced an ethos of mastery and control that was self-consciously cultivated as part of their status of religious authorities who were legitimized.

The Charismatic Catholic predicadores, on the other hand, cultivated an ethos of spontaneity that I would argue was enacted through their bodily movements as well as through their code-switching between Spanish and Q'eqchi'. La Renovación's formulation of religious authority depended on the idea that predicadores were legitimated by divine inspiration, which was ultimately subject to the will of the Holy Spirit. That inspiration could come quickly or be delayed, when and how it arrived was unpredictable. To facilitate it, though, carismáticos employed a number of techniques including code alternation, call-and-response routines, prayers for guidance and

---

9. They would certainly not be the first culture to create these expectations. In the Classical world the careful cultivation of gestural styles was part and parcel of oratorical training (Corbeill 2004; Graf 1991). Analyses of more recent American political speech, likewise, show what appear to be some deliberate regimentation (Streeck 2008) and flouting of gestural style in political oratory (Hall, Goldstein, and Ingram 2016), although the rules now are tacit, and cultivation of styles is not programmatic as it was in Classical oratory.

10. The few times when a highly visible manual gesture was performed were meaningful precisely because conventions were being flouted. Similarly, when Spanish language terms were introduced, the obvious flouting of an implicit rule of code consistency only served to highlight the meaningfulness of the code-switch.

knowledge, and myriad other practices meant to give the sense that their meetings were free-flowing and unplanned. Glossolalia, which was rare but highly desirable, similarly operated on the logic that extraordinary, heavenly language could suddenly erupt in the mundane world by virtue of the Holy Spirit's bestowal of grace on an individual. Although frequent gesturing and code-switching were not exactly the same thing as either divine inspiration or glossolalia, they all shared a common sensibility—namely, an emphasis on spontaneity, by which I simply mean a sense that personal control was loosened and that an openness to the unexpected was cultivated. Doing this, in principle, displaced personal agency and paved the way for the Holy Spirit to infuse people's words and actions. The free-flowing movement of words and limbs, which was in marked contradistinction to Mainstream Catholic norms, evidenced that sense of openness to the uncontrolled irruption of divine power into the world.

The observable facts that catequistas' bodily stillness was accompanied by linguistic code consistency and that predicadores' bodily movement was accompanied by code-switching thus help us to better understand the communicative ethos that guided each group's public performance of language. Evidence that these norms carried over into the practices of the congregation at large can be found in how people prayed.

Praying: Habits and Critiques

When Mainstream Catholics criticized the Charismatics, they were wont to throw their hands up to mimic the latter's prayer posture. Coupled with a rapid and slightly nasal "amén, amén, amén," the gesture would reliably draw both sardonic laughs and knowing nods, and thus serve neatly to both lampoon the carismáticos' religiosity and critique everything that catequistas perceived was wrong with them. On the other hand, when I asked members of La Renovación about what had led them to leave their old Mainstream Catholic CEBs, carismáticos would often fold their arms across their chest and lightly hunch their shoulders recalling a characteristic prayer posture of Mainstream Catholics that for carismáticos gave the sense that those other Catholics' faith was cold and listless. In both cases these pantomimes served simultaneously as iconic representations of the other group's religious practices as well as an index of their putatively bad behavior. It is telling that both were imitations of what people (supposedly) did while praying.

While prayer is often thought of as an "oral rite" that is first and foremost a linguistic act (Mauss 2003, 56), it is difficult to ignore the fact that religious communities also tend to establish bodily norms for how to pray. Ironically, what was most observable about prayers to me as an ethnographer was their bodily dimensions, not their verbal or linguistic ones, especially when compared to the other genres of speech discussed here. During sermons I tried to focus intently on what was being said as an active listener, and during hymns (see the following discussion) I gave myself over (if reluctantly at first) to the task of singing as an active vocalist. During prayers, however, the linguistic aspects of what was going on tended to recede to the background of my attention. This was because in the context of both Mainstream and Charismatic Catholic services, prayers were spoken aloud by everyone at once. It was thus impossible to make out what any individual person was saying, and even prayer leaders' electronically amplified voices were often completely drowned out by the great wave of sound that washed over the space as each person simultaneously engaged in their own oration. My inability to focus on linguistic aspects of collective prayer, however, offered an opportunity to focus on what parishioners did with their bodies. While everyone else was busy speaking to God, I was left standing with my feet firmly planted in one place but with my head and torso swiveling and my eyes scanning the room to see what everyone else was doing.

It should, of course, not come as a surprise that I saw a lot of people embodying the characteristic prayer postures that parishioners mimicked in their cross-congregational critiques. Mainstream Catholics by and large did stand with their arms folded at chest level and heads bowed while praying, just like the carismáticos said they did when critiquing that group's "dull" faith. Charismatic Catholics often did stand with their arms raised high with their palms flattened and faces turned skyward, just like the catequistas said they did when complaining about that group's unseemly boisterousness. However, congregants did not simply adopt one of these postures and remain immobile while the rest of their energy was channeled into the spoken elements of prayer. Rather, those embodied stances (along with a few others) served as "primary positions" or moments of relative rest around which a larger kinetic flow of bodily movement was organized (Schilder cited in Weiss 1999, 18). Thus, to fully understand how San Felipe's parishioners used their bodies in church we need to pay attention not just to those moments when their religious ethos crystallized in these iconic prayer postures but also to what happened around and between them.

FIGURE 8 Carismáticos praying at a vigilia

I regularly observed carismáticos standing with their arms raised high, their palms flattened, and faces turned skyward, but this action was not the totality of a prayer. In fact, people often began prayers with their arms bent at the elbow with their hands close to their belly button or solar plexus—a stance that would not have been out of place at a Mainstream Catholic service. They might say the first line of their prayer with their heads leaning back and face turned upward or bowed down, their eyes might be open or closed. Whatever posture a person adopted at the start of prayer, it rarely took long for them to begin to shift their weight and then move their hands, arms, torsos, and faces. Hands clasped at the start of prayer would separate from each other, then wrists would turn so that their palms faced upward. Fingers that were lightly curled on a cupped hand might extend and tense convexly for a moment before relaxing again. A right hand then would close into a fist, resting for a moment in a cradle made by the left hand, before rising to the level of the person's jawline. From that fist a finger might extend, pointing skyward, that arm would perform two, three, four beats with increasing vigor and then shoot up in a full extension as the fist relaxed, blooming into an open palm with fingers spread wide. The left hand meanwhile had moved to touch the person's chest, fingers spread widely, before joining its counterpart in the air. The arms would hang in the air for a moment as the person's torso swayed lightly back and forth; their head lolling from side to side several times, the balls of the feet serving as rockers. Through all this their lips would have been moving, sometimes just barely, suggesting circumspect speech aimed at an intimate divinity who can hear one's softest whispers, other times opening and closing quite visibly in accompaniment of full-throated vocal enunciations and forceful proclamations of glory intended for the whole world to hear. The eyes, too, evidenced a dynamic interaction. A person's eyes might begin closed, then open up to look at some point in the mid-distance; they might later close partway as if in concentration or widen in excitement. Even with closed eyelids a person's brows would suggest varying and alternating degrees of intensity—sometimes creases emerged on the forehead that hinted at a deliberate and forceful attempt to shut out the outside world, other times a light fluttering of lashes on closed eyes suggested a more relaxed state in which the eyes might slowly and gradually open once again. After a time, eyes might open wide for a moment, letting the fullness of light in, and then gently close one more time as the head tilted downward and hands finally stopped reaching skyward to return to chest level. This could be the end of all that this person needed to say to God that day and all that was left was a quiet catharsis; or it could have just as likely been a pause taken to briefly reflect, take a breath, and wet the lips before launching into another period of verbal thanksgivings, petitions, and invocations accompanied by another series of gestures and shifts in postures. Sometimes laughter took over, too, and sometimes tears streamed down faces, and every so often a person was lucky enough to experience a fit of involuntary shaking that signaled that the Holy Spirit was indeed very near to them. In any case, in due time each person would conclude their prayer and begin to relax, standing silently until every voice had intoned, "Amén."

Mainstream Catholics' prayers were likewise active embodied performances, though their limbs, torsos, heads, and faces moved less dramatically than the carismáticos' did. Nevertheless, if one watched closely, one would see that they likewise moved through a range of actions. Arms that were held tightly against the torso with the palm of the hands open and facing upward at the start of a prayer would soon shift and those hands would come together in a loose clasp. They might remain that way for a few seconds, perhaps moving lightly up and down and then separate again to follow the rhythm of what their owner was saying. More subtly, a single finger from that pair of clasped hands might tap against its partner in short staccatos to help enumerate a list of specific petitions, and then straighten, pointing ever so slightly upward to signal the heavenly beings who could make those things happen. Clasped hands might come upward as the person's head simultaneously lowered, until the lips and hands were within range of touching each other, though perhaps it was only breath that connected them. These small movements could be minimized even further. Some people folded their arms and placed each hand under the opposite armpit in a sort of self-hug that gave the appearance of drawing the whole of a parishioner's body close into itself. Yet even in that constrained position, eyebrows arched, and the wrinkling and smoothing of a forehead hinted at the narrative and poetic ebbs and flows of a prayer. One could see a person's level of concentration fluctuating and intuit changes to the subjective stances they took in prayer until they finally uttered, *"Jokan taaxaq"* (amen). All of that would be accompanied by subtle, gentle rocking back and forth on the balls of their feet. To conclude a prayer, a person touched the outstretched index and middle fingers of their right hand to their forehead, sternum, left and right shoulders, and then raised their hand to their lips to seal the prayer with a light kiss. Speech steadily accompanied these bodily movements, and even if the lips sometimes seemed to barely be moving, behind them a tongue articulated words for a deity who dwelled close to the person's ch'ool (heart). Though at first these prayers seemed to be borne of stillness, there was an intense animacy to them that was mostly directed inward but that was nonetheless perceptible to the outside observer. The movement was especially palpable once individual persons ceased to pray, as they began to stand up straighter and relax their shoulders. Having ended their prayers, some of them now pinched the bridge of their noses or gently wiped away the moisture that had accrued at the corner of an eye. As more and more people ended their prayers, a distinct feeling of calm—peace, we might even call it—took over the space.

In both Mainstream and Charismatic Catholic spaces people were fully and deeply engaged in prayer as an embodied activity as much as a linguistic one. Mainstream Catholics' movements may have been smaller and less dramatic than Charismatics', but they were no less constant or meaningful. As with the conventions of what counted as good oratory when preaching,

FIGURE 9   Mainstream Catholics praying at a Celebration of the Word

these observable differences between congregations suggest that a distinct ethos underlay each congregation's communicative styles. The Mainstream Catholic style focused on constraint. Their prayers were performed close to the body in a circumscribed space, giving the impression of speech directed at an intimate deity who dwelled near people's hearts and who was best addressed with circumspect respect. The Charismatic Catholic style, on the other hand, was effusive. Each person's prayer seemed directed at a resplendent deity who dwelled expansively in the surrounding ether and who was best addressed with vigorous joy.

These characterizations of prayer as constrained and as effusive help us understand something of the metadiscursive elaboration of gesture that served as a point of critique across the congregations. We can interpret each congregation's gestural critique of the other as part of a protracted and spatially dispersed example of what Yolanda Covington-Ward has called a "performative encounter," which is to say a situation, "when the body is used strategically in everyday life to transform interpersonal relationships in meaningful ways, impacting the social and political positions of the people interacting" (Covington-Ward 2016, 9). Although Mainstream Catholics and Charismatic Catholics were rarely co-present in the intimate spaces of ritual life, they were always aware that they were each only one part of a heteroglot religious landscape in which their own voicings of piety vied for legitimacy against those of others, and thus, these gestures became a meaningful part of how the larger social reality of Catholicism as a contested category became real. Mainstream Catholics' bodily constraint when praying, which from their perspective was a way of respectfully engaging in an intimate dialogue with God, contravened Charismatic Catholics' belief that prayer should be as much a vociferous proclamation of God's glory as anything else. From La Renovación's perspective, to fail to pray in that way was to fail to adequately give oneself over to God's immanent power. From their perspective, a stilled and constrained body was one which had not (yet) really experienced the Holy Spirit and was thus not really a faithful and pious one. Conversely, Charismatic Catholics' bodily effusiveness, which from their perspective was a necessary way of communicating and communing with God, seemed like a flagrant violation of the ethos that regulated Mainstream Catholics' notions about how to speak to God with the deference and respect He above all others deserved. From the catequista's perspective, an effusively gesticulating body belonged to a person who lacked mature humility and thus could not seriously engage with the divine mystery of God. Of course, carismáticos did find times for intimate encounters with God, and there were times when Mainstream Catholics' faith was more openly on display, but when we understand the specific valences that they attached to prayer more generally we can better see why those primary postures became such ripe signs of difference.

Singing: Affect and Morality

One of the aspects that I least expected about being a participant-observer at Catholic Charismatic services was enjoying myself when singing and clapping along to hymns. When I first started going to their services I stood still during the songs, but the music was infectious. It was not hard to understand what Hermano Rigo had meant when he told me that music was what initially drew him into La Renovación and kept him going back until he finally felt the Holy Spirit (see chapter 5). Initially I used the ethnographer's toolkit of pen and notebook to inhibit my full embodied participation in the alabanzas because I was self-conscious that it would somehow violate the norms of ethnographic objectivity I strove for, not to mention that I would be adding to the noise that Qawa' Emanuel said kept him awake at night. But once I set down those tools and began to join in singing, I found that my experiences of these services changed significantly. The difference came not from the vocal act of singing itself (by then I had already sung plenty of hymns in Mainstream Catholic services) but rather from the full embodied act of the performance.

The rhythm of the music that accompanied the alabanzas lent itself to clapping along with the music on the downbeat (i.e., the first and third beats in 4/4 time), and it was clear that full participation in hymn singing as defined by the community included making one's body a percussive instrument in that way. No one in this congregation abstained from clapping, although it is true that not everyone could be said to hit the beats exactly on time. The group's leadership, moreover, often explicitly expressed the expectation that everyone should participate fully, telling the assembled congregants that they needed to stand up and be "*alegres*"—that is, joyful—during this part of the service. Herman Rigo would also sometimes call out, "*A ver las palmas!*" (lit. "let's see the palms!") during song bridges as an encouragement to clap.[11] As such, when the time came to sing alabanzas, all members of the congregation gave themselves over to the task of producing a collective sung voice and embodied percussion.

As this chapter's opening vignette illustrates, and as I discussed in the previous chapter, certain songs called for even more embodied participation. Several of the most popular songs in the carismáticos' songbook were performed with specific bits of choreography in which the congregants would mimic the content of the lyrics. So, for example, when the singer's body, which had been stiff like a metronome until then, was moved when the Holy Spirit touched it, they were meant to sway it back and forth. Another song (which I quoted in chapter 5) spoke of expressing one's love for Jesus through a list of bodily activities that included dancing, jumping, walking, and laughing, among others, each of which were iconized through bodily movements—doing a little shimmy, jumping in place, walking in a tight circle, and throwing one's head back while holding one's hand with fingers extended on either side of one's stomach to mimic a hearty belly laugh. In yet another song, the lyrics spoke of God's blessings filling a person's body parts (hands, ears, face, arm), which were then used to pass on those blessings to other hermanos by corresponding actions that could be performed through dance (for example, touching, listening, smiling, and hugging).

---

11. There is an intertextual link here to the talk one might hear from DJs at secular parties, who are also figured as animadores. In both cases the inducement to clap and make noise is positively linked with feelings of joy.

Conversely, Mainstream Catholic congregants did not clap, dance, or even necessarily sing along with the choir band. As we saw in the previous chapter, music was a valued part of Mainstream Catholic religious practices, but catequistas never enjoined their congregations to sing loudly, nor did they talk about the importance of loudly adding one's voice to the choir's. Instead, the proper way to participate was to sing along, *sotto voce*, reading along in one's hymnal if a copy was on hand; otherwise, it was perfectly acceptable to simply stand, listening. The primary parts of the body people engaged in singing were their mouths and throats.[12] Music filled the church and village chapels, and there was a certain physical intensity to the movements of the marimba players who provided accompaniment, but congregants were otherwise still while this was going on. No adult that I ever saw gave themselves over to a rhythmic swaying to the music, although children might be seen swinging their arms, bobbing their heads, or moving their torsos along with the beat. This is not to say that the music played would not have lent itself to dancing. Mainstream Catholics' music was by no means somber; much of it was quite up-tempo and based on musical genres that were locally understood as dance music (notably, the *Son Chapín*). Rather, what this relative stillness suggests is that the minimization of bodily movement by adult members of the congregation was a deliberate choice, a stance cultivated for specific cultural reasons and to which parishioners were socialized over time.

If both stillness and movement were deliberately cultivated dispositions and their performance a product of socialization, then why did bodily movement feature so prominently in Charismatic hymn singing and not in Mainstream Catholic singing? Half of our answer lies in how Charismatic Catholicism (and we could say Pentecostal/Charismatic Christianity more generally) ideologically links piety to movement. This connection is twofold. First, there is a strong emphasis on joy as an emotional stance, and clapping and dancing are a means of displaying joyfulness. This was evident when Hermano Rigo, Hermano Guillermo, and other leaders of these communities called out to their congregation to be joyful, asking them to produce a *"grito de júbilo"* (shout of joy) to show their love of God. Joy was cultivated as the ideal affective stance that a person needed to take when in church, and songs were arguably the moment in the meetings when joy could most clearly be embodied, since during

---

12. Mainstream Catholics tended to sing from the upper larynx, not the diaphragm, giving their voices a bit of flat nasal tonal quality.

sermons congregants still had to perform being an attentive audience, and during prayers the weight of one's problems could overwhelm other feelings.

Second, one of the central theological tenets of this form of Christianity is that people can feel the immanent power of the Holy Spirit firsthand as a bodily experience. These bodily feelings are at once experienced as joyful and a cause for joy. Tanya Luhrmann's discussion of the role of "metakinesis" in the lives of US Third Wave Pentecostals is apropos here. Luhrmann argues that part of the process of becoming this kind of Christian comes from individuals learning "to identify bodily and emotional states as signs of God's presence in their life" (Luhrmann 2004, 519). New converts are socialized to interpret their subjective and idiosyncratic mind–body states within the framework of that group's understanding of how God can show His presence to them, and in doing so they come to new understandings of their own bodies and the nature of the world around them (522). The embodied affects cultivated through prayer and other discrete religious techniques are thus a consequential part of how the supernatural becomes real to people. The musicking (Small 1998) that carismáticos did through their singing, clapping, and dancing was thus not just a symbolic activity, it undergirded their affective state and was thus a constitutive part of their experience of being Catholic (Hoenes del Pinal 2011).

Interpreting Mainstream Catholics' stillness is a bit trickier since it is not always easy to find meaning in an apparent absence. Yet, our earlier discussion of preaching and prayer has prepared us to understand that Mainstream Catholics' relative stillness was not in any way a "natural" disposition but rather, like their code consistency, a performative choice organized by an ethos of control and constraint. As we saw above in the context of preaching, the controlled, gesturing body articulated a kind of mastery of the self that reproduced the catequista's authority as orator. In the context of prayer, bodily constraint demonstrated a certain kind of spiritual maturity that led the person to be humble before God. When individuals stilled their bodies in response to music that they might in another context move to, they reproduced this pattern of bodily discipline. As Saba Mahmood has persuasively shown in her ethnography of Egyptian women's participation in an Islamist piety movement, adherence to prescribed forms of ritual conduct is a crucial means through which religious actors develop their ethical and moral selves and is thus inseparable from what it means to be a religious subject (Mahmood 2005). Though it was nowhere near as evident as it was among carismáticos for whom júbilo served as the key affective state that linked music, affect, and piety, the musicking of Mainstream Catholics also served as a means of cultivating an affective disposition that was constitutive of the larger way people experienced being Catholic—namely, a state of respectful humility enacted through deference.

In *The Logic of Practice*, Pierre Bourdieu notes that "the attention paid to staging in great collective ceremonies derives..., as many uses of singing and dancing show, from the less visible intention of ordering thoughts and suggesting feelings through the rigorous marshalling of practices and the orderly disposition of bodies" (1990, 69). Beyond representing distinct aesthetics for religious music, then, the ways that the body was recruited in musicking evidenced distinct constructions of what proper Catholic comportment meant to the two congregations. As I have alluded to, members of both congregations had to be socialized to perform songs in these distinct ways, but they fundamentally operated according to the same logic in which outward bodily behavior could be read as a reliable index of ethical, affective, and ultimately moral stances. By consciously working to enact their ideal forms of bodily behavior, members of these congregations both cultivated the moral dispositions they sought to inhabit and refined the norms of behavior that they believed would help them achieve those moral states. This suggests that parishioners' bodily actions in ritual contexts, and perhaps more specifically their habituated forms of bodily behavior (or "*hexis*," to use Bourdieu's terminology), were subject to reflexive adjustment and refinement, with the self-conscious monitoring and evaluation of both in-group and out-group actions serving as a critical site for developing and reinforcing congregational identities, too.

Conclusion: Gesture and Body Movement in Discourse

One of the most famous and widely read essays in the anthropological cannon—Clifford Geertz's "Thick Description: Towards an Interpretive Theory of Culture" (1973)—hinges on the question of how a minute bodily action is interpreted. When is the rapid closing and opening of an eye a blink and when is it a wink? What are students of human behavior to make of that distinction? Geertz proposes that our interest should be not in the intention behind the blink/wink but rather in the consequences that follow from it. It matters less why the first boy's eyelids closed than whether the second boy determines whether he has been winked at or not. That determination of meaning would be based as much on the larger context of the interaction as anything else and will condition his response and help set the terms for any actions that follow.

We might well subject the actions of San Felipe's Catholics' preaching, dancing, and praying bodies to a similar kind of scrutiny. What is, after all, the meaning of a shaking body? Is it an indexical sign that the Holy Spirit is present and acting upon the person as an outside force? Or is it, rather, an iconic representation of that idea? If it is the latter, is its performance deliberate, staged, or otherwise subject to the person's control? And if it is so, is it performed in the idiom of praise or of parody? Perhaps more vexingly, what is the meaning of a still body? Does its immobility come from a sense of solemnity or insouciance? Does an absence of motion bespeak an absence of spirit? Or is it, on the contrary, a purposeful sublimation of the mundane human needs and habits to some greater spiritual end? Whatever stance a person in San Felipe might take with regard to these questions and their potential answers will speak to how they position themselves in relation to a much larger discursive field of what it means to be Catholic. It will, of course, also have deep implications for how that person him- or herself experiences that meaning individually, with their co-congregants, and in relation to the large institutional bodies with which they identify or are interpellated into.

Beyond being something to be interpreted à la Geertz, gestures and other learned techniques of the body are the catalyst for creating much of the reality of social life (Covington-Ward 2016). As Carrie Noland has argued, "culture is both embodied and challenged through . . . kinetic acts" (2009, 2). If we understand that cultures are not static, but rather assemblages that are always in flux due to the way distinct voices jockey for influence against each other, then we can understand that gesturing bodies can play deeply consequential roles in both prompting change and resisting it. It should not be surprising then that many of Sa'xreb'e's carismáticos seemed to have so much trouble dancing along to the song about the stiff body that came to life through divine intervention, even though they also adamantly believed that such things could and should happen for those who were truly faithful. Their bodies were simultaneously primed for those experiences and resistant to them, and their halting attempts to sway from here to there were a collective attempt to dance their truth into being.

CHAPTER 7

Bearing the Collective Cross
The Body in Public Piety

During *Semana Santa* (Holy Week) Guatemala seems to especially live up to its reputation as an exceptionally colorful country. The main attraction is the cycle of processions of santos depicting various scenes from the Passion story that wend their way through the streets of every city and town. For the occasion, most notably on Good Friday and Easter Sunday, streets are carpeted with *alformbras* made by arranging dyed sawdust and flower petals into elaborate patterns. During the processions, men, traditionally dressed in purple robes and white headcloths modeled after an imagined version of first-century clothing from the Levant, bear the weight of the massive *andas* (biers or litters) that carry the santos on their shoulders, while others fashioned as Roman centurions, complete with bronze-colored breastplates and tall spears, escort them to the sounds of brass bands playing funereal dirges. The low rumbling of sousaphones, baritone horns, trombones, and bass drums set the lumbering pace of the processions, while the accompanying trumpets, French horns, and clarinets play sweeping melodies that are at once mournful and majestic. As the music crescendos, piccolos trill agonizingly, and snare drums roll dramatically; glockenspiels ring out anxious exclamations and cymbals clash violently. Then the music seems to crash down like a wave in a clatter. It subsides into a sorrowful lull that lasts just a moment, before building back up again. As with any Catholic ritual in Guatemala (and most secular ones, for that matter), fireworks accompany the processions, announcing their movements with percussive blasts that leave small clouds of gray-black smoke high in the sky. Traces of the unmistakable scent of burned gunpowder mix with the pungent odor of copal pom incense emanating from the silver censer swung at the front of the procession.

The processions are spectacular; their sights, sounds, and smells can be enrapturing. They are also a burden on the city as their movement requires that major thoroughfares be closed to traffic. The performance of the full cycle of Semana Santa processions and the demands they place on the city's population by closing streets and suspending much of regular commerce and business are a way that the Catholic Church as an institutional body establishes its ascendancy over public space. While it is clear that the Catholic Church's authority has never been absolute or unchallenged in Latin America, from the Church's perspective the legitimacy of this use of public space is unproblematic. Indeed, the spatial arrangement of Latin American cities founded during the colonial period, like Cobán, with an open plaza at their center surrounded by buildings housing secular and religious authorities, including city hall, the palace of arms, the courthouse, and the church, reinforces the Roman Catholic Church's position as a central public institution.[1] Holy Week processions are oriented toward the church on the central plaza (either starting there, ending there, or both), and the proximity of buildings

---

1. As urban centers have grown, this spatial arrangement has remained important with the *centro* (center of town), retaining at least symbolic importance though, of course, the dynamics of church-state relations are less clear-cut today than they would have been at their foundation. The growth of evangélico Christianity has reshaped many aspects of Latin American society, but one thing that has not changed are the physical spaces that Catholic churches occupy at the center of cities. Evangélico churches have at best been able to set up at the peripheries of city centers. In Cobán the closest that a Protestant church got to occupying a space on the central plaza in 2005 was when the Universal Church of the Kingdom of God (*Igreja Universal do Reino de Deus*)—a major Brazilian Pentecostal organization with congregations world-wide—rented out the all-but-abandoned theater just off the parque central. The Pentecostal congregation had the theater's marquee refitted with a sign bearing their logo of a white dove superimposed on a bright red heart and the slogan "*Pare de sufrir*" (stop suffering). Signs promised healing and redemption at the foot of a miraculous cross daily, and though large crowds attended, they never filled the plaza as Catholics did during Semana Santa or Santo Domingo's day. Their occupation of the space was temporary, as well; the IURG's time spent there paled in comparison to the centuries that a Catholic church had stood on the ridge at the center of Cobán. The next closest evangélico churches were several blocks away and no longer in direct sight of the plaza, although sometimes one could hear them. Evangélico groups occasionally held events for a few hours in the parque and street preachers would also occasionally offer testimony from there, but the old cathedral building still dominated the space.

FIGURE 10 Semana Santa procession

representing state authorities also means that these tend to be co-opted in the performance of a ritual that links the physical space of contemporary Guatemala to the sacred space of first-century Jerusalem.

On Easter Wednesday in 2005 I watched the procession sponsored by San Felipe's Hermandad amble to a stop in front of a prominent family's restaurant on one of the city's main throughfares. Drawn by the throngs of spectators and the sounds of music and fireworks that drifted down the street, a handful of children crowded around me on the sidewalk and jockeyed to get a better look at the spectacle. In the bright light of the vernal sun the visual details of the procession were striking. The bier featured an image of Jesus shouldering the cross on his way to the crucifixion. As the procession drew nearer, the details became clearer. A crown of thorns held down a wig of chestnut hair that blew in the breeze. His royal purple satin robe, which was crumpled at the waist by a golden cord that hung past his knees to keep it secured, shone in the sunlight. The expression on his frozen face spoke of pain and resignation as he carried the apparently excruciating burden of his cross, which had been carefully molded out of plaster with make-believe knots and darkened lines to give the appearance of a natural wood grain. Crimson rivulets seemed to trickle down his forehead and across his brow. Though the santo's deep, dark eyes looked downward, his expression suggested he could not see the colorful arrangements of flowers—some of which were artificial and had accompanied him on previous years' marches to Calvary, and some of which had been cut just the day before—at his feet, nor the fabric-wrapped signs bearing gold letters proclaiming the miracle of his sacrifice and resurrection, which were propped on each side of the mahogany bier upon which he stood.

As the santo and his companions neared our position, the music got louder, and we could smell the rich incense smoke that emanated in curling whisps from the silver censer the man at the very head of the procession swung back and forth. The experience was enthralling, and the children clambered onto the back of a parked pickup truck to get a better look. And then, quite suddenly, a man with slicked-back hair and wearing a crisp white dress shirt and navy slacks burst from the building behind us, scolding the kids and ushering them inside. "¡Métanse pa' dentro! ¡Apúrense! ¡Eso no es para ustedes!" (Get inside! Hurry up! That isn't for you!) The building behind us was an evangélico church. With the children ushered safely inside, the man shut the metal door behind him. Inside, a praise band struck the first few notes of an up-tempo *alabanza* that briefly dueled with the sounds of the procession but was ultimately drowned out by the heavy dirge that played from the speakers mounted on the back of Qawa' Walter's Toyota pickup. The processions ambled to a stop so that the santo and his bearers could rest and members of the family who had helped sponsor the procession could spend a moment of prayer with the santo. After a few minutes, the procession moved on, continuing its peregrination through the streets of Cobán, which, like those of so many others throughout the region, was experiencing its annual mimetic transformation into the *Via Crucis* of Jesus's final earthly days.

This event, which lasted but a moment, allows us to take up a slightly different perspective on Catholic heteroglossia in Cobán by bringing into view the larger social world that San Felipe's parishioners inhabit, even if some of it only does so fleetingly at the periphery of our vision. The evangélico man's sudden actions, the clear annoyance he expressed that his congregation's children (perhaps one of them was his son) were being drawn in by the Catholic spectacle, the slamming of a door, and the musical counter-discourse his band played from inside their sanctuary all spoke to the contested nature of religion in Guatemala's public sphere. The rich, enveloping sensorium that the processions produce for participants and bystanders, not to mention the great investment of both material and human resources needed for their performance, are clear indices of the value that religious actors place on intervening in public life through regimentations of the senses. The procession, after all, depended not just on an organizing leadership, but also crucially on the devotional labor (Peña 2011, 10) of the myriad individuals who performed it and who were willingly swept up in its grand spectacle of public religiosity—exactly what the Pentecostal man feared might happen to his congregation's children should they stay on the street. So, this is also an opportunity to think through what it is like to participate in these kinds of rituals and how doing so creates particular kinds of subjective investments in one's sense of religious being and belonging. To bring together these multiple themes, I will use the idea of body in both its literal and metaphorical senses.

Guatemala's Semana Santa rituals have been well studied by anthropologists for decades (see, for example, Moore 1973; Watanabe 1992; Cook 2010). Most analyses have emphasized how the symbolism of the rituals dramatize social relationships and offer a critique of interethnic inequalities (Nash 1968). A prime example of this is Allen Christenson's masterful and detailed analysis of the Holy Week cycle in Santiago Atitlán, Sololá (Christenson 2016) in which he demonstrates that the Semana Santa ritual cycle there, while ostensibly commemorating Jesus's death and resurrection, also recapitulates the pre-invasion Maya *wayeb'* ceremonies of world renewal. Christenson explains how elements of Holy Week in Santiago—which include a mock raid on plantations in Guatemala's coastal region to procure fresh fruit, all-night barefoot races in which drunken young men carry San Juan (St. John) to meet Mary, symbolizing sexual intercourse between the two, the decoration of Jesus's cross with green fronds, and the significant role that the folk saint *cum* Mayan deity known as both Maximón and Rilaj Mam plays as a counterpart to Jesus in the ritual cycle's narrative—tell a Mayan story about cyclical deaths and rebirths consistent with a Mesoamerican cosmology and decidedly different from the more orthodox Catholic story about the singular event of Jesus's crucifixion and resurrection.

My discussion of Semana Santa in this chapter departs from the existing literature on the processions in two ways. First, as I have been doing through this book, I want to foreground the Catholic element of the processions. Although Cobán and Santiago Atitlán are both places with deep Maya roots, they are culturally and historically distinct from each other and it should not surprise us to find that people perform Semana Santa quite differently in each town. Moreover, my interlocutors were especially concerned with their identities as Catholics, and so I highlight that aspect of their practices.

Second, in emphasizing the symbolic dimensions of the rituals, the existing literature has tended to not pay as much attention to how these spectacular rituals are organized (though to be fair, Christenson does go into significant detail about the rituals that must be performed in preparation of Semana Santa) or to the phenomenological dimensions of their performance, both of which I highlight here. The related concepts of intersubjectivity and intercorporeality (Csordas 2008) provide us greater insight into what makes these rituals so meaningful for participants, and a theoretical grounding for discussing the central role of bodies—that is, both social bodies and personal physical bodies—in the production and meaning of these rituals. As Gail Weiss has noted, "the experience of being embodied is never a private affair but is always already mediated by our continual interactions with other human and nonhuman bodies" (1999, 5). As we saw in the previous chapter, embodied behaviors are meaningful and subject to ideological regimentation in religious practice, and here we will further investigate why this was so consequential for people's collective experiences of religion in San Felipe. Examining the intercorporeal dimensions of the Semana Santa processions allows us to more clearly understand how religious meaning is constituted through collective action.

Bodies that Organize

Performing the complete cycle of processions representing the story of Jesus's entry into Jerusalem, his arrest, crucifixion, death, and resurrection required the collaboration of a number of institutional bodies in Cobán, including parishes, lay groups, and other parachurch organizations. Each of these organizations had to marshal its members' resources and coordinate their actions to mount the part of the ritual cycle that they were responsible for. At the most basic level, the responsible parties were the Hermandades that sponsored the individual processions. Because each of these groups was attached to a different parish, the duties for performing the ritual cycle were distributed across the city's Catholic landscape. Each Hermandad was charged with making the necessary arrangements for its own procession, including procuring, storing, and maintaining the material objects needed for the ritual, which included the santos, their clothing and wigs, the *anda* and its decorations, the uniform robes that the sodality's ranking members wore, and a number of indispensable consumables such as incense and fireworks. They also needed to secure musicians[2] to accompany the procession and enlist people to perform specific duties like censing the air and managing the fireworks. All of this took money and labor, and so the sodality also had to fundraise and manage volunteers' efforts to ensure that everything was ready well before Holy Week began. There were, in fact, also a number of smaller processions that had to be arranged and performed during Lent (see the following discussion). All of this was done without any central oversight or organization (though of course the Catholic Church's liturgical calendar established the dates for Lent and Easter and ensured that the themes appropriate to the season were prominently featured in Masses and Celebrations of the Word); rather, due in part to the fact that these rituals had been performed annually for generations and to the tacit understandings that existed among the sodalities, Semana Santa came together in an altogether ad hoc, but also largely predictable, manner.

Though talk about the upcoming season began just days after the feast of El Señor de Esquipulas was celebrated (and which itself followed closely on the heels of New Year's Day), the process of mounting these rituals began in earnest about a week before Lent, when several men from the Hermandad's directorate gathered to build a temporary shelter out of wood planks and corrugated tin that served as their workshop. There the santos' andas could be cleaned, assembled, polished, decorated, and otherwise prepared for the

---

2. In an indigenous parish like San Felipe there are two separate musical needs to be met. The first is the one they share with Ladino processions—the funereal dirges I described above. Ideally this music should be performed live by a brass band. However, if it isn't possible to secure the cooperation of live musicians, recorded music can be used, in which case arrangements have to be made to get a gas-powered generator, speakers, and portable music source that can follow the procession either mounted on a truck or in some cases pushed along on carts. In the mid-2000s, CD-Rs of the music could be easily purchased for fifteen or twenty quetzales from street vendors, and professionally distributed recordings on cassette or CD could be bought at stores for five times that price. The second kind of music, which Ladino processions do not feature, comes from drum and *flauta* or *chirimía*, which is coded as indigenous sacred music. The *flauta* is a simple woodwind instrument similar to a recorder, which is played by blowing into a mouthpiece carved into a straight wooden cylinder and whose sound changes by placing one's fingers over a combination of six open holes. A *chirimía* is also a woodwind instrument, but with a double reed mouthpiece like an oboe's, attached via a metal tube to the wooden frame with open finger holes. Both instruments produce a sort of high-pitched whine, although the chirimía's tone also has a distinct buzz to it. The drum and woodwind combo leads the procession, while the brass band (or its digital analogue) trails behind the santos.

upcoming processions.³ Activity in the workshop was slow at first, since there wasn't much to do after the biers were pulled out of storage and put together. Nonetheless, some of the qawachineb' would come in once or twice a week to perform minor maintenance tasks on the andas, and the space also hosted sessions to plan for the Easter processions and strategize how they might find the money to fund them.

There were four sources of funds. The first of these were the contributions that each of the parish's comunidades were expected to make. Most of these contributions were slow to come in and difficult to collect, so much so that the Hermandad made repeated pleas for the money over the radio. A second source of funds was donations that individual households in the vicinity of San Felipe made. These were usually reciprocated by a visit of the santo's Lenten procession to the house; although sometimes the donations were given, and no stop was made, as was the case with one household that donated in memory of a deceased family member who had been a devout Catholic but who themselves were now evangélicos and thus did not participate in the processions. Getting these donations involved drafting letters of request—appropriately sealed with the group's official stamp—and hand-delivering them, as well as making (often multiple) return visits to collect the money. A third source of funds was the collection box that the Hermandad placed in the nave of the church beginning on Ash Wednesday, in which attendees to church services and other visitors could place coins or small bills. The fourth source of funds bears a bit more discussion, as they were themselves small-scale ritual events.

On the morning of *Lunes Santo* (the Monday before Easter) a small group from the Hermandad met at the church to take a small bier with a half-size santo (again an image of Jesus bearing his cross) to visit homes around the town. The anda was small enough that it could be carried by just four men, and for the next ten hours the Hermandad took the santo through Cobán's streets. Qawa' Walter followed in his truck on which they had mounted a gas-powered generator and speaker system that played a CD of the season's signature dirges. Upon hearing the distinctive music, people came out of their homes or businesses and flagged down this miniature procession to stop. The bier was then placed on the sidewalk or road, and while its bearers

---

3. The rest of the year the santos remain in their respective niches inside the church, while the disassembled andas are kept in a storage space in the parish center.

rested, the home's resident knelt in prayer before the santo for a few minutes. The devotees tenderly touched the hem of the santo's garments and crossed themselves to secure His blessings as they finished praying. For this privilege they made a small donation to the Hermandad, placing a few quetzales in the slot of a little wooden box that was attached to the bier. These *visitas de hogares* (visits to homes) rituals were deeply meaningful for people as intimate encounters with the sacred images, but they were also a crucial source of money that helped pay for the materials and supplies needed for the Hermandad's Holy Wednesday's procession. The year I joined them, the visitas de hogares lasted well into the night, at which point the santo was loaded into the back of the pickup and driven back up to the church, where the donations were counted and logged in the Hermandad's ledger. This is all to say that behind the successful performance of the spectacular Semana Santa rituals lay an often-overlooked flurry of activities driven by the practical material necessities of mounting them.

Just after the temporary workshop was built and funds started to trickle in during the second week of Lent, the Hermandad helped build a sort of portico or gateway around the entrance to the church. It was fashioned out of bamboo canes lashed together with rope and festooned with palm fronds, flowers, and colored streamers that were tied into bows or cut into geometric patterns. The portico was a striking visual reminder that we were entering a holiday season.[4]

Every Friday afternoon during Lent, a procession bearing Jesús Nazareno and the Virgen de Dolores passed under the portico and made the precarious descent down the steps to the streets below.[5] The Hermandad oversaw these processions, but they also called on specific comunidades to help co-sponsor each week's event, ensuring that there would be enough people to help carry the santos. Over the course of the season these processions would travel different routes through the city's streets. Private homes along the route

---

4. These porticos are built for other holidays and special occasions, too, although they may be smaller and less elaborate. They are put up at village chapels as well. Besides Lent, I saw them during All Saints and All Souls days in early November, for El Señor de Esquipulas in January, and for the celebration of Qawa' Emanuel's and Qana' Esmeralda's fiftieth wedding anniversary.

5. Similar processions would simultaneously exit other churches in the city and make their own peregrinations. Some evenings while we walked, we could briefly hear the sounds or even see the lights of another Jesus and Mary's company as they traveled their own routes through Cobán's streets.

were designated as stops where a station of the cross would be recited and prayers offered. The houses' residents set up altars to receive the procession. Sometimes these altars were just small tables placed on the sidewalk and decorated with a pretty piece of cloth, candles, some flowers, and their own statuette or picture of a santo; other times the heavy metal doors that face streets in Cobán would be thrown open to reveal elaborate scenes with flowers and potted plants, candles and colored lights, decorative banners and garlands surrounding a whole coterie of santos dressed in taffeta and velvet. At some of these stops, after the station of the cross was read and prayers were said, women from the household would offer the visitors a light snack—pan dulce or a packet of store-bought cookies accompanied by small Styrofoam cups of weak coffee, a tostada slathered with refried black beans and topped with a crumbling of *queso seco*, and sweetened artificial *frescos* served out of plastic bags, or a cup of sweet, warm *atol de elote*. Like the visitas de hogares, these stops along the Via Crucis were opportunities for Catholics to be physically nearer the images of Jesus and Mary, chances to bridge between home and church, and to cultivate relationships of intimacy with the santos as a means of securing their blessings.

Of course, all of this was just a prelude, and, as Semana Santa drew nearer, the pace of devotional labor picked up. The makeshift workshop became a hub of activity as plans for decorating the Easter andas were finalized and materials acquired. Men, women, and *jóvenes* would come for hours to put together the main bier and help craft decorations. Inevitably someone had to be sent on an errand to buy some supply that had run out or to see if someone with a special skill could come lend a hand. In those last few days before Semana Santa, various families sent food up to the church to feed the workers, offering them tortillas accompanied by *pacaya envuelta*—palm fronds whose tendrils look like a cross between baby corn and squid tentacles, and which is fried in egg batter and topped with a runny tomato salsa. The first time I tried the pacaya, I commented on its bitter flavor, and Qawa' Hugo told me that the flavor was meant to remind you of the bitterness of Jesus's sacrifice, making this seasonal delicacy another sensory marker of the holiday season. The parish cook, Qana' Julia, made sure that coffee and sugary frescos were in full supply, too. The presence of food and friends meant that the space was used not just for devotional labor but also for amicable socialization and fellowship. People traded stories, gossip, and jokes while they worked, and some of the jóvenes started to show up more often once they realized that this was an opportune time to flirt with young ladies from other comunidades.

The jovial nature of the work belied a certain sense of anxiety, though, since having enough people to carry the santos on the actual day of the processions was neither *fait acompli* nor taken for granted. Though one might expect that the Hermandad could generally count on people being present to perform this important public ritual, there was a feeling that the Catholic community was not as strong as it had once been. As my interlocutors liked to point out, neither the hermanos separados nor the carismáticos understood the value of the processions and thus didn't participate in them anymore. Conversion to these "sects" meant fewer people came to the processions than they had in their parents' and grandparents' times. So, significant efforts were made to ensure wide participation among católicos (which in this case excluded La Renovación). The Hermandad expected that each *chinam* (ranking member of the group) as well as other lay leaders would activate interpersonal networks to ensure that enough people were present for the entirety of the procession. They were especially interested in having them recruit católicos who did not regularly attend Masses or actively participate in their local CEBs, but who were also not otherwise affiliated with another religious group. The sodality also leased airtime on the diocesan radio station to publicize their events and called upon the faithful, especially those living in remote villages and hamlets, to come take part in the rituals (Hoenes del Pinal 2019). Finally, the leadership of each Hermandad sent formal invitations to participate in their procession to the leadership of every other sodality in town and they all likewise expected to receive reciprocal invitations from each other. My own invitation to participate in the Good Friday procession, which I discuss in more detail later, was an extension of the one received by San Felipe's Hermandad.

There was, however, a double edge to this kind of inter-group recruitment, since one group's ability and efforts to draw participants to its own procession could negatively impact another's. In the lead up to Semana Santa, Qana' Esperanza confided that she was worried that a group of jóvenes from her CEB, including her eldest son, were not going to help carry the santo on Holy Wednesday because, she said gesturing toward La Catedral in the center of town,

They only want to carry over there. They're not interested in helping us here [in San Felipe], because we are just humble people. They think that carrying over there [at La Catedral] is, I don't know, more important because they're going to be with the rich people, with people who have money, so it must be better. But it isn't like that, because there are some people there who don't carry because they have faith, they carry just to be seen. But what can I tell them? Maybe they need to go see and then they will understand that our faith here is [something] very special.

While the boys' participation in more than one parish's activities might not have in and of itself been a bad thing—and indeed could have been interpreted as a desire to be more fully engaged in Catholic life under slightly different circumstances—Qana' Esperanza lamented that their impetus to do so seemed to stem from the ethnic and class differences between two parishes. In her assessment, the boys were drawn to the more prestigious parish in the center of town because it was not coded as an "indigenous," and hence, poor, humble parish like her own. Though the boys ultimately did carry in San Felipe's processions, and a few (including her sons) were even coaxed to come work on decorating the *anda* the day before the procession, this episode illustrated the ways in which the distribution of the ritual cycle across parishes was marked by conflict as well as cooperation.

The conflicts stemmed precisely from the fact that these independent social bodies were interdependent insofar as they relied on each other to perform the complete ritual cycle of Holy Week. Each Hermandad acted individually to produce its own procession, but they also reacted to each other by virtue of being involved in the larger task of producing the whole ritual cycle. That they ultimately drew on the same finite pool of human and material resources to successfully reach their own goals only complicated the process and made the fact that year in and year out they jointly accomplish the task all the more remarkable. Echoes of these tensions were present in the experience of performing the rituals themselves.

Bodies that Carry

The chinames of San Felipe's Hermandad invited me to accompany them to be part of the Good Friday procession sponsored by the Hermandad de La Catedral. I agreed to go that day less because I saw it as an opportunity to further my research, and more because I was curious about what it was like to carry the santos. I had been busy observing and documenting the ritual activities carried out by San Felipe's Hermandad and the parish through Lent and into Semana Santa, dutifully taking notes, pictures, and video of the proceeding, but San Felipe wasn't sponsoring any events that day, and so my schedule was clear. I figured I'd earned a day off from formal research, anyway.[6] So, on *Viernes Santo* (Good Friday) I left the satchel that carried my notebooks and camera at home and headed a few short blocks from my family's home to the parque central to meet up with the qawachineb' as they joined the procession leaving La Catedral.

As it turned out, that was not a day off from research at all. As a number of scholars influenced by phenomenological approaches to embodiment have noted, the ethnographer's own bodily experiences—the kinesthetic and sensual processes that one participates in during fieldwork—are vital sources of knowledge about other cultures and forms of lived religion (see, for example, Jackson 1989; Stoller 1997; Okely 2007; and Nabhan-Warren 2011). In this section I draw on some of the insights I gained through my own embodied experience of carrying a santo.

When one carries a santo's anda, one assumes the role of a penitent.[7] The weight of the anda is borne over one shoulder, recalling the image of Jesus carrying the cross (which on some days during Holy Week is precisely the image that stands atop the anda). In Cobán there were no formal requirements for who could help carry the santo in a procession, though of course the presumption was that one was at least a nominal Catholic who had been baptized. Typically, the first turn at carrying was reserved for active members of the sponsoring sodality, and on Good Friday and Easter Sunday some spots were also reserved for other important townspeople such as the mayor and members of the municipal government and courts (if they were católicos, of course). People who lined up to carry were expected to be if

---

6. I had only ever been in Guatemala once for Holy Week since emigrating as a child in 1984, but the processions always held a certain mystique as distinctive and salient symbols of the country's cultural traditions that I could never adequately access during my summer trips.

7. *Penitente* in Spanish, although the term used colloquially in Guatemala is *cucurucho*—literally "cone," in reference to the pointed hats that were traditionally worn in Iberian manifestations of the ritual but that are no longer used in Guatemala. The term has stuck, although today it is the color purple that is most closely associated with penitent's garb. To wear purple in Guatemala is to invite teasing that one is dressed as a cucurucho.

not entirely in a pure moral state, at the very least not actively flouting the community's mores. One Cobanero I knew joked that he no longer carried in processions because if he did, he would surely get seriously ill, and then his wife would definitely find out about his girlfriend! Whether he sincerely thought that was the case (or if he really was having an affair), I don't know, but the joke resonated with the idea that this kind of devotional labor is serious business and should only be undertaken by pious people, or at the very least those who are seeking to absolve themselves of sin and intending to behave morally after doing so. Nonetheless, parishioners also said that anyone who wanted to participate in the ritual out of good intentions could do so (which is why the qawachineb' thought it would be alright if I joined their party on Good Friday despite not being a self-identified, much less baptized, Catholic), and in principle, everyone was welcome to queue up in the two rows that trailed the procession to take their turn under the anda.[8]

This point was made quite clear during the visita de hogares when a visibly intoxicated man attached himself to San Felipe's procession and seemed to go through an emotionally charged spiritual transformation with the group. The man, whose name I never learned, was not a member of the Hermandad, nor, to the best of my knowledge or that of the qawachineb', even a member of the parish. One of my consultants said he knew him only by sight as a ne'er-do-well who hung out by the bus terminal market looking to make just enough money—either through informal labor or petty thievery—to buy alcohol, marijuana, or crack cocaine from the dingy cantinas in the area. However, when this man approached us and asked if he could help them carry the santo, he was allowed to put his shoulder under the santo despite being quite visibly inebriated. At first, he simply helped carry the santo from one stop to the next and eagerly received the snacks and soft drinks that people sometimes brought out for the group. Within the hour, however, his demeanor had

---

8. This is not necessarily the case everywhere in Guatemala. In the larger, much more elaborate and well-known processions in Guatemala City and Antigua Guatemala, parishioners must pay a fee in order to participate. Payment entitles them to a spot in the procession at a specific time and for a specific turn. Penitents receive numbered badges to pin to their clothes that indicate that they are registered participants, and which grant access to the street. At some of these processions dress codes are, if not overtly enforced, at least tacitly monitored so that the bearers of the santo are wearing at least suits if not the traditional satin *cucurucho* robes. None of this was the case with San Felipe's procession, although the men who joined La Catedral's Good Friday procession's *turno de honor* (shift of honor, which was reserved for local dignitaries) did dress for the occasion.

changed. At one of our stops, he dropped to his knees in front of the santo and, with tears streaming down his face, began to pray for forgiveness. For the next couple of hours, he helped bear the santo through the streets and at each stop we made he would again fall to his knees and pray intensely, audibly asking Jesus to forgive him for his past sins and swearing that he would change his ways. At one point, another man, likewise dressed in stained pants and dirty T-shirt and no doubt also in a less-than-sober state approached him and tried to coax him into leaving the procession so that they could go to a cantina. This other man went so far as to try to pull our new penitent up to his feet by the back of his pants and drag him away, but he was rebuked by his former drinking buddy. "*Dejamé vos, ahora voy con Jesusito*" (Leave me, now I'm going with [little] Jesus), he slurred with his chest slightly puffed out in defiance. I don't know what ultimately happened to that man—he eventually peeled away from the procession, and I never saw him again—but it was clear from his actions and demeanor that his participation in the ritual was an intensely affective experience. Members of the Hermandad explained to me later that such occurrences were, if not exactly frequent, not uncommon either. More important, although some of them dismissed the man as a drunk taking advantage of the free refreshments and thought that he may well have ended up at one of his usual haunts drinking and getting high after he left us; several others thought that we might have witnessed the start of a genuine conversion that would set him on the path of moral reform. Qawa' Luis explained that carrying a santo had that effect on people because by physically suffering just a little bit like Jesus had when carrying the cross, one could better understand His sacrifice and hence God's love for humanity. With that taste of suffering and grace one could sincerely repent for one's past sins and be mindful not to commit more.

San Felipe's Catholics clearly believed that the physical act of carrying the santo through the city streets had a soteriological effect, and I would argue that this belief stemmed not just from the mimetic resemblance that the ritual created between the penitent and Christ but also from the ways the ritual performance itself regimented bodily agency, forcing an embodied experience of humility and submission to a force larger than oneself. Taking part in these processions constituted a technique of moral self-formation because carrying the santo was predicated on giving up personal agency and falling into a supra-individual order of action. In doing so the penitent entered into a distinct set of intersubjective and intercorporeal relations that marked the experience as extraordinary. To better explain this, I need to discuss some of the physical and material aspects of carrying a santo in more detail.

Processions were organized by *turnos*—"turns" of people who took on the weight of the biers on their shoulders for an indefinite (but finite) amount of time along the route. With the exception of the *turnos de honor*, which were reserved for church and civic leaders and occurred at the very beginning and end of the procession, the turns were managed ad hoc. In Cobán it was up to the ranking members of the procession's sponsoring sodality to direct the procession and determine when and where a change of turnos would happen (although there were places along the route where it made more sense to do so than others, such as at the homes of prominent families who donated to the Hermandad and were known to provide refreshments for the penitents, as well as on flat streets before the route hit steep inclines that practically demanded a fresh set of legs to climb even when one wasn't shouldering a sacred image).

During a change of turno, the bier was not simply set down by one group and picked back up by another; instead, it remained aloft while one group of bodies swapped in for the other. It was a delicate and somewhat chaotic process. Once a change was initiated, the procession's guides had to act quickly and decisively to identify the next set of penitents from the trailing crowd and direct the appropriate number of them next to the anda. Participants were arranged by height on the fly, with the shortest at the front and the tallest at the rear, so that ideally the weight of the bier would be distributed relatively evenly on their shoulders. Once the penitents were in place next to the anda, they and the guides had to collectively manage the transition of bodies underneath the heavy wooden structure with those who were carrying stepping out from under it one by one and fresh individuals replacing them. Those about to start their turn had to negotiate taking their place and holding the weight of the bier just as the previous turno's members left, which was no mean task since there was not much space for extra bodies in the lineup. Those at the very front of the bier switched out first, then the ones behind them, and so on in sequence until the last person took their respective place at the very back of the structure. As people sidled in sideways carefully but quickly past the body of their predecessors, the bier swayed and tilted in response to the variable support it received from underneath. The men charged with "steering" the anda strained to keep it steady by holding on to two rods that extended from the front and back of the wooden structure, but their efforts, heroic though they might have been, did little to steady the santo, who seemed to be impatiently dancing from side to side and eager to continue His march. It was in these chaotic moments that people entered the ritual as full-fledged penitents.

It was a seasonally warm and sunny day and we had already been walking for over two hours before the time came to fulfill the Hermandad de La Catedral's invitation to carry the Viernes Santo anda, which featured Jesus lying in state after His death. We walked trailing behind the santo in the procession's tail, and at each change of turno our group got closer and closer to the santo's bier until it was finally our time. As the tallest person by several inches in my group, I was shuttled to the very last place on the left-hand side of the bier and watched as one by one my companions took their spots. Then it was my turn to slide my right shoulder into place under the bier. The physical experience of carrying the santo came as a shock. I immediately felt the tonnage of the anda pressing down on my shoulder. The wood was hard; there was no padding, and its edges, though slightly rounded, felt sharp.

When you join the procession, it takes a moment to adjust to both the sensation of carrying the massive structure on your shoulder and the confined space you now occupy alongside your fellow penitents. Your knees cannot help but bend a little under the weight. You can try to use your hands and arms to support the bier as it presses against your shoulder, but it does little to diminish the pressure and the best you can hope for is to steady yourself in place.

When you first start your turno, the anda tilts and sways forcefully, but once everyone is in place it assumes a rhythmic side-to-side motion that forces you into step with it. The bier exerts a tremendous amount of force on your upper body and to resist it is to find yourself impotent at best and pushed off balance and falling at worst. The anda demands that you move with it, and when the call goes out to walk, each step is little more than a shuffle forward. Every so often your head knocks against the bier until you acclimate yourself to its rhythmic movements. Though you are carrying the santo, you have no agency to determine where it is headed, how long you will be carrying it, or even the length of your gait. There is no way of altering the procession's direction or pace. As the procession moves, so do you; you become part of a moving assemblage of flesh and wood that at once depends on your efforts to stay animated, but also subsumes them into a supra-individual collectivity. Your efforts are at once necessary and inconsequential.

The musical movements of the dirge ebb and flow, but they never quite match the lumbering motion of the bier or the rhythm of your shuffling steps. As you walk you are meant to contemplate Jesus's sacrifice, and the physical discomfort you feel makes it hard to do much else. It takes a real physical effort to keep the anda aloft and steadied on your shoulder. Some of the strain is on the upper body, but it is really your legs that do the heavy lifting (and I imagine it is more so if you happen to be taller than your nearest co-penitents, as was my experience). The sun beats down for most of the day, and there is little shade in the streets. Heat radiates from the sun-warmed wood next to your face and the bodies of your co-penitents. The edge of the wooden platform digs in deeper into your trapezius muscle with each step, and you feel pains both dull and sharp in various parts of your body. People have gathered on the city's uneven sidewalks to watch, but their eyes look above you to the figure of Jesus, ignoring your efforts to bear Him aloft, so there is a sense of social isolation even while you are packed into a tight crowd of bodies. The lumbering music, shuffling steps, and growing physical discomfort become all-encompassing sensory stimuli leading you into a contemplative frame of mind. It is a humbling experience.

Eventually the call comes for a change, not that you hear it over the music. The bier just stops moving forward and you find yourself held back by your own physical attachment to the hard wooden structure and the body of the penitent in front of you, which now becomes a barrier to forward movement. The side-to-side swaying of the bier never stops, though, and in fact its motion feels more intense now. Other bodies shuffle around the bier, and those few seconds become more agonizing. As the person in front of you is replaced, the bier becomes temporarily heavier. Finally, someone comes to take your place. You duck slightly to relieve yourself of the weight. It is almost disconcerting to be able to stand and move according to your own will again. You are then ushered back to the double-file line that trails behind the anda to wait for another turn bearing the santo.

Of course, some people used this opportunity to join family members and friends and head home to eat, rest, and enjoy the rest of the day after having fulfilled their penitential duties, but the great collectivity of the procession continued on its path around Cobán well past nightfall, until finally the santo found His way back home to the church to finally rest for the night. Some of the penitents, but especially the members of the sponsoring sodality, would have walked with the santo for eight or ten hours at this point. The exhaustion was palpable when they finally brought the santo inside and knelt before the altar to offer a final prayer. The most dedicated of them would need to be up early the next day to help prepare that day's devotional labors.

Enacting the Passion was meant to hurt, and it did. It was meant to give the penitent a taste of Jesus's suffering. The performance of the ritual was a means of reflecting on the meaning of Christ's sacrifice, and of realizing, in both senses of the word, its importance in one's own spiritual life. There were also, of course, other customs that helped reinforce this, such as the dietary restrictions that accompanied Lent and the absence of instrumental music in Mass during Holy Week. Symbols of privation and suffering abounded, elaborating a general aesthetic that lent the Semana Santa a distinct aesthetic and affective feel as time apart from everyday life.[9] Certainly, though, that feeling found its strongest expression in the embodied experience that penitents had while carrying their santos, where each person subsumed themself in the great movement of the procession, stripped of individual agency, but also part of something spectacular, as part of "a circulation of affects of shame and pride that [brought] up associations with servitude, magnitude, and glory" (Napolitano 2017a, 252). I have gone into detail describing the physical experiential details of carrying a santo because I think they shed light on how the subjective experience of penitence is formed intersubjectively.

Intersubjectivity

Intersubjectivity, like many scholarly terms of art, has several meanings, and it is worthwhile unpacking them here a bit before proceeding. Intersubjectivity has often been used as a shorthand for the processes that lead social actors to be able to intuit each other's intentions and respond to them appropriately by accessing a "theory of mind"[10] (Luhrmann 2011). By this sort of cognitive model intersubjectivity is the precondition for culturally

---

9. The week of Semana Santa is also a holiday week in a more secular sense. The season is warm and sunny, and educational and commercial activities are suspended to accommodate Catholic traditions, so it is also a week when people who can afford to do so take vacations to the country's beaches, lakes, and *balnearios* (swimming spots). Families and friends also gather for meals, and despite the somber mood that the processions cultivate, nightlife venues do good business that week, taking advantage of the fact that most people don't have to go to work the next day.

10. Theory of mind refers to the ability to attribute to others the same kinds of mental states and abilities that one's own self has, and to understand that another person's perspectives, desires, and beliefs may differ from one's own even if they are of the same kind.

appropriate social interaction. However, anthropologists have critiqued this approach's emphasis on "mind reading" for uncritically reproducing and naturalizing Western language ideological models of intentionality (Duranti 2006) and selfhood that may not in fact be universal (Rumsey and Robbins 2008). Rather than formulating the question of intersubjectivity in terms of how it is that human beings can seemingly "read other minds," these scholars instead propose that the key to understanding intersubjective relations lies in asking how it is that we regularly manage to jointly accomplish tasks (Goodwin 2004; Danziger 2006).

This last approach to the problem of intersubjectivity is, I think, useful for discussing the mechanics of carrying a santo in a Semana Santa procession as well as the effect that performing that action has on participants. The key question raised by the literature on intersubjectivity is, How is it that human beings constitute shared common ground for complex collective actions such as religious rituals? In the absence of explicit direction and without much preplanning, how do people coordinate spectacular performances like Holy Week processions? To put it just a little too bluntly and a bit flippantly, how was it that the penitents didn't drop the anda every time the turno changed? As anyone who has had the pleasure of trying to move a sofa into a walk-up apartment has no doubt experienced, accomplishing tasks of this kind has less to do with clearly articulating directions and expectations and more to do with how we adjust our body's position and movements in response to the unexpected and unpredictable pushes, pulls, and pivots of the shared bulk. The material object acts as the "intercorporeal hinge" between parties (Csordas 2008, 111), and both success and failure in such a task come from an unspoken willingness and ability to give oneself over to the physicality of the task as an embodied experience.

Alessandro Duranti has argued that Husserl's formulation of intersubjectivity offers some insight into these questions (Duranti 2010). According to Duranti, there are at least six discrete levels of intersubjectivity in Husserl's theory ranging from, on the one hand, the baseline assumption that we share our world with other beings whose experience of the world are roughly the same as our own, to, on the other hand, our ability to jointly perform actions with these others through complex symbolic systems like language. These multiple levels of intersubjective understanding are possible because in recognizing others as beings with capacities for action similar to our own, we intuit that we could theoretically "trade places" with those others, and that it is this potentiality for swapping places and perspectives that allows us to work together to jointly accomplish the complex tasks that social life demands. The core of intersubjectivity is thus neither communication nor mutual recognition per se, but rather the "*possibility* of human interaction and human understanding" (Duranti 2010, 11, emphasis in original) afforded by people's ability to, if even in extremely limited ways, take another's perspective. Prior to symbolic representation, prior to the cognition, maybe even prior to the affective experience, then, it is a sense of potential interexchange between alters that grounds human social and cultural life.

Intersubjectivity, as this kind of potential to position oneself as another, is at the core of the Guatemalan Holy Week procession. At a very broad, symbolic level the ritual is structured around the idea that the penitent "trades places" with the bearer of the cross.[11] In this sense, the ritual is predicated on the possibility of intersubjectivity between the human actor and a sacred figure. Carrying a santo through Cobán is an embodied technique for taking up (in a limited way to be sure) the perspective of Jesus carrying the cross in Jerusalem. Carrying the santo is understood as having soteriological power precisely because the pain that the penitent experiences in performing this limited version of the Calvary march places him in a sympathetic relationship to Jesus, whose sacrifice is the ultimate reason that sin can be expiated.

A great deal of coordination of embodied action is required to jointly accomplish the ritual task of carrying the anda through the streets. The logistics and mechanics of the processions requires that many people coordinate their actions without explicit direction or instruction. That this is routinely done without major mishaps is on the one hand remarkable, and on the other, completely mundane. Year after year, the directorates of Hermandades come together to prepare the santos, build their andas, and assemble groups of penitents to carry them. Households along well-trod routes, too, organize their resources and labor and then carefully craft the delicate alfombras that the processions trample, all without direct instruction, planning, or oversight. Individuals come together to carry in the processions, bearing on their shoulders the weight of both the santo and the continued traditions of this spectacular Catholic ritual.

---

11. Usually this is understood to be Jesus, but some people said that it is Simon of Cyrene— who the synoptic Gospels say was pressed into service to help Jesus carry the cross on the way to Calvary—whom one should model oneself after. They said that at best, human beings can help Christ, but they cannot actually carry His sacred burden.

The idea that carrying the santo changes a person's religious and moral standing by humbling them before something greater than themself is made experientially real when an individual penitent submits their bodily agency to the supra-individual energy of the corporate body of the procession. By conscripting the penitent's subjective experience to the assemblage of the santo's anda, processions make suffering and humility affectively real. If these rituals are efficacious, and there is no reason to believe that Cobán's católicos do not find them to be so, it is in part (1) because of the way that they coordinate the actions of so many people in the public performance of piety and (2) because their very performative structure demands the kinds of perspective-taking and "trading of places" that generates a kind of "empathetic responsiveness" that can serve as a shared ground for religious experience (Ziegler 2006). The processions are thus much more than spectacles; their intersubjective and intercorporeal dimensions make them deeply affecting and effective because they make religious values experientially real.

Perhaps it was that potential of those spectacular rituals to be deeply affecting in this way that worried the evangélico pastor and spurred him to usher the children off the street and into the safety of his church. The shared spaces of streets and sidewalks lent themselves to encounters between religious bodies, making manifest the heteroglossia of religious life in Cobán. At another moment on that very same block, it could well have been a católico father worrying that his children would be drawn by evangélicos' shouts of joy; that they would be fascinated by the infectious rhythms of those alabanzas and want to join the exuberant dancing and clapping of their worship services. For that congregation's members, those sensory stimuli and embodied acts would likewise have been techniques for collectively invoking their love of God and calling forth the blessings of the Holy Spirit, which they understood had the power to effect deep personal transformations in themselves and a few fortunate passersby. In either instance the crux of the problem would lay with the essential commensurability of the parties involved, who, as sensate beings, could be drawn in and swept up by the affective power of collective rituals. Caught up in the enveloping sensorium of religion, one might well see oneself as another, and even be tempted to adopt another's voice as one's own.

Conclusion
Leaving, Returning, and the Dialectics of Change

There is a long tradition in ethnographic writing of telling the story of how the anthropologist arrived at their research site, but stories about leaving are rarer. Sometimes, though, exits illuminate things better than entrances. That was the case for me on the second Wednesday of January 2006.

My research funds and time were depleted, and I was due to leave Cobán in two days, so I went to see the carismáticos in Sa'xreb'e one last time to say my goodbyes, thank them for allowing me to join their services over the past year, and leave them with what I thought would be a good and useful gift—a couple of the handheld microphones that I had bought with my research funds twenty months earlier. I wryly imagined that the Mainstream Catholics in the village who thought that the carismáticos were too loud already would probably not appreciate them having more devices with which to amplify their voices, but the carismáticos themselves would certainly find a use for the mics.

I arrived a bit early and went to greet Hermano Rigo and Hermano Guillermo. They already knew that that evening would be my last one with them and agreed to let me address the congregation near the end of the service before the closing prayer. Knowing that the hermanos still had several things to do to get ready, I went to say hello to a few of the other people I had gotten to know and then took a seat in one of my usual spots on the right side of the aisle. As was typical, the band tuned their instruments and tested out the sound system by playing a few bars, while everyone else took their seats and gradually shifted their focus to the front of the chapel. Hermano Rigo welcomed us and led the opening prayer. Except for the fact that I was slated to talk directly to the congregation during the announcement period at the end of the service, everything indicated that this service would be just like any other with its mixture of song, prayer, and sermonizing. I settled in to be more of a participant than observer. Although I did set up my audio and video recorders to squeeze just a little bit more data out of my time in the field, I didn't really expect anything new or interesting to happen. And yet, as a senior anthropologist of religion quipped at dinner at a conference about nine months later, "A lot of fieldwork is just waiting for the second coconut to fall" (Webb Keane, personal communication).

Back in Sa'xreb'e, the proverbial second coconut fell in about the middle of the evening's first alabanza, when Qawa' Emanuel strolled into the chapel and took a seat next to me.[1] To my knowledge this was the first time that Qawa' Emanuel—who was one of the most vociferous critics of the Charismatics—entered one of their meetings. He greeted me and shook my hand with the soft grip that Q'eqchi'-Mayas use to show respect but otherwise sat mostly quietly, breaking his silence only to recite the *Pater Noster* and the Apostle's Creed in Spanish along with the congregation. Something must have moved him, though, because about twenty minutes later, he stood up, walked to the front of the chapel, and pulled Hermano Rigo aside for a quick conversation. From my seat I could not hear what either man said, but I did see Hermano Rigo give a slight nod that indicated some form of assent to whatever Qawa' Emanuel had said to him. He then retook his seat next to me and went back to watching the service. After all the hymns had been sung and all prayers save the closing one had been prayed, Qawa' Emanuel was invited to take the microphone. He addressed the congregation in Q'eqchi'.

> *¿Ma saa sa' lee ch'ool?* ["Are your hearts content?" i.e., a standard greeting] Thanks to the Lord God we are gathered here together at this time. We are beginning a new sacred year and I want to ask a favor of you. We will be at the holy Mass on Saturday at San Felipe and you are also invited on Sunday to Raxru Choxa [i.e., another chapel nearby] for Mass as well. I don't know if anyone has told you to go [to the Mass] yet.[2]

---

1. For a more nuanced discursive analysis of this incident and its implications for understanding ritual action, see Hoenes del Pinal (2016a). My transcription here differs a bit from the one presented there because I have opted to edit it for clarity here rather than to highlight the discursive elements that are the focus of that piece.

2. Translated from Q'eqchi' and edited for clarity and concision.

Conclusion

So far, this seemed like a rare instance of ecumenism on his part. He had come to explicitly invite the carismáticos to the services that would be held in honor of El Señor de Esquipulas who, though He is a nationally and ethnically coded santo, is nonetheless a representation of Jesus Christ crucified and thus well within the parameters of the sacred figures that La Renovación held to be important. So, even though there would be elements of the larger celebrations that they might have objected to (such as the *Baile del venado* masked dance that would be performed before the Mass), his invitation was a welcoming one.

Qawa' Emanuel continued. "There are brothers who study the Word of God to give us His message. Their work is good. It is good to take up that sacred work." The speech was beginning to stray from being a simple invitation to participate in the patron saint's festivities but could still be interpreted as generally friendly, since Qawa' Emanuel was clearly extolling the importance of knowing scripture, which was something that Charismatics certainly valued. But then it took a turn. "There are many things in the Bible, but not all the things that happened to Our Lord Jesus are in there. Many things happened to Jesus just so on Earth, and those things are in the *tradición* [tradition][3] that was left to us. The sacred tradition explains them exactly. These are things that the prophets left to us. They lived hundreds and hundreds of years ago before our lives."

For the next seven minutes, Qawa' Emanuel laid out his belief that life today was harder than it had been for people forty, eighty, a hundred years ago. He explained that this was because people had forgotten the wisdom left by our ancestors (*qaxe' qatoon*), who had known things about God and the nature of the world that people today had forgotten. People today suffered because they trusted too much in modern things and had forgotten or willfully ignored the traditions left by the ancestors. By the time Qawa' Emanuel spoke these words, it was clear to everyone in the room that far from being an invitation to reconcile across the church aisle, this was a thinly veiled critique of the carismáticos' absenteeism at certain events. Carismáticos emphasized the Bible and the direct inspiration from the Holy Spirit as the lynchpins of religious knowledge and authority and found fault with the notion that the Catholic Church's structures and traditions were in themselves

---

3. He pointedly used the Spanish term *tradición* here, switching from Q'eqchi' to emphasize the word.

adequate paths to piety. Qawa' Emanuel's preferred form of Catholicism required both scriptural knowledge and participation in the church community's traditional collective events, such as the patron saint's celebrations. He was effectively scolding them for failing to meet his, and by extension their ancestors', ideal of Catholic piety.

Hermano Rigo and the other Charismatics were not able to respond directly to Qawa' Emanuel's criticisms because not only was he holding the microphone, but his seniority in the parish and status as official caretaker of and keyholder to the chapel would have made challenging him both awkward and imprudent. This is not to say that they agreed with him, of course, and they employed some subtle methods of expressing their displeasure with his intervention. The congregation mostly sat silently during the speech in stark contrast to how they had participated in the parts of service that had just preceded it (Hoenes del Pinal 2016a). Congregants slumped and shifted around in their seats, looking anywhere but at the speaker—actions that anyone who has given or sat through a bad lecture should instantly recognize as the physical embodiment of boredom and inattention. They provided none of the usual verbal or bodily back-channel cues that they performed as part of being engaged and spirit-filled Catholics. Ironically, however, this form of silence and stillness was likely read by Qawa' Emanuel as an appropriate response that signaled not just the congregation's respect for his standing as a catequista and elder member of the community but also their assent to what he was saying.

A few minutes into the speech, Hermano Juan Pablo moved to the Yamaha keyboard and began softly playing notes that were not quite random, but also not quite coherent enough to be a melody. The sounds of the keyboard—which were similar to what Hermano Rigo sometimes played in the background while people prayed—were a reminder to the congregation that despite who was speaking and what he was saying, the chapel was for the time being a carismático space. Qawa' Emanuel eventually ran out of things to say. Without any more ways of reiterating his points about the value of tradición and having laid out the schedule of upcoming Masses and Rosaries no less than three times, he ceded the microphone back to Hermano Rigo, who thanked him rather curtly for his message and promptly switched the event back to a Charismatic frame by performing a few short call-and-response routines to which congregants responded with rousing *améns* and *aleluyas* and *gritos de júbilo* (shouts of joy). He then called me up to the front to say my goodbyes. As I took the microphone, I saw Qawa' Emanuel exit the church and turn right to head back home.[4]

On the drive home in my Honda Civic, just as I had fifty-three and a half weeks earlier in Padre Agustino's Suzuki Samurai when I had first visited the Charismatics, I was left to puzzle over what I had witnessed in the chapel at Sa'xreb'e. A year earlier I had been stunned when that same group of Catholics seamlessly switched their style of religiosity as an act of accommodation to the priest's presence. Now I was witnessing a rare instance of the two styles coming into direct conflict with each other. Qawa' Emanuel had tried to impose his voicing of Catholicism on the carismáticos, who had resisted in a way that was legible to them, but likely appeared as acquiescence to their antagonist. What had motivated Qawa' Emanuel to act in that way on that night? Had it been a genuine desire to see more participants at the patron saint's festivities the next week? Had his invitation been a sincere but poorly framed olive branch? Or a thinly veiled harangue? Did he feel that those annual venerations were in peril somehow and that adding the carismáticos to their numbers would help? Or had it just been that the noise of the drums and keyboards had finally gotten on his last nerve, and he decided to try to do something about it in person? Had he hoped to recruit me to finally join in his critique of La Renovación before I left Cobán?

I had no time to visit Qawa' Emanuel again to ask him about that night[5] or to follow up with Hermano Rigo on these questions. Less than thirty-six hours later I was on a bus back to Guatemala City, and on an airplane back to California a couple of days after that. Nonetheless, that night stuck with me as a clear example of the multiple ways that San Felipe's parishioners attempted to establish and articulate what it meant for them to be Catholic. It highlighted the ways big and small that people embodied those distinct

---

4. In my own speech, I thanked the congregation for allowing me to be with them at the services over the previous months. As I had done with the Mainstream groups, I told them that I had learned a lot both personally and professionally from them and that they'd helped me understand a lot about being católico. I said a few words wishing them success in the future and hoping that they would always find new ways of helping each other get ahead. In response, this group offered to pray over me, which I accepted. They asked the Holy Spirit to watch over me as I traveled back to my country.

5. The next time I got to talk to Qawa' Emanuel was sadly at his wife's funeral in 2017. Qana' Esmeralda was an incredibly warm person, who always seemed to be smiling unless she was praying. The couple had been important and very well-respected people in their community, and it is no exaggeration to say that their village benefitted from their presence.

visions and voicings, and of course recapitulated the terms of the conflict I had become familiar with over the course of a year and half. Even if the conflict between catequistas and carismáticos had seemingly become more muted than it had been two years earlier, the divide between them seemed like it would continue to grow.

I would not have an opportunity to go back to Cobán for almost a decade; when I finally did get back there, I found that it and San Felipe had changed quite a bit.[6] The city had continued to grow, and its streets seemed busier than ever. Atop its pine-covered hill San Felipe's main church still felt a world away from the bustle of the city, but it too had been transformed. El Señor en Agonía had recently returned from a sojourn to Guatemala City where He had been extensively studied and carefully restored by the National Institute of Anthropology and History. The experience had left Him noticeably paler. That may have also had to do with the new floor tiles that had been installed inside the church. Signs posted on the church's columns enjoined people to use the votive stands and not place burning candles directly on the floor, which limited how much smoke rose into the air to help carry prayers heavenward and tint the ceiling gray.

Padre Agustino had left years ago. The work had taken its toll on him, and I was told that he went back to his home country very ill and dejected. No one had heard from him in years, they told me. Padre Manuel, who had joined the parish about two-thirds of the way through my original fieldwork was wrapping up a decade of service and had been joined by several other priests—one each from Cameroon, Congo, and Haiti—who had brought new energy and perspectives to the parish. Tellingly, there was a schedule of events posted at the front of the church that announced a number of events and workshops as well as daily Masses in Spanish alongside the sole Sunday morning Mass in Q'eqchi'. Some Ladinos who had formerly belonged to other parishes, including my aunt, now made the hike up those 134 stairs to attend services at San Felipe. The parish was still overwhelmingly Q'eqchi'-Maya, but it was no longer exclusively so, and people at Mass prayed as much in Spanish as they did in Q'eqchi'.

---

6. My first visit back came as part of a family obligation in 2014, and I returned to conduct formal periods of field research on changes in the parish in the summers of 2015 and 2017.

Many of the catequistas who I had known were still working closely with the parish and their comunidades, but now they kept talking about *las santas misiones* (the holy missions). *Las santas misiones en la Verapaz*, I would learn, was a wide-sweeping diocesan evangelization project instituted in response to CELAM's call at its fifth general meeting in Aparecida for lay Catholics to become disciple-missionaries who would carry out a "Great Continental Mission" of Catholic renewal (Consejo Episcopal Latinoamericano 2007, 147). To do this, the Diocese of the Verapaz took up the framework of *las santas misiones populares* or "holy missions of the people" that followed the work of Father Luís Mosconi, an Italian priest who has worked in Brazil since the late 1960s.

As Mosconi tells it, he formulated the program as a response to the apparent failure of Catholicism in the face of the explosive growth and activity surrounding Pentecostal churches. He felt as though there was something missing that was keeping Catholicism "sterile," and eventually concluded that what was needed was a prophetic and mystic missionary practice that would put them in closer contact with the needs of the people. The central idea of las santas misiones populares was to foment conditions through which lay people could become closer to God through their relations with each other, and in doing so create a new experience of being a Catholic community (Mosconi 2008).

Creating Las santas misiones en la Verapaz necessitated translating and adapting it to the Q'eqchi'-Maya cultural context and several of San Felipe's catequistas were tapped to help with the project of making Catholicism more public-facing and socially responsive. Qana' Esperanza and Qawa' Luis, for example, aided in producing some of the translations of the basic didactic materials into Q'eqchi'. They and others had also accompanied the priests to make week-long visits to some of the larger rural communities. Those *semanas misioneras* (missionary weeks) were packed with activities meant to awaken católicos' spirituality and sense of pride in their religious identity. Many of San Felipe's parishioners were quite enthusiastic about las santas misiones and threw themselves wholeheartedly into the task of rethinking what it meant to practice their religion in the contemporary world. Qawa' Eduardo, who had been deeply involved with the parish but not a catequista during my original fieldwork, spoke about the energy that las santas misiones brought to his community, and was quite proud of his outreach work through it. He said he had personally visited every household in the peri-urban *colonia* where he lived and had managed to encourage three families of lapsed católicos to start participating in their comunidad again. Qana' Esperanza told me about a time she and another catequista were invited into an evangélico pastor's home and how he had questioned them about the Bible, presumably as a sort of challenge. "We answered all his questions," she reported proudly, "He thought we didn't know the Bible because we were católicas. For two hours we talked to him and when we left, he said to us, 'You really do understand [the Bible]', and he even invited us to come see him again." She was clearly pleased with the outcome of that interaction, since it proved that she was indeed a good disciple-missionary for her church.

The carismáticos had also undergone internal changes that had led them to reevaluate their own sensibilities and stances with regard to what it meant to be Catholic. While the explosive growth that had characterized the movement's first few years in the parish had slowed significantly, the carismáticos' congregations had grown to the point where their numbers plus the time that they had been active had secured their place in the parish. Las santas misiones' core ideas about a renewal of Catholic evangelization also fit nicely with their self-conception as "renewers" of Catholicism, as did its discourse of developing a more mystical relationship with God. Even if the forms of spirituality las santas misiones tended to foster were not exactly like their own, the carismáticos could see the larger project as sympathetic to their own goals and this had prompted many of them to become more involved in parish life.

As Hermano Federico put it, "We hadn't understood things well before, but the santas misiones came to motivate us. . . . Now we really know how to be with our brothers in the [Catholic] Church and not fight." What they had not understood before, he elaborated, was why it was important to be active with the parish and not just the local group; the parish made sure that you didn't get confused about your religion and helped you be stronger in your faith, he said. What las santas misiones had motivated them to do was be proud to be *católicos* as well as *renovados*. He liked the new events that came with las santas misiones, too, especially the *caminatas* (walks) in which parishioners would gather and walk from one point in the city to another, because then other people could see that católicos were also proud of their faith. Caminatas weren't like the santos' procesiones (although those still happened), he said, because the aim wasn't to blindly follow what had come before but rather to help bring people to God and the Church. It wasn't just the evangélicos who did that, now católicos were doing it, too.

Conclusion

None of this meant that La Renovación was any less charismatic than it had been before—in fact, the Holy Spirit had seemingly become more generous in parsing out its spiritual gifts. When I visited the Sa'xreb'e services again, I saw several people manifesting intense glossolalia, something that had been exceedingly rare a decade earlier. Their numbers had not continued to grow exponentially, but at their prayer meetings I recognized only about half of the congregation, and there were several people in leadership positions who I had never met before, too, suggesting that the group continued to attract new members even if some had also left. Notably, Hermano Rigo had stepped back from his duties a bit. He still played keyboard, but he preached less frequently than he had a decade earlier and was no longer the group's de facto leader. When I had a chance to speak with him one-on-one, he told me that there had been a lot of problems in the community a few years after I left. People had been fighting amongst themselves, and a few families had left altogether. Unsure of how else they could address the problems in the congregation, they decided to hold a special prayer meeting to ask God for help. At that meeting, he said, the Holy Spirit's power poured down on them so that many people spoke in tongues and others fell down. "It was something really very amazing. . . . In the end, everyone cried and those who were fighting asked for forgiveness and, thanks to God, we came out ahead from that because that night He showed us many of the errors we had been making." After that, he said, the Holy Spirit's gifts had come more easily, and the group had gotten stronger again. This had all happened before the parish had adopted las santas misiones, but Hermano Rigo thought that both his congregation's revival and the parish's commitment to the new project of evangelization were positive signs for La Renovación. The former meant that their faith was stronger now and the latter that the Catholic Church more generally was following in their footsteps of being loud and proud about their faithfulness to a living and powerful God. Perhaps this was evidence that San Felipe was undergoing a sort of "incipient pentecostalization" that would fundamentally shift how Catholicism was practiced in the parish (Thorsen 2015, 2).

However, not everyone was enamored with las santas misiones' new voicing of the religion. Qawa' Hugo, who had been a catequista for decades and had worked tirelessly for the Hermandad in 2005, chafed at the new aesthetics introduced by las santas misiones. The banners and flags that seemed to be ubiquitous in the parish proclaiming the initiative, the new songs they were asked to sing, and the clerical directive that catechists should try to dress in suit jackets when they preached, all seemed like unnecessary impositions of Ladino culture to him. "If I have to wear a suit and if they tell me to start hopping around [i.e., like carismáticos], I'm not going to feel comfortable, because that's not [part] of my culture. Those are things of the 'urban sector' [i.e., Ladinos]," he said. None of these things had anything to do with the real meaning of being católico to a Q'eqchi'-Maya person. It was a shame, too, because young people seemed to be less and less interested in their culture and they were losing their values, he said. In Hugo's estimation, las santas misiones had forgotten all the important work of inculturation they had struggled to establish two decades before. He and a few others had been talking to the priests to make sure that at least some of those ideas were kept alive and central to the parish's work, but he lamented that

> Sometimes it is hard for us to talk about our culture while being in the Catholic Church. Sadly, we sometimes have a mentality where we take radically what the Bible says, and we forget what the *Popol Vuh*[7] says. [But] the *Popol Vuh* and the Bible are one single book. True, they are two different stories, but in reality what the *Popol Vuh* talks about is the creation of a kingdom of love, of unity, [and] for everyone to advance. So that's the fundamental thing that we're trying to do—to keep people from losing their identity, so that our culture is maintained.

In his estimation, the parish was in danger of losing sight of its core mission of ensuring that Maya people had a place to authentically practice their unique voicing of Catholicism. He and his grandparents and their grandparents had shared a specific religious sensibility that was attuned to spiritual realities that were not always accessible to *kaxlanes* (foreigners), who often misinterpreted things like the miraculous appearance of a santo guarded by two jaguars in the midst of a forest hill, who misjudged how best to interact with God, and who did not recognize the real spiritual depth of his Maya culture.

Thus, as they had in the mid-2000s, so again in the mid-2010s, San Felipe's Catholics were engaging in debate and contestation over how to be

---

7. The *Popol Vuh* ("Book of Counsel" or "Book of the People") is a K'iche'-Maya text known from an early colonial era manuscript that tells the Maya story of creation and the exploits of the hero twins Jun Ajpu' (Hunahpu) and Ixb'alamke (Xbalanque), who learned the secret to defeating death and became enshrined in the stars. The text is sometimes colloquially referred to as the "Maya Bible."

Catholic in the best way, even though the specific issues that concerned them and that they thought merited debate had changed.

What does it mean to be Catholic and indigenous in postwar Guatemala? How do San Felipe's parishioners construct distinctive senses of their religious subjectivity from a position of social marginality? How do they reconcile histories of colonialism and exclusion with drives to be protagonists of their spiritual lives? The answers to these questions seem to be ever shifting, and the terms of the debates that they prompt are contingent on a range of factors both internal and external to the parish.

If in the 2000s San Felipe's catequistas and carismáticos seemed to be locked in a struggle over the future of their parish that figured communicative practices as key markers of internal difference, a decade later the stakes of that debate seemed far less pressing. Las santas misiones had displaced those concerns and replaced them with new ones about how to represent being an engaged Catholic to a larger non-Catholic public. Las santas misiones asked San Felipe's parishioners to think of themselves as actors in a much larger sphere of Catholic life, one that had national and continental implications, even if doing so meant leaving aside local matters that had once seemed critically important. However, we should not take the fact that those conflicts over language and gesture were dropped as a sign that they were ever fully resolved or that they were ultimately inconsequential. Howling winds and crashing waves are no less threatening because one experiences them aboard a miniature ship inside a teapot rather than on the decks of a frigate on the open seas. The scale of the consequences in no way diminishes the intensities of feelings around them. The issues of language mattered so much in San Felipe for a time because they indexed larger concerns about the intersection of their religious and ethnic identities. The new debates that emerged around whether las santas misiones' public-facing actions came at the expense of the cultivation of a distinctive Q'eqchi'-Maya spiritual sensibility were likewise at their core about two distinct visions of what it meant to be a Catholic in the Verapaz. In both instances there were forces averring toward local specificity and toward a transnational cosmopolitanism; toward the parochial and toward the catholic. To voice a position on how to be Catholic and Maya in Guatemala is and has always been to engage in a perennial dialogue about the meaning of those terms.

If we take seriously the idea that religion is as much about the practices and discourses of common people as it is about pronouncements of elites, then the vicissitudes of Catholicism in this corner of highland Guatemala are as consequential for our understanding of what Catholic Christianity is as are the writings of American social scientists, the pronouncements of theologians, or the encyclicals of popes. Of course, there are imbalances of power and influence—a bishop's opinions on a given issue may move things in ways that those of a rural catechist can never hope to—but taking the perspective of religion as something that is contested and not just declaimed demands that we consider that the layperson's position is as worthy of attention as that of the prelate.

If, as some have argued, anthropologists of religion have something to learn by dialoguing with theologians (see, e.g., Robbins 2006; Lemons 2018), I think it is incumbent on us to think expansively about who belongs in that latter category of intellectuals. It cannot simply be the work of elites in the North Atlantic world that we count as theology. John Milbank's writings may be useful to think with about otherness, but so are Qawa' Emanuel's and Hermano Rigo's words and actions. These lay leaders are not just practitioners of a lived religion, their practices constitute the lived theologies of their respective communities. It is through their dialogue with each other as well as with African clergy, colonial saints, and emigrant scholars (among others) that we can come to understand the meaning of religion in the contemporary world.

In this book I have adopted the perspective that Roman Catholicism, despite all the grandeur that its claim to be the "one, holy, catholic, apostolic church" projects, is far from settled, static, or uniform. If (at least some of) the Roman Catholic Church's institutional forms appear to be imbued with a sort of timelessness, anthropological examinations of how Catholics actually practice their religion provide ample evidence that Catholicism is continually being produced dialogically in an assemblage that resembles Mikhail Bakhtin's model of heteroglossia. Adopting this model allows us to think about how distinct forces and impulses work to both pull members of the same religion apart and bring them together in their shared spiritual projects. This perspective, I think, is not just a good way to conceive of the transnational, multilevel, at once centralized and broadly dispersed bodies of the Catholic Church, it also opens up new ways to think about how religions more generally are dialogically constituted through discourse and practice.

WORKS CITED

Abreu, Maria José de. 2021. *The Charismatic Gymnasium: Breath, Media, and Religious Revivalism in Contemporary Brazil*. Durham, NC: Duke University Press.
Allert, Tilman. 2008. *The Hitler Salute: On the Meaning of a Gesture*. Translated by Jefferson S. Chase. New York: Picador.
Althoff, Andrea. 2014. *Divided by Faith and Ethnicity: Religious Pluralism and the Problem of Race in Guatemala*. Berlin: Walter de Gruyter.
Annis, Sheldon. 1987. *God and Production in a Guatemalan Town*. Austin: University of Texas Press.
Arnold, David. 2009. "Salutation and Subversion: Gestural Politics in Nineteenth-Century India." *Past and Present* 203 (suppl. 4): 191–211. https://doi.org/10.1093/pastj/gtp009.
Asad, Talal. 1993. *Genealogies of Religion: Discipline and Reasons of Power in Christianity and Islam*. Baltimore, MD: Johns Hopkins University Press.
Assmann, Hugo. 1976. *Theology for a Nomad Church*. Translated by Paul Burns. Maryknoll, NY: Orbis Books.
Austin-Broos, Diane, Andrew Buckser, and Stephen D. Glazier. 2003. "The Anthropology of Conversion: An Introduction." In *The Anthropology of Religious Conversion*, edited by Andrew Buckser and Stephen D. Glazier, 1–12. Lanham, MD: Rowman & Littlefield Publishers.
Ayobade, Dotun. 2015. "Fela's Clenched Fists: The Double 'Black Power' Salute and Political Ideology." In *Body Talk and Cultural Identity in the African World*, edited by Augustine Agwuele, 37–57. Sheffield, UK: Equinox.
Baker, Geoffrey. 2008. *Imposing Harmony: Music and Society in Colonial Cuzco*. Durham, NC: Duke University Press.
Bakhtin, Mikhail M. 1981. *The Dialogic Imagination: Four Essays*. Edited by Michael Holquist. Translated by Caryl Emerson and Michael Holquist. Austin: University of Texas Press.

Bakhtin, Mikhail. 1984. *Problems of Dostoevsky's Poetics*. Translated by Caryl Emerson. Minneapolis: University of Minnesota Press.

Bandak, Andreas. 2017. "Opulence and Simplicity: The Question of Tension in Syrian Catholicism." In *The Anthropology of Catholicism: A Reader*, edited by Kristin Norget, Valentina Napolitano, and Maya Mayblin, 155–69. Oakland: University of California Press.

Baquedano-López, Patricia. 2008. "The Pragmatics of Reading Prayers: Learning the Act of Contrition in Spanish-Based Religious Education Classes (*doctrina*)." *Text & Talk* 28 (5): 581–602. https://doi.org/10.1515/TEXT.2008.030

Barth, Fredrik. 1998. "Introduction." In *Ethnic Groups and Boundaries: The Social Organization of Culture Difference*, edited by Fredrik Barth. Long Grove, IL: Waveland Press.

Bastos, Santiago, and Manuela Camus. 2003. *Entre el mecapal y el cielo: Desarrollo del movimiento Maya en Guatemala*. Guatemala: FLACSO, Cholsamaj.

Bateson, Gregory. 1936. *Naven: A Survey of the Problems Suggested by a Composite Picture of the Culture of a New Guinea Tribe from Three Points of View*. Cambridge: Cambridge University Press.

Bauman, Richard. 1983. *Let Your Words Be Few: Symbolism of Speaking and Silence among Seventeenth-Century Quakers*. Cambridge: Cambridge University Press.

Bendaña Perdomo, Ricardo. 2001. *Ella es lo que nosotros somos y mucho más: Síntesis histórica del Catolicismo Guatemalteco. II parte: 1951–2001*. Guatemala: Librerías Artemis-Edinter.

Bendaña Perdomo, Ricardo. 2011. *La iglesia en la historia de Guatemala, 1500–2000*. 5th ed. Guatemala: Librerías Artemis-Edinter.

Berryman, Phillip. 1984. *The Religious Roots of Rebellion: Christians in Central American Revolutions*. Maryknoll, NY: Orbis Books.

Berryman, Phillip. 1994. *Stubborn Hope: Religion, Politics, and Revolution in Central America*. Maryknoll, NY: Orbis Books.

Bialecki, Jon, Naomi Haynes, and Joel Robbins. 2008. "The Anthropology of Christianity." *Religion Compass* 2 (6): 1139–58.

Bialecki, Jon, and Eric Hoenes del Pinal. 2011. "Introduction: Beyond Logos: Extensions of the Language Ideology Paradigm in the Study of Global Christianity(-ies)." *Anthropological Quarterly* 84 (3): 575–93.

Bielo, James S. 2011. *Emerging Evangelicals: Faith, Modernity, and the Desire for Authenticity*. New York: NYU Press.

Birdwhistell, Ray L. 1970. *Kinesics and Context: Essays on Body Motion Communication*. Philadelphia: University of Pennsylvania Press.

Blom, Jan-Petter, and John J. Gumperz. 1986. "Social Meaning in Structure: Code-Switching in Norway." In *Directions in Sociolinguistics: The Ethnography of Communication*, edited by John J. Gumperz and Dell Hymes, 407–34. New York: Basil Blackwell.

Blommaert, Jan, ed. 1999. *Language Ideological Debates*. Berlin: Walter de Gruyter.

Bourdieu, Pierre. 1977. *Outline of a Theory of Practice*. Translated by Richard Nice. Cambridge: Cambridge University Press.

Bourdieu, Pierre. 1990. *The Logic of Practice*. Translated by Richard Nice. Stanford, CA: Stanford University Press.

Boylston, Tom. 2018. *The Stranger at the Feast: Prohibition and Mediation in an Ethiopian Orthodox Christian Community*. Oakland: University of California Press.

Braddick, Michael J. 2009. "Introduction: The Politics of Gesture." *Past and Present* 203 (suppl. 4): 9–35. https://doi.org/10.1093/pastj/gtp001.

Brandist, Craig. 2002. *The Bakhtin Circle: Philosophy, Culture and Politics*. London: Pluto.

Brandist, Craig, and Galin Tihanov, eds. 2000. *Materializing Bakhtin: The Bakhtin Circle and Social Theory*. New York: St. Martin's Press.

Brennan, Vicki L. 2018. *Singing Yoruba Christianity: Music, Media, and Morality*. Bloomington: Indiana University Press.

Bricker, Victoria R. 1981. *The Indian Christ, the Indian King*. Austin: University of Texas Press.

Briggs, Charles L. 1993. "Personal Sentiments and Polyphonic Voices in Warao Women's Ritual Wailing: Music and Poetics in a Critical and Collective Discourse." *American Anthropologist* 95 (4): 929–57.

Brookes, Heather. 2004. "A Repertoire of South African Quotable Gestures." *Journal of Linguistic Anthropology* 14 (2): 186–224.

Brubaker, Leslie. 2009. "Gesture in Byzantium." *Past and Present* 203 (suppl. 4): 36–56. https://doi.org/10.1093/pastj/gtp002.

Brusco, Elizabeth E. 1995. *The Reformation of Machismo: Evangelical Conversion and Gender in Colombia*. Austin: University of Texas Press.

Bucholtz, Mary and Kira Hall. 2016. "Embodied Sociolinguistics." In *Sociolinguistics: Theoretical Debates*, edited by Nikolas Coupland, 173–97. Cambridge: Cambridge University Press.

Burdick, John. 1993. *Looking for God in Brazil: The Progressive Catholic Church in Urban Brazil's Religious Arena*. Berkeley: University of California Press.

Burdick, John. 1998. *Blessed Anastácia: Women, Race, and Popular Christianity in Brazil*. New York: Routledge.

Calbris, Geneviève. 1990. *The Semiotics of French Gestures*. Translated by Owen Doyle. Bloomington: Indiana University Press.

Calder, Bruce J. 2004. "Interwoven Histories: The Catholic Church and the Maya, 1940 to the Present." In *Resurgent Voice in Latin America: Indigenous Peoples, Political Mobilization, and Religious Change*, edited by Edward L. Cleary and Timothy J. Steigenga. New Brunswick, NJ: Rutgers University Press.

Cannell, Fanella. 2006. "Introduction: The Anthropology of Christianity." In *The Anthropology of Christianity*, edited by Fanella Cannell, 1–50. Durham, NC: Duke University Press.

Carayon, Céline. 2019. *Eloquence Embodied: Nonverbal Communication among French and Indigenous Peoples in the Americas*. Chapel Hill: University of North Carolina Press.

Carmack, Robert M., ed. 1988. *Harvest of Violence: The Maya Indians and the Guatemalan Crisis.* Norman: University of Oklahoma Press.

Carrasco, Davíd. 2014. *Religions of Mesoamerica.* 2nd ed. Long Grove, IL: Waveland Press.

Centro Ak'Kutan. 1994. *Evangelio y culturas en Verapaz.* Cobán, Guatemala: Centro Ak'Kutan.

Chesnut, R. Andrew. 2003. *Competitive Spirits: Latin America's New Religious Economy.* New York: Oxford University Press.

Chesnut, R. Andrew. 2007. "Specialized Spirits: Conversion and the Products of Pneumacentric Religion in Latin America's Free Market of Faith." In *Conversion of a Continent,* edited by Timothy Steigenga and Edward L. Cleary, 72–92. Ithaca, NY: Rutgers University Press.

Chojnacki, Ruth J. 2010. *Indigenous Apostles: Maya Catholic Catechists Working the Word in Highland Chiapas.* Studies in World Christianity and Interreligious Relations, no. 46. Amsterdam: Rodopi.

Christenson, Allen J. 2016. *The Burden of the Ancients: Maya Ceremonies of World Renewal from the Pre-Columbian Period to the Present.* Austin: University of Texas Press.

Clark, Katerina, and Michael Holquist. 1984. *Mikhail Bakhtin.* Cambridge, MA: Harvard University Press.

Cleary, Edward L. 1985. *Crisis and Change: The Church in Latin America Today.* Maryknoll, NY: Orbis Books.

Cleary, Edward L. 2011. *The Rise of Charismatic Catholicism in Latin America.* Gainesville: University Press of Florida.

Cleary, Edward L., and Timothy J. Steigenga. 2004. "Resurgent Voices: Indians, Politics, and Religion in Latin America." In *Resurgent Voices in Latin America: Indigenous Peoples, Political Mobilization, and Religious Change,* edited by Edward L. Cleary and Timothy J. Steigenga, 1–24. New Brunswick, NJ: Rutgers University Press.

Cojtí Cuxil, Demetrio. 1994. *Políticas para la reivindicación de los Mayas de hoy.* Guatemala: Editorial Cholsamaj.

Cojtí Cuxil, Demetrio. 1996. "The Politics of Maya Revindication." In *Maya Cultural Activism in Guatemala,* edited by Edward F. Fischer and R. McKenna Brown, 19–50. Austin: University of Texas Press.

Comisión Nacional de Pastoral Indígena. 2003. *Inculturación del evangelio.* Guatemala: Ediciones San Pablo.

Conferencia Episcopal de Guatemala. 1997. *Al servicio de la vida, la justicia y la paz: Documentos de la Conferencia Episcopal de Guatemala, 1956–1997.* Guatemala: Ediciones San Pablo.

Consejo Episcopal Latinoamericano. 1992. *Nueva evangelización, promoción humana, cultural cristiana: IV conferencia general del Episcopado Latinoamericano (Santo Domingo).* Guatemala: Ediciones San Pablo.

Consejo Episcopal Latinoamericano. 2007. "Concluding Document of the 5th General Conference of the Episcopal Council of Latin America and the Caribbean (Aparecida)." *Consejo Episcopal Latinoamericano.* https://www.celam.org/aparecida/Ingles.pdf.

Cook, Garrett W. 2010. *Renewing the Maya World: Expressive Culture in a Highland Town.* Austin: University of Texas Press.

Cooper, Travis Warren. 2018. "The Uncanniness of Missionary Others: A Discursive Analysis of a Century of Anthropological Writings on Missionary Ethnographers." *Religion and Society* 9 (1): 68–85.

Corbeill, Anthony. 2004. *Nature Embodied: Gesture in Ancient Rome.* Princeton: Princeton University Press.

Cordes, Paul Josef. 1997. *Call to Holiness: Reflections on the Catholic Charismatic Renewal.* Collegeville, MN: The Liturgical Press.

Covington-Ward, Yolanda. 2016. *Gesture and Power: Religion, Nationalism, and Everyday Performance in Congo.* Durham, NC: Duke University Press.

Csordas, Thomas J. 2007. "Global Religion and the Re-Enchantment of the World: The Case of the Catholic Charismatic Renewal." *Anthropological Theory* 7 (3): 295–314.

Csordas, Thomas J. 2008. "Intersubjectivity and Intercorporeality." *Subjectivity* 22 (1): 110–21.

Csordas, Thomas J. 2017. "Possession and Psychopathology: Faith and Reason." In *The Anthropology of Catholicism: A Reader,* edited by Kristin Norget, Valentina Napolitano, and Maya Mayblin, 293–304. Oakland: University of California Press.

Danziger, Eve. 2006. "The Thought That Counts: Interactional Consequences of Variation in Cultural Theories of Meaning." *Roots of Human Sociality: Culture, Cognition and Interaction,* edited by N. J. Enfield and Stephen C. Levinson, 259–78. London: Routledge.

De Theije, Marjo, and Cecília L. Mariz. 2008. "Localizing and Globalizing Processes in Brazilian Catholicism: Comparing Inculturation in Liberationist and Charismatic Catholic Cultures." *Latin American Research Review* 43 (1): 33–54.

Dolar, Mladen. 2006. *A Voice and Nothing More.* Cambridge, MA: MIT press.

Dorian, Nancy C. 1982. "Defining the Speech Community to Include Its Working Margins." In *Sociolinguistic Variation in Speech Communities,* edited by Suzanne Romaine, 25–33. London: Edward Arnold.

Du Bois, J. W. 1992. "Meaning without Intention: Lessons from Divination." In *Responsibility and Evidence in Oral Discourse,* edited by Jane H. Hill and Judith T. Irvine, 48–71. Cambridge: Cambridge University Press.

Du Bois, John. 2007. "The Stance Triangle." In *Stancetaking in Discourse: Subjectivity, Evaluation, Interaction,* edited by Robert Englebretson, 139–82. Amsterdam: John Benjamins Publishing Company.

Duranti, Alessandro. 2006. "The Social Ontology of Intentions." *Discourse Studies* 8 (1): 31–40.

Duranti, Alessandro. 2009. "The Relevance of Husserl's Theory to Language Socialization." *Journal of Linguistic Anthropology* 19 (2): 205–26.

Duranti, Alessandro. 2010. "Husserl, Intersubjectivity and Anthropology." *Anthropological Theory* 10 (1–2): 16–35.

Early, John D. 2006. *The Maya and Catholicism: An Encounter of Worldviews.* Gainesville: University Press of Florida.

Early, John D. 2012. *Maya and Catholic Cultures in Crisis.* Gainesville: University Press of Florida.

Eisenlohr, Patrick. 2018. *Sounding Islam: Voice, Media, and Sonic Atmospheres in an Indian Ocean World.* Oakland: University of California Press.

Elisha, Omri. 2018. "Dancing the Word: Techniques of Embodied Authority among Christian Praise Dancers in New York City." *American Ethnologist* 45 (3): 380–91. https://doi.org/10.1111/amet.12672.

England, Nora C. 2003. "Mayan Language Revival and Revitalization Politics: Linguists and Linguistic Ideologies." *American Anthropologist* 105 (4): 733–43.

Falla, Ricardo. 2001. *Quiché Rebelde: Religious Conversion, Politics, and Ethnic Identity in Guatemala.* Austin: University of Texas Press.

Farnell, Brenda. 2002. "Dynamic Embodiment in Assiniboine (Nakota) Storytelling." *Anthropological Linguistics* 44 (1): 37–64.

Farnell, Brenda M. 2009. *Do You See What I Mean? Plains Indian Sign Talk and the Embodiment of Action.* Lincoln: University of Nebraska Press.

Fischer, Edward F. 2001. *Cultural Logics and Global Economies: Maya Identity in Thought and Practice.* Austin: University of Texas Press.

Fischer, Edward F., and R. McKenna Brown, eds. 1996. *Maya Cultural Activism in Guatemala.* Austin: University of Texas Press.

Fox Tree, Erich. 2009. "Meemul Tziij: An Indigenous Sign Language Complex of Mesoamerica." *Sign Language Studies* 9 (3): 324–66.

Friedlander, Judith. 2007. *Being Indian in Hueyapan: A Revised and Updated Edition.* New York: Palgrave Macmillan.

Gandarias, Igor de. 2014. "Acercamiento al son Guatemalteco tradicional desde una perspectiva histórica." *ÍSTMICA. Revista de la facultad de filosofía y letras,* no. 17: 29–43.

Gandarias, Igor de. 2015. "Aspectos fenomenológicos del son Guatemalteco tradicional phenomenological: Aspects of the Traditional Guatemalan Son." *Ciencias sociales y humanidades* 2 (1): 9–18.

Garrard-Burnett, Virginia. 1998. *Protestantism in Guatemala: Living in the New Jerusalem.* Austin: University of Texas Press.

Garrard-Burnett, Virginia. 2004. "'God Was Already Here When Columbus Arrived': Inculturation Theology and the Maya Movement in Guatemala." In *Resurgent Voices in Latin America: Indigenous Peoples, Political Mobilization, and Religious Change,* edited by Edward L. Cleary and Timothy J. Steigenga, 125–53. New Brunswick, NJ: Rutgers University Press.

Garriott, William, and Kevin Lewis O'Neill. 2008. "Who Is a Christian? Toward a Dialogic Approach in the Anthropology of Christianity." *Anthropological Theory* 8 (4): 381–98.

Garzon, Susan, R. McKenna Brown, and Julia Becker Richards. 1998. *The Life of Our Language: Kaqchikel Maya Maintenance, Shift, and Revitalization.* Austin: University of Texas Press.

Geertz, Clifford. 1973. *The Interpretation of Cultures*. New York: Basic Books.
Goffman, Erving. 1981. *Forms of Talk*. Philadelphia: University of Pennsylvania Press.
Goldin-Meadow, Susan. 2003. *Hearing Gesture: How Our Hands Help Us Think*. Cambridge, MA: The Belknap Press of Harvard University Press.
Gómez, Ileana, and Manuel Vásquez. 2001. "Youth Gangs and Religion among Salvadorans in Washington and El Salvador." In *Christianity, Social Change, and Globalization in the Americas*, edited by Anna Peterson, Manuel Vásquez, and Philip Williams, 165–87. New Brunswick, NJ: Rutgers University Press.
Goodwin, Charles. 1980. "Restarts, Pauses, and the Achievement of a State of Mutual Gaze at Turn-Beginning." *Sociological Inquiry* 50 (3–4): 272–302.
Goodwin, Charles. 2000. "Action and Embodiment within Situated Human Interaction." *Journal of Pragmatics* 32 (10): 1489–1522.
Goodwin, Charles. 2004. "A Competent Speaker Who Can't Speak: The Social Life of Aphasia." *Journal of Linguistic Anthropology* 14 (2): 151–70.
Goodwin, Marjorie Harness, Charles Goodwin, and Malcah Yaeger-Dror. 2002. "Multi-Modality in Girls' Game Disputes." *Journal of Pragmatics* 34 (10–11): 1621–49.
Gooren, Henri. 2010. *Religious Conversion and Disaffiliation: Tracing Patterns of Change in Faith Practices*. Basingstoke, UK: Palgrave Macmillan.
Gossen, Gary H. 1976. "Language as Ritual Substance." In *Language in Religious Practice*, edited by William J. Samarin, 40–60. Rowley, MA: Newbury House.
Graf, Fritz. 1991. *Gestures and Conventions: The Gestures of Roman Actors and Orators*. Cambridge, UK: Polity Press.
Gumperz, John J. 1982. *Discourse Strategies*. Cambridge: Cambridge University Press.
Gutiérrez, Gustavo. 1988. *A Theology of Liberation: History, Politics, and Salvation*. Translated by Caridad Inda and John Eagleson. Maryknoll, NY: Orbis Books.
Hager, Anna. 2019. "The Emergence of a Syriac Orthodox Mayan Church in Guatemala." *International Journal of Latin American Religions* 3 (2): 370–89.
Hall, Edward T. 1969. *The Hidden Dimension*. New York: Anchor Books.
Hall, Kira, Donna M. Goldstein, and Matthew Bruce Ingram. 2016. "The Hands of Donald Trump: Entertainment, Gesture, Spectacle." *HAU: Journal of Ethnographic Theory* 6 (2): 71–100. https://doi.org/10.14318/hau6.2.009.
Handman, Courtney. 2015. *Critical Christianity: Translation and Denominational Conflict in Papua New Guinea*. Berkeley: University of California Press.
Hanks, William F. 2006. "Joint Commitment and Common Ground in a Ritual Event." In *Roots of Human Sociality: Culture, Cognition and Interaction*, edited by N. J. Enfield and Stephen C. Levinson, 299–328. New York: Berg.
Hanks, William F. 2010. *Converting Words: Maya in the Age of the Cross*. Berkeley: University of California Press.
Hann, Chris. 2007. "The Anthropology of Christianity per se." *Archives Européennes de Sociologie: European Journal of Sociology* 48 (3): 383–410. https://doi.org/10.1017/S0003975607000410.

Hann, Chris, and Hermann Goltz. 2010. *Eastern Christians in Anthropological Perspective*. Berkeley: University of California Press.

Harkness, Nicholas. 2014. *Songs of Seoul: An Ethnography of Voice and Voicing in Christian South Korea*. Berkeley: University of California Press.

Haviland, John B. 2011. "Musical Spaces." In *Embodied Interaction: Language and Body in the Material World*, edited by Jürgen Streeck, Charles Goodwin, and Curtis LeBaron, 289–304. Cambridge: Cambridge University Press.

Haviland, John B. 2013. "The Emerging Grammar of Nouns in a First Generation Sign Language: Specification, Iconicity, and Syntax." *Gesture* 13 (3): 309–53. https://doi.org/10.1075/gest.13.3.04hav.

Hawkins, Richard John. 2005. "Language Loss in Guatemala: A Statistical Analysis of the 1994 Population Census." *Journal of Sociolinguistics* 9 (1): 53–73.

Heo, Angie. 2018. *The Political Lives of Saints: Christian-Muslim Mediation in Egypt*. Oakland: University of California Press.

Hernández Sandoval, Bonar L. 2018. *Guatemala's Catholic Revolution: A History of Religious and Social Reform, 1920–1968*. Notre Dame, IN: University of Notre Dame Press.

Hill, Jane H. 1986. "The Refiguration of the Anthropology of Language." *Cultural Anthropology* 1 (1): 89–102.

Hoenes del Pinal, Eric. 2009. "How Q'eqchi'-Maya Catholics Become Legitimate Interpreters of the Bible: Two Models of Religious Authority in Sermons." In *The Social Life of Scriptures*, edited by James S. Bielo, 80–99. New Brunswick, NJ: Rutgers University Press.

Hoenes del Pinal, Eric. 2011. "Towards an Ideology of Gesture: Gesture, Body Movement, and Language Ideology among Q'eqchi'-Maya Catholics." *Anthropological Quarterly* 84 (3): 595–630.

Hoenes del Pinal, Eric. 2016a. "A Ritual Interrupted: A Case of Contested Ritual Practices in a Q'eqchi'-Maya Catholic Parish." *Journal of Contemporary Religion* 31 (3): 365–78.

Hoenes del Pinal, Eric. 2016b. "From Vatican II to Speaking in Tongues: Theology and Language Policy in a Q'eqchi'-Maya Catholic Parish." *Language Policy* 15 (2): 179–97.

Hoenes del Pinal, Eric. 2019. "The Promises and Perils of Radio as a Medium of Faith in a Q'eqchi'-Maya Catholic Community." *Journal of Global Catholicism* 3 (2): 4. https://doi.org/10.32436/2475-6423.1055.

Holleran, Mary Patricia. 1949. *Church and State in Guatemala*. New York: Columbia University Press.

Horst, Oscar H., Robert N. Thomas, and John M. Hunter. 2010. "Difusión del culto al Cristo negro crucificado de Esquipulas." *Mesoamérica* 31 (52): 143.

Hughes, Jennifer Scheper. 2010. *Biography of a Mexican Crucifix: Lived Religion and Local Faith from the Conquest to the Present*. New York: Oxford University Press.

Ingalls, Monique M., and Amos Yong. 2015. *The Spirit of Praise: Music and Worship in Global Pentecostal-Charismatic Christianity*. University Park, PA: Penn State University Press.

Instituto Nacional de Estadística de Guatemala. 2002. "XI censo nacional de población y VI de habitación (CENSO 2002)." Instituto Nacional de Estadística de Guatemala.

International Catholic Charismatic Renewal Services. 2005. "The Catholic Charismatic Renewal." *International Catholic Charismatic Renewal Services*. http://www.iccrs.org/ccr.php.

Irarrázaval, Diego. 2000. *Inculturation: New Dawn of the Church in Latin America*. Translated by Phillip Berryman. Maryknoll, NY: Orbis Books.

Irvine, J., and Susan Gal. 2000. "Language Ideology and Linguistic Differentiation." In *Regimes of Languages. Ideologies, Polities, and Identities*, edited by Paul V. Kroskrity, 35–83. Santa Fe, NM: School of American Research Press.

Jackson, Michael. 1989. *Paths toward a Clearing: Radical Empiricism and Ethnographic Inquiry*. Bloomington: Indiana University Press.

Jenkins, Timothy. 2012. "The Anthropology of Christianity: Situation and Critique." *Ethnos* 77 (4): 459–76. https://doi.org/10.1080/00141844.2012.669775.

Jorio, Andrea de. (1832) 2000. *Gesture in Naples and Gesture in Classical Antiquity: A Translation of La Mimica Degli Antichi Investigata Nel Gestire Napoletano, Gestural Expression of the Ancients in the Light of Neapolitan Gesturing*. Edited by Adam Kendon. Advances in Semiotics. Bloomington: Indiana University Press.

Keane, Webb. 2007. *Christian Moderns: Freedom and Fetish in the Mission Encounter*. Berkeley: University of California Press.

Kendall, Carl. 1991. "The Politics of Pilgrimage: The Black Christ of Esquipulas." In *Pilgrimage in Latin America*, edited by N. Ross Crumrine and Alan Morinis. New York: Greenwood Press.

Kendon, Adam. 1990. *Conducting Interaction: Patterns of Behavior in Focused Encounters*. Cambridge: Cambridge University Press.

Kendon, Adam. 1997. "Gesture." *Annual Review of Anthropology* 26 (1): 109–28.

Kendon, Adam. 2004. *Gesture: Visible Action as Utterance*. Cambridge: Cambridge University Press.

Kendon, Adam, and Cornelia Müller. 2001. "Introducing Gesture." *Gesture* 1 (1): 1–7. https://doi.org/10.1075/gest.1.1.01ken.

King, Arden R. 1974. *Coban and the Verapaz: History and Cultural Process in Northern Guatemala*. New Orleans: Middle American Research Institute, Tulane University.

Kistler, S. Ashley. 2014. *Maya Market Women: Power and Tradition in San Juan Chamelco, Guatemala*. Urbana: University of Illinois Press.

Konefal, Betsy. 2010. *For Every Indio Who Falls: A History of Maya Activism in Guatemala, 1960–1990*. Albuquerque: University of New Mexico Press.

Kratz, Corinne A. 1994. *Affecting Performance: Meaning, Movement, and Experience in Okiek Women's Initiation*. Washington, D.C.: Smithsonian Institution Press.

Kroeber, Alfred Louis, and Clyde Kluckhohn. 1952. *Culture: A Critical Review of Concepts and Definitions*. Cambridge, MA: Peabody Museum Papers.

Kuper, Adam. 1999. *Culture: The Anthropologists' Account.* Cambridge, MA: Harvard University Press.
Labov, William. 1969. "The Logic of Nonstandard Dialect." *School of Languages and Linguistics Monograph Series* 22: 1–43.
Lange, Barbara Rose. 2003. *Holy Brotherhood: Romani Music in a Hungarian Pentecostal Church.* New York: Oxford University Press.
Latour, Bruno. 1993. *We Have Never Been Modern.* Cambridge, MA: Harvard University Press.
LeBaron, Alan. 1993. "The Creation of the Modern Maya." In *The Rising Tide of Cultural Pluralism: The Nation State at Bay?*, edited by Crawford Young, 265–85. Madison: University of Wisconsin Press.
Lehmann, David. 2003. "Dissidence and Conformism in Religious Movements: What Difference – If Any – Separates the Catholic Charismatic Renewal and Pentecostal Churches." *Concilium* 3: 122–38.
Lemons, J. Derrick. 2018. *Theologically Engaged Anthropology.* Oxford: Oxford University Press.
Lempert, Michael P. 2005. "Denotational Textuality and Demeanor Indexicality in Tibetan Buddhist Debate." *Journal of Linguistic Anthropology* 15 (2): 171–93.
Lempert, Michael P. 2019. "What Is an Anthropology of Gesture?" *Gesture* 18 (2–3): 173–208. https://doi.org/10.1075/gest.19019.lem.
Levine, Daniel H. 1992. *Popular Voices in Latin American Catholicism.* Princeton: Princeton University Press.
Lomax, Alan, and Forrestine Paulay. 2008. *Rhythms of Earth: Dance and Human History.* DVD. Documentary Educational Resources (DER).
Luhrmann, Tanya M. 2004. "Metakinesis: How God Becomes Intimate in Contemporary US Christianity." *American Anthropologist* 106 (3): 518–28.
Luhrmann, Tanya M. 2011. "Toward and Anthropological Theory of Mind." *Suomen Antropologi: Journal of the Finnish Anthropological Society* 36 (4): 5–13.
MacKenzie, C. James. 2016. *Indigenous Bodies, Maya Minds: Religion and Modernity in a Transnational K'iche' community.* Boulder: University Press of Colorado.
Mahmood, Saba. 2001. "Rehearsed Spontaneity and the Conventionality of Ritual: Disciplines of Şalat." *American Ethnologist* 28 (4): 827–53.
Mahmood, Saba. 2005. *Politics of Piety: The Islamic Revival and the Feminist Subject.* Princeton, NJ: Princeton University Press.
Mandelker, Amy, ed. 1995. *Bakhtin in Contexts: Across the Disciplines.* Rethinking Theory. Evanston, IL: Northwestern University Press.
Mauss, Marcel. 1979. "Body Techniques." In *Sociology and Psychology: Essays,* 95–123. London: Routledge.
Mauss, Marcel. 2003. *On Prayer.* Edited by William Stuart Frederick Pickering. Translated by Susan Leslie. New York: Durkheim Press.
Maxwell, Judith. 1996. "Prescriptive Grammar and Kaqchikel Revitalization." In *Maya Cultural Activism in Guatemala,* edited by Edward F. Fischer and R. McKenna Brown, 195–207. Austin: University of Texas Press.

Mayblin, Maya. 2010. *Gender, Catholicism, and Morality in Brazil: Virtuous Husbands, Powerful Wives*. New York: Palgrave Macmillan.

Mayblin, Maya, Kristin Norget, and Valentina Napolitano. 2017. "Introduction: The Anthropology of Catholicism." In *The Anthropology of Catholicism: A Reader*, edited by Kristin Norget, Valentina Napolitano, and Maya Mayblin, 1–30. Oakland: University of California Press.

McGuire, Meredith B. 1982. *Pentecostal Catholics: Power, Charisma, and Order in a Religious Movement*. Philadelphia: Temple University Press.

McNeill, David. 1992. *Hand and Mind: What Gestures Reveal about Thought*. Chicago: University of Chicago Press.

McNeill, David. 2000. *Language and Gesture*. New York: Cambridge University Press.

Mead, Margaret, and Gregory Bateson. 1942. *Balinese Character: A Photographic Analysis*. New York: New York Academy of Sciences.

Medvedev, Pavel N., and M. M. Bakhtin. (1928) 1978 *The Formal Method in Literary Scholarship: A Critical Introduction to Sociological Poetics, Trans*. Translated by Albert J. Wehrle. Baltimore, MD: Johns Hopkins University Press.

Melgar, Rafael. 2003. "Historia de la iglesia de Verapaz. Ultimos 50 años." In *Rescatando la memoria del camino: Diócesis de Verapaz 1935–2003*, 2–25. Materiales Ak' Kutan 14. Cobán, Guatemala: Centro Ak' Kutan.

Mitchell, Nathan D. 2009. *The Mystery of the Rosary: Marian Devotion and the Reinvention of Catholicism*. New York: NYU Press.

Montejo, Victor. 2005. *Maya Intellectual Renaissance: Identity, Representation, and Leadership*. Austin: University of Texas Press.

Moore, Alexander. 1973. *Life Cycles in Atchalan: The Diverse Careers of Certain Guatemalans*. New York: Teachers College Press.

Moore, Leslie C. 2008. "Body, Text, and Talk in Maroua Fulbe Qur'anic Schooling." *Text & Talk* 28 (5): 643–65.

Moran, Michelle. 2013. "The Spirituality at the Heart of the Catholic Charismatic Renewal Movement." *Transformation: An International Journal of Holistic Mission Studies* 30 (4): 287–91. https://doi.org/10.1177/0265378813500424.

Mosconi, Luís. 2008. *Santas misiones populares: Una experiencia de evangelización al servicio del pueblo*. Mexico City: Ediciones Dabar.

Mosse, David. 2017. "'Complexio Oppositorum?' Religion, Society, and Power in the Making of Catholicism in Rural South India." In *The Anthropology of Catholicism: A Reader*, edited by Kristin Norget, Valentina Napolitano, and Maya Mayblin, 105–21. Oakland: University of California Press.

Muehlebach, A. 2009. "Complexio Oppositorum: Notes on the Left in Neoliberal Italy." *Public Culture* 21 (3): 495–515. https://doi.org/10.1215/08992363-2009-005.

Murga Armas, Jorge. 2006. *Iglesia Católica, movimiento indígena y lucha revolucionaria: Santiago Atitlán, Guatemala*. Guatemala: Impresiones Palacios.

Nabhan-Warren, Kristy. 2011. "Embodied Research and Writing: A Case for Phenomenologically Oriented Religious Studies Ethnographies." *Journal of the American Academy of Religion* 79 (2): 378–407.

Napolitano, Valentina. 1998. "Between 'Traditional' and 'New' Catholic Church Religious Discourses in Urban, Western Mexico." *Bulletin of Latin American Research* 17 (3): 323–39.

Napolitano, Valentina. 2015. *Migrant Hearts and the Atlantic Return: Transnationalism and the Roman Catholic Church*. New York: Fordham University Press.

Napolitano, Valentina. 2017a. "On a Political Economy of Political Theology: El Señor de los Milagros." In *The Anthropology of Catholicism: A Reader*, edited by Kristin Norget, Valentina Napolitano, and Maya Mayblin, 243–55. Oakland: University of California Press.

Napolitano, Valentina. 2017b. "The Sacred Heart and the Religious in Movement." *Material Religion* 13 (2): 237–39.

Nash, June. 1968. "The Passion Play in Maya Indian Communities." *Comparative Studies in Society and History* 10 (3): 318–27.

Needham, Rodney. 1967. "Percussion and Transition." *Man* 2 (4): 606–14.

Nelson, Diane M. 1999. *A Finger in the Wound: Body Politics in Quincentennial Guatemala*. Berkeley: University of California Press.

Ness, Sally Ann. 1992. *Body, Movement, and Culture: Kinesthetic and Visual Symbolism in a Philippine Community*. Philadelphia: University of Pennsylvania Press.

Noland, Carrie. 2009. *Agency and Embodiment*. Cambridge, MA: Harvard University Press.

Norget, Kristin. 2004. "'Knowing Where We Enter': Indigenous Theology and the Popular Church in Oaxaca, Mexico." In *Resurgent Voices in Latin America: Indigenous Peoples, Political Mobilization, and Religious Change*, edited by Edward L. Cleary and Timothy J. Steigenga, 154–86. New Brunswick, NJ: Rutgers University Press.

Norget, Kristin. 2017. "The Virgin of Guadalupe and Spectacles of Catholic Evangelism in Mexico." In *The Anthropology of Catholicism: A Reader*, edited by Kristin Norget, Valentina Napolitano, and Maya Mayblin, 184–200. Oakland: University of California Press.

Norris, Sigrid. 2004. *Analyzing Multimodal Interaction: A Methodological Framework*. New York: Routledge.

O'Hara, Matthew D. 2009. *A Flock Divided: Race, Religion, and Politics in Mexico, 1749–1857*. Durham, NC: Duke University Press.

Okely, Judith. 2007. "Fieldwork Embodied." *The Sociological Review* 55: 65–79.

O'Neill, Kevin Lewis. 2010. *City of God: Christian Citizenship in Postwar Guatemala*. Berkeley: University of California Press.

O'Neill, Kevin Lewis. 2015. *Secure the Soul: Christian Piety and Gang Prevention in Guatemala*. Berkeley: University of California Press.

Ong, Aihwa. 1988. "The Production of Possession: Spirits and the Multinational Corporation in Malaysia." *American Ethnologist* 15 (1): 28–42.

Oosterbaan, Martijn. 2009. "Sonic Supremacy: Sound, Space and Charisma in a Favela in Rio de Janeiro." *Critique of Anthropology* 29 (1): 81–104.

Orta, Andrew. 2004. *Catechizing Culture: Missionaries, Aymara, and the "New Evangelization."* New York: Columbia University Press.

Padden, Carol A., Irit Meir, So-One Hwang, Ryan Lepic, Sharon Seegers, and Tory Sampson. 2013. "Patterned Iconicity in Sign Language Lexicons." *Gesture* 13 (3): 287–308.

Pavlick, Elizabeth-Jane. 2010. "John Paul II's Statements on Music in the Church: A Fulfillment of the Theology of Vatican II." *Sacred Music* 137 (1): 6–24.

Peña, Elaine A. 2011. *Performing Piety: Making Space Sacred with the Virgin of Guadalupe*. Berkeley: University of California Press.

Perrino, Sabina M. 2002. "Intimate Hierarchies and Qur'anic Saliva (Tëfli): Textuality in a Senegalese Ethnomedical Encounter." *Journal of Linguistic Anthropology* 12 (2): 225–59.

Pujolar, Joan. 2000. *Gender, Heteroglossia and Power: A Sociolinguistic Study of Youth Power*. Berlin: Mouton de Gruyter.

Rampton, Ben. 2011. "From 'Multi-Ethnic Adolescent Heteroglossia' to 'Contemporary Urban Vernaculars.'" *Language & Communication* 31 (4): 276–94.

Ratzinger, Joseph Cardinal. 1984. "Instruction on Certain Aspects of the 'Theology of Liberation.'" Congregation for the Doctrine of the Faith. https://www.vatican.va/roman_curia/congregations/cfaith/documents/rc_con_cfaith_doc_19840806_theology-liberation_en.html.

Reina, Ruben E. 1966. *The Law of the Saints: A Pokomam Pueblo and Its Community Culture*. Indianapolis, IN: Bobbs-Merrill Company.

REMHI (Proyecto Interdiocesano de Recuperación de la Memoria Historica). 1998. *Guatemala, nunca más: Informe del proyecto Interdiocesano Recuperación de la Memoria Histórica (REMHI)*. Guatemala: Oficina de Derechos Humanos del Arzobispado de Guatemala.

Reyes Narcisco, Francisco. 1998. *Lem ha' (espejos de agua): Estampas y tradiciones cobaneras*. Cobán, Guatemala: Corporación Municipal de Cobán.

Reynolds, Susan Bigelow. 2019. "Fieldwork in Ecclesial Borderlands: Culture, Community, and Belonging in a Multiethnic Boston Parish." *Exchange* 48 (3): 225–35.

Robbins, Joel. 2003. "What Is a Christian? Notes toward an Anthropology of Christianity." *Religion* 33 (3): 191–99.

Robbins, Joel. 2006. "Social Thought and Commentary: Anthropology and Theology: An Awkward Relationship?" *Anthropological Quarterly* 79 (2): 285–94.

Robbins, Joel. 2014. "The Anthropology of Christianity: Unity, Diversity, New Directions: An Introduction to Supplement 10." *Current Anthropology* 55 (S10): S157–71.

Rommen, Timothy. 2007. *Mek Some Noise: Gospel Music and the Ethics of Style in Trinidad*. Berkeley: University of California Press.

Rothschild, N. Harry. 2017. "Flouting, Flashing, and Favoritism: An Insouciant Buddhist Monk Bares His Midriff before the Confucian Court; Or Smile, You've Been Tanfu'ed!" In *Behaving Badly in Early and Medieval China*, edited by N. Harry Rothschild and Leslie V. Wallace, 154–68. Honolulu: University of Hawaii Press.

Rumsey, Alan, and Joel Robbins, 2008. "Social Thought and Commentary Section: Anthropology and the Opacity of Other Minds." *Anthropological Quarterly* 81 (2): 407–94.

Ruthrof, Horst. 2000. "Globalisation and the Theorisation of Language." *Social Semiotics* 10 (2): 187–200.

Sacks, Harvey. 1984. "On Doing 'Being Ordinary.'" *Structures of Social Action: Studies in Conversation Analysis*, edited by J. Maxwell Atkinson and John Heritage, 413–29. Cambridge: Cambridge University Press.

Salamone, Frank A. 1977. "Anthropologists and Missionaries: Competition or Reciprocity?" *Human Organization* 36 (4): 407–12.

Samson, C. Mathews. 2007. *Re-enchanting the World: Maya Protestantism in the Guatemalan Highlands*. Tuscaloosa: The University of Alabama Press.

Samuels, David W. 2004. *Putting a Song on Top of It: Expression and Identity on the San Carlos Apache Reservation*. Tucson: The University of Arizona Press.

Schegloff, Emanuel A., and Harvey Sacks. 1973. "Opening up Closings." *Semiotica* 8 (4): 289–327.

Schmitt, Carl. (1923) 1996. *Roman Catholicism and Political Form*. Translated by G. L. Ulmen. Contributions in Political Science, Global Perspectives in History and Politics, no. 380. Westport, CT: Greenwood Press.

Segundo, Juan Luis. 1985. *Theology and the Church: A Response to Cardinal Ratzinger and A Warning to the Whole Church*. Minneapolis, MN: Winston Press.

Selka, Stephen. 2007. *Religion and the Politics of Ethnic Identity in Bahia, Brazil*. Gainesville: University Press of Florida.

Shoaps, Robin A. 2002. "'Pray Earnestly': The Textual Construction of Personal Involvement in Pentecostal Prayer and Song." *Journal of Linguistic Anthropology* 12 (1): 34–71.

Small, Christopher. 1998. *Musicking: The Meanings of Performing and Listening*. Middletown, CT: Wesleyan University Press.

Soulaimani, Dris. 2017. "Embodiment in Moroccan Arabic Storytelling: Language, Stance and Discourse Analysis." *Text & Talk* 37 (3): 335–57. https://doi.org/10.1515/text-2017-0008

Stasch, Rupert. 2009. *Society of Others: Kinship and Mourning in a West Papuan Place*. Berkeley: University of California Press.

Stewart, Charles. 1999. "Syncretism and Its Synonyms: Reflections on Cultural Mixture." *Diacritics* 29 (3): 40–62.

Stewart, Stephen. 1980. *Gramática Kekchí*. Guatemala City: Editorial Académica Centro Americana.

Stokes, Martin. 1994. "Music in Human Life: Anthropological Perspectives on Music." *Man* 29 (3): 721–23.

Stoll, David. 1990. *Is Latin America Turning Protestant?: The Politics of Evangelical Growth*. Berkeley: University of California Press.

Stoller, Paul. 1997. *Sensuous Scholarship*. Philadelphia: University of Pennsylvania Press.

Streeck, Jürgen. 2008. "Gesture in Political Communication: A Case Study of the Democratic Presidential Candidates during the 2004 Primary Campaign." *Research on Language and Social Interaction* 41 (2): 154–86.

Stromberg, Peter G. 1993. *Language and Self-Transformation: A Study of the Christian Conversion Narrative*. Cambridge: Cambridge University Press.
Suenens, Léon Joseph. 1975. *A New Pentecost?* Translated by Francis Martin. New York: Seabury Press.
Sullivan-González, Douglass. 1998. *Piety, Power, and Politics: Religion and Nation Formation in Guatemala, 1821–1871*. Pittsburgh, PA: University of Pittsburgh Press.
Sullivan-González, Douglass. 2016. *The Black Christ of Esquipulas: Religion and Identity in Guatemala*. Lincoln: University of Nebraska Press.
Tarr, Bronwyn. 2017. "Social Bonding through Dance and 'Musiking.'" In *Distributed Agency*, edited by N. J. Enfield and Paul Kockelman, 151–58. New York: Oxford University Press.
Taussig, Michael. 1977. "The Genesis of Capitalism amongst a South American Peasantry: Devil's Labor and the Baptism of Money." *Comparative Studies in Society and History* 19 (2): 130–55.
Terga Cintrón, Ricardo. 1991. *Almas gemelas: Un estudio de la inserción Alemana en las Verapaces y la consecuente relación entre los alemanes y los k'ekchíes*. Cobán, Guatemala: Imprenta y Tipografía "El Norte."
Thornton, Brendan Jamal. 2016. *Negotiating Respect: Pentecostalism, Masculinity, and the Politics of Spiritual Authority in the Dominican Republic*. Gainesville: University Press of Florida.
Thorsen, Jakob Egeris. 2015. *Charismatic Practice and Catholic Parish Life: The Incipient Pentecostalization of the Church in Guatemala and Latin America*. Global Pentecostal and Charismatic Studies 17. Leiden, Netherlands: Brill.
Tsitsipis, Lukas D. 1998. *A Linguistic Anthropology of Praxis and Language Shift: Arvanitika (Albanian) and Greek in Contact*. Oxford: Clarendon Press.
Turner, Terence S. 2012. "The Social Skin." *HAU: Journal of Ethnographic Theory* 2 (2): 486–504.
Turrent, Lourdes. 1993. *La Conquista Musical de México*. Mexico City: Fondo de Cultura Econòmica.
Urban, Greg. 1988. "Ritual Wailing in Amerindian Brazil." *American Anthropologist* 90 (2): 385–400.
U.S. Department of State. 2018. "Guatemala 2018 International Religious Freedom Report." US Department of State. https://www.state.gov/wp-content/uploads/2019/05/GUATEMALA-2018-INTERNATIONAL-RELIGIOUS-FREEDOM-REPORT.pdf.
Van Oss, Adriaan Cornelis. 1986. *Catholic Colonialism: A Parish History of Guatemala, 1524–1821*. Cambridge: Cambridge University Press.
Velho, Otávio. 2007. "Missionization in the Post-Colonial World: A View from Brazil and Elsewhere." *Anthropological Theory* 7 (3): 273–93.
Verhelst, Daniël, and Nestor Pyke. 1995. *CICM Missionaries, Past and Present, 1862–1987: History of the Congregation of the Immaculate Heart of Mary (Scheut/Missionhurst)*. Lueven: Leuven University Press.
Villacorta, Lola. 1977. *Leyendas del calvario de Cobán*. Cobán, Guatemala.

Vološinov, V. N. (1929) 1986. *Marxism and the Philosophy of Language*. Translated by Ladislav Matejka and I. R. Titunik. Cambridge, MA: Harvard University Press.

Warren, Kay B. 1978. *The Symbolism of Subordination: Indian Identity in a Guatemalan Town*. Austin: University of Texas Press.

Warren, Kay B. 1998. *Indigenous Movements and Their Critics: Pan-Maya Activism in Guatemala*. Princeton, NJ: Princeton University Press.

Warren, Kay B. 2002. "Lessons from the 1999 Referendum." In *Indigenous Movements, Self-Representation, and the State in Latin America*, edited by Kay B. Warren and Jean E. Jackson, 149–80. Austin: University of Texas Press.

Watanabe, John. 1992. *Maya Saints and Souls in a Changing World*. Austin: University of Texas Press.

Weiss, Gail. 1999. *Body Images: Embodiment as Intercorporeality*. New York: Routledge.

Wharry, Cheryl. 2003. "Amen and Hallelujah Preaching: Discourse Functions in African American Sermons." *Language in Society* 32 (2): 203–25.

Wightman, Jill M. 2007. "Healing the Nation: Pentecostal Identity and Social Change in Bolivia." In *Conversion of a Continent: Contemporary Religious Change in Latin America*, edited by Timothy J. Steigenga and Edward L. Cleary, 239–55. New Brunswick, NJ: Rutgers University Press.

Wilk, Richard R. 1991. *Household Ecology: Economic Change and Domestic Life among the Kekchi Maya in Belize*. Tucson: University of Arizona Press.

Williams, Philip. 2000. "The Limits of Religious Influence: The Progressive Church in Nicaragua." In *On Earth as It Is in Heaven: Religion in Modern Latin America*, edited by Virginia Garrard-Burnett. Jaguar Books on Latin America 18. Wilmington, DE: SR Books.

Wilson, Richard. 1995. *Maya Resurgence in Guatemala: Q'eqchi' Experiences*. Norman: University of Oklahoma Press.

Wolf, Eric R. 1957. "Closed Corporate Peasant Communities in Mesoamerica and Central Java." *Southwestern Journal of Anthropology* 13 (1): 1–18.

Wolseth, Jon. 2011. *Jesus and the Gang: Youth Violence and Christianity in Urban Honduras*. Tucson: University of Arizona Press.

Woolard, Kathryn A. 1998. "Simultaneity and Bivalency as Strategies in Bilingualism." *Journal of Linguistic Anthropology* 8 (1): 3–29.

Woolard, Kathryn A. 2004. "Codeswitching." *A Companion to Linguistic Anthropology*, 73–94.

Wright-Rios, Edward. 2009. *Revolutions in Mexican Catholicism: Reform and Revelation in Oaxaca, 1887–1934*. Durham, NC: Duke University Press.

Ziegler, Joanna E. 2006. "Scholarship and/as Performance: The Case of Johan Huizinga and His Concept of 'Historical Sensation.'" In *Practicing Catholic: Ritual, Body, and Contestation in Catholic Faith*, edited by Bruce T. Morrill, Joanna E. Ziegler, and Susan Rodgers, 247–55. New York: Palgrave Macmillan.

INDEX

Acción Católica Rural. *See* Catholic Action
aj ilonel. *See* Maya priest
altars: in homes, 37, 46; in village chapels, 183
Alta Verapaz, 36–38. *See also* Verapaz
ancestors (*qaxe' qatoon*), 56, 58, 83, 93n6, 225–26. *See also* elders
andas. *See* biers
animation of religious services, 44n8, 47–48, 96, 100n10, 136, 161–63, 176; secular uses, 196n11
animation of voices, 113–14, 141, 169, 183
anthropologists in relation to: missionaries, 14n9; theologians, 234
anthropology of: body movement, 181n5, 199; Catholicism, 17–18, 17n13, 234; Christianity, 11, 14–17, 14n10, 32; gesture, 180–82; Guatemala, 16, 59, 205; language, 13, 23, 27, 179–80; music, 169; voice, 172n16
Aparecida. *See* CELAM
Asad, Talal, 94
authority, 93, 94–96, 114; catechists, 102–3, 107–8, 109, 111–13, 188; competing structures of, 6–8, 50–51, 62–63, 65–66, 225–26; embodiment of, 183–84, 188; in heteroglossia, 24–25; preachers, 106, 108, 109, 113–16, 188; priests, 10, 102n12, 121

Bakhtin, Mikhail M., 20–25, 20n15. *See also* chronotope; dialogism; heteroglossia; voicing
Barrio Minuto de Dios, 75
Barrios, Justo Rufino (president), 61
Belgium, 42
Benedict XVI (pope), 69
Bible: catechist uses of, 47, 98–99, 100, 102, 107, 110; Charismatic uses of, 104–6, 108, 110, 115–16; exegesis of, 96–97, 109, 116; knowledge of, 230; reading, 47, 96, 98, 99, 101, 165–66, 183; relation to ancestral Maya religion, 56, 225, 232; translations in Q'eqchi', 98n8
biers (*andas*), 201, 208n3; act of carrying, 213–14, 216–18; assembly, 206, 207–8, 210, 222. *See also* processions
Black Christ of Esquipulas (Cristo Negro de Esquipulas). *See* El Señor de Esquipulas

body: body movement, 161, 177–79, 180, 181n5, 182–200 *passim*; body stillness, 183, 184, 188, 189, 193, 197–99, 226; in communication, 12–13, 179–82 (*see also* gesture); embodiment of Christian subjectivity, 161, 178, 190, 213, 226; in ethnography, 213; posture, 179, 180, 183, 189, 191; in religion, 161, 178, 198, 213–15, 221–22; sensations, 166, 217–18. *See also* hexis; intercorporeality; metakinesis

Bogotá. *See* Barrio Minuto de Dios

Bourdieu, Pierre, 199

call-and-response routines, 106, 109, 110n14, 136–37, 139, 188, 226; use by Mainstream Catholics, 141n16

Cameroon, 9, 42n42, 228

carismáticos. *See* Charismatic Catholics

Carrera Turcios, José Rafael (president), 61n3

Casariego y Acevedo, Mario (archbishop), 76

Castillo Armas, Carlos (president), 67

catechists (*catequistas*), 3, 6, 10, 63–67, 84–86; duties, 44n8, 47–48, 50n11, 101, 162, 229; gender, 112n15; performance, 183–84, 186; as pseudonym for Mainstream Catholics, 8–9; qualities of, 46, 102, 107–8, 111–13, 165, 198, 230; relationship to clergy, 10, 49, 70–71, 102–3, 103n12, 109, 182n6; training (*cholob'ank*), 97–100; training program origins, 100n11, 150n3. *See also* authority, catechists; sermons, catechists

Catholic Action, 63–67, 80–81, 85

Catholic Charismatic Renewal (*La Renovación*), 48, 48n10, 74–79, 80–81; global origins of, 74–76, 75n13; in Guatemala, 48n10, 76–77, 115; in San Felipe, 5, 48–51, 116–17, 230–31. *See also* Charismatic Catholics

Catholic Church, 13, 17–18, 47, 56, 63, 76, 96, 101–2, 112; in Guatemala, 10, 17, 59n2, 61, 61n3, 67, 73, 202–3, 232; hierarchy, 6–7, 18, 70, 76, 96, 107–9, 156; in Latin America, 15, 61, 64n7, 67, 68–70 (*see also* CELAM); Pentecostalization of, 18, 231; renewal of, 77–78, 231 (*see also* Catholic Charismatic Renewal). *See also* Diocese of Verapaz; San Felipe parish; Vatican II

CEB (ecclesial base community, *comunidad eclesial de base*, *ch'utam*), 45–48, 69; compared to Charismatics, 49–50, 106; variability of, 45n9

CELAM (Episcopal Conference of Latin America, *Consejo Episcopal Latinoamericano*): 1st general meeting, Rio de Janeiro (1955), 68n10; 2nd general meeting, Medellín (1968), 41, 68–69, 71; 3rd general meeting, Puebla (1979), 70–71; 4th general meeting, Santo Domingo (1992), 71, 81n17; 5th general meeting, Aparecida (2007), 229

Celebration of the Word (*Celebración de la Palabra, Xnimqehinkil li Raatin*), 45, 47, 100–1, 107, 132; compared to Mass, 98, 100; music, 156

centrifugal force, 22

centripetal force, 22, 88

chapels, 10, 35, 40, 46, 50; as contested spaces, 4–7, 50n11, 149–50, 168n15, 224–26

charismata. *See* gifts of the spirit

Charismatic Catholics (*carismáticos, católicos renovados*), 4–10, 13, 17–18, 48–51, 55, 87, 96, 104–6, 108, 109–10, 115, 118, 133–34, 175–78, 188, 211, 223–26, 230–31; conversion, 48, 50, 146, 147, 166–68, 170; in Guatemala City, 18, 115, 157; language (*see also* code, mixing), 82–83, 119–21, 123–25, 126, 134–42; music and song, 149–50, 157–58, 160–62, 161n11, 163–64, 166–67, 169–70, 177, 195–96, 197–98; prayer, 190–92, 194,

195. *See also* Catholic Charismatic Renewal; hymnals, Charismatic Catholic; preachers
Charles V, Holy Roman Emperor, 35
cholob'ank. See catechists, training program
chronotope, 25
CICM (Congregation of the Immaculate Heart of Mary, *Congregatio Immaculati Cordis Mariae*), 42, 42n6, 97, 150
clapping, 10, 119–20, 169, 170, 171, 195–97, 198
Cobán, Alta Verapaz, 34–52 *passim*; central plaza (parque central), 36, 202, 202n1; economy, 37–38, 39–40; geography, 36–37, 202; history, 35; peri-urban areas, 40–41; in relation to other parts of Guatemala, 35, 38; soundscape, 147–50. *See also* Verapaz; villages
code: choice, 82–83, 120–21, 124–26, 124, 125, 126, 137–38, 173; consistency, 83, 125–26, 132, 142–43, 188, 189, 198; mixing, 134–37, 142; switching, 83, 121, 123, 126, 129, 133–34, 139, 141–44, 188–89
cofradías, 34–35, 37, 40, 51–52, 74, 87, 127n5, 152n6; Catholic Action and, 63–66; Costumbre and, 61–63, 80; history of, 62n5; Inculturation and, 72; social function of, 59–60. *See also* Costumbre; Hermandad de San Felipe
complexio oppositorum (complex of opposites), 18–19
comunidad eclesial de base. *See* CEB
Congo: Belgian, 42n6; Democratic Republic of, 9, 42n6, 97, 228
conversion narratives, 167–68
copal pom (incense), 35, 53, 62, 89, 128, 202
Costumbre (traditionalist Maya Catholicism), 48, 61–62, 65, 74, 80–82, 83, 117, 225, 232. *See also* cofradías
creolization. *See* syncretism

dance, 168–71, 177–78, 196–98, 199, 200; Inculturation and, 73; in Mainstream Catholicism, 126, 126n4, 152n6, 225
dialogism, 23, 73, 88, 94. *See also* monologism
Diocese of Verapaz, 36, 45, 153, 157, 164, 229; as Diocese of Verapaz y Petén, 63; and indigenous peoples, 41–42, 42n5, 73; and music, 153, 157; structure of, 42n5, 164
Dominicans (Order of Preachers), 36, 73, 90–92, 145, 146n1. *See also* missionaries
Duquesne University, (Pittsburgh, PA), 74
Durou y Sure, Luis (archbishop), 63

Easter. *See* Holy Week
ecclesial base community. *See* CEB
elders, community (*ancianos*), 74, 93n6, 123. *See also* ancestors; cofradías
El Señor de Esquipulas, 45, 92n5, 207, 209n4; history of, 127n5; rituals in honor of, 45, 126–32, 207, 224–25
El Señor en Agonía, 90–93, 228
embodied sociocultural linguistics, 180–81
embodiment. *See* body; intercorporeality
Episcopal Conference of Latin America. *See* CELAM
Esquipulas, Chiquimula, 127n5. *See also* El Señor de Esquipulas
esquisuche tree, 91n3
Evangélicos (Protestant Christians), 4, 6, 7n5, 13–14, 15–16, 24, 36, 40, 49, 59–60, 138, 148, 168, 202n1, 204–5, 208, 222, 229, 230; compared to Charismatic Catholics, 9–10, 75, 77, 119, 123, 124, 139, 149–50; history in Guatemala, 59n2, 63–64, 66n9; media, 115, 147, 157. *See also* Pentecostal Christianity

fireworks, 126, 129–32, 203, 207; *torito*, 126n4

Flores Reyes, Gerardo Humberto (bishop), 42
food and drink, 33, 35, 37–38, 39, 40, 62, 119n1, 127, 176, 210
footing, 129

Gálvez, Mariano (president), 59n2
García Herreros, Rafael. *See* Barrio Minuto de Dios
Geertz, Clifford, 199–200
Gerardi Conedera, Juan José (bishop), 41n4, 71
gesture, 12–13, 178–95 *passim*, 199–200; anthropology of, 181–82; categorization, 184–85n7; historiography of, 181n4; ideology, 13, 179; language and, 178–79, 179n3, 180–81, 184–86, 198; linguistics and, 185n8; methodological problems, 179–80, 185n8; performative encounter, 194; phrases, 185n8, 186–87; units, 185n8, 186–87
gifts of the spirit (charismata, *dones*), 74–75, 78, 78n15, 104, 106, 108, 109–10, 113–16, 161, 166–67, 231
glossolalia, 77n14, 114, 178, 189, 231. *See also* gifts of the spirit
Guatemalan Civil War, 10, 16–17, 39, 41n4, 57, 71, 81, 85–86, 146
Gutiérrez, Gustavo, 68–70. *See also* Liberation Theology

Haeserijn, Esteban, 150n3
hauntings, 38n3
Hermandad de San Felipe, 126–32, 128n6, 128n7, 203, 206–12, 213–15, 217; leadership of, 127–28. *See also* cofradías
Hermano Pedro de San José Betancur (saint), 91
heteroglossia, 20–23, 88, 94, 144, 149, 204–5; as model for Catholicism, 23–25, 26, 56–57, 95, 234; as model for religious life in Cobán, 204–5, 222; as sonic reality, 148

hexis, 199. *See also* body
Hoenes family, 30–31, 31n16
holy missions of the people. *See las santas misiones populares*
Holy Spirit (*Espíritu Santo, Santil Musiq'e*), 49, 77n14, 78n16, 81, 104, 108, 144, 148, 161, 171, 175, 177–78, 188–89, 198, 222, 225, 231; baptism in, 74–75, 78; experience of, 166–68, 189, 192, 195–96, 231; songs about, 151, 170, 174, 177. *See also* gifts of the spirit
Holy Week (*Semana Santa*), 45, 61, 201–3, 212, 219; Easter Wednesday, 203–4; Good Friday, 213, 217; in Guatemala City, 214n8; in Santiago, Atitlán, 205. *See also* processions
hybridization. *See* syncretism
hymnals, 147, 150–55 *passim*; Charismatic Catholic, 153–55; Mainstream Catholic, 150–53, 151n5, 155, 156, 197; as tool for literacy, 151n4
hymns (alabanzas), 4, 8, 10, 19, 24, 98, 100, 101, 106, 119–20, 128, 133–35, 147–74 *passim*, 231–32; circulation of, 155–57; embodied performance, 195–99; pragmatics, 169–71; structure and content, 157–61. *See also* hymnals; music; singing

ICM (Missionary Sisters of the Immaculate Heart of Mary, *Immaculati Cordis Mariae*), 97n7
Inculturation theology, 48, 56, 71–74, 79, 80–81, 83, 87, 124–25, 232
indigenous languages, Diocese of Verapaz, 42n4, 42n5; Inculturation and, 73, 81; language rights, 84; sign languages, 185n7. *See also* Q'eqchi' language
intercorporeality, 206, 215, 220, 221–22
intersubjectivity, 206, 219–22
Irarrázaval, Diego, 72. *See also* Inculturation Theology

Jesus, 12, 203–5, 206, 224–25; identification with, 83, 210, 213–14, 217–19, 221, 221n11; Inculturation Theology, 72; intimacy with, 208–10, 215; language spoken by, 83, 141–42; Liberation Theology, 70; Mesoamerican versions, 93; songs about, 157–60, 170. *See also* El Señor en Agonía; El Señor de Esquipulas
John Paul II (pope), 70, 91, 148
jóvenes (youth), 155, 165, 210, 211

Kendon's continuum. *See* gesture, categorization

Ladinos (mestizos), 7, 18, 31–32, 42, 48, 58, 62, 64–65, 82, 123n3, 127, 146, 164n13, 176, 228, 231–32; as *kaxlan*, 7n5, 232
language. *See* anthropology of, language; Charismatic Catholics, language; code; gesture, language and; glossolalia; indigenous languages; Jesus, language spoken by; Mainstream Catholics, language; Mass, language of; multilingualism; prayer, language; Q'eqchi' language; sign language
language ideologies, 13, 23, 172, 179, 220, 233
language shift, 123
La Renovación. *See* Catholic Charismatic Renewal; Charismatic Catholics
las Casas, Bartolomé de, 35, 145–46
las santas misiones populares, 229–33
La Virgen del Rosario (Our Lady of the Rosary), 34n1
Lent, 45, 207–10, 213, 219
leyendas populares (folk tales), 91
Liberation Theology, 48, 67–71, 72, 74, 78–79, 80–81, 85–86
literacy, 47, 69, 96, 107, 151; programs, 64; texts, 98, 151n4

Mainstream Catholics, 8–9, 11–13, 44–48, 49–51, 55, 82–83, 96, 132, 168n15, 173; language, 83, 122–26, 129–32, 142–43, 188, 189, 198 (*see also* code, consistency); music and song, 158–59, 162–64, 171, 197, 198–99; prayer, 190, 192–93, 195. *See also* catechists; CEB; hymnals, Mainstream Catholic
Maldonado, Alonso de (governor), 145
Maryknoll (Catholic Foreign Mission Society of America), 64n6, 67
Marroquín, Francisco (bishop), 145
Mass, 9, 44–45, 47, 48, 50, 98, 148, 151, 162; Charismatic Catholics and, 48n10, 118–21, 143–44; language of, 120–21, 122–23, 139n12, 228; music in, 148, 149, 156, 165, 219
Maya cultural activism, 57–60, 81–82, 83–87; and religion, 58, 86–87
Maya priest (*sacerdote Maya, aj ilonel*), 53–56, 58, 72, 87
mayejak (offering ceremony), 53, 55–56; Catholic Church and, 56, 83
Medellín. *See* CELAM
Medvedev, Pavel, 20, 20n15
mestizos. *See* Ladinos
metakinesis, 198
missionaries, 61, 63–64, 102; anthropologists and, 14n9; lay people as disciple-missionaries, 229–30; Protestant, 59n2, 63, 64. *See also* CICM; Dominicans; ICM; Maryknoll
monologism, 24, 94
Mosconi, Luís, 229
multilingualism, 10, 122–24, 123n3
music, 145–74 *passim*; as claim on space, 147–48; conversion through, 166, 174; evangelization through, 145–47, 146n1, 168n15; genres, 150n3, 152, 156, 163–64; instruments, 119, 145, 147, 149, 152n6, 155–56, 161, 164, 165–67, 201, 207n2; literacy, 152, 155; media, 147, 150, 154–55, 157 (*see also* hymnals); morality of, 146n1; of processions, 201, 207n2. *See also*

music (*continued*)
    Charismatic Catholics, music and song; Mainstream Catholics, music and song; singing
musicians, 35, 48, 133, 146n1, 149, 157, 176, 197, 207; in church hierarchies, 165–67. *See also* Renacer en Cristo (band)
musicking, 168–71, 198–99

Nahuales (Maya day spirits), 58
New Year's celebrations, 45, 118–22, 175–77

Orthodox Christians, 16n12

Pan-Maya Movement. *See* Maya cultural activism
Parishes: heterogeneity within, 8–10, 81n17, 83, 87–89, 173; *parroquias de indios*, 42n7; relations among, 42n5, 48, 209n5, 211–12; as unit of analysis, 25–26. *See also* San Felipe parish
Paul (apostle), 12, 78n15
Paul VI (pope), 69, 77
Pentecost, 77n14
Pentecostal Christianity, 6, 15–16, 157, 161n11, 169, 197, 202, 204–5, 229; Catholic Charismatic Renewal and, 74–77, 78n15; sounds of, 119–20, 147, 205. *See also* Evangélicos
Peter (apostle), 12, 167
Philippines, 42, 97, 181
Pittsburgh. *See* Duquesne University
Pius V (pope), 34
Pop, Francisco, 90–91, 90n2
Popol Vuh, 232n7
positionality of author, 30–33
prayer, 9–11, 13, 45, 47, 56, 98, 134–36, 161, 166, 171, 175, 176n2, 182, 189–95, 198, 204, 209, 210, 215, 227n4; embodied, 190–95, 198; inspiration, 104–5, 106, 113, 114; language, 82–83, 119, 123–25, 228; Maya priests', 53, 55; *Pater Noster*, 98, 148, 151, 224; postures, 190; Rosary, 34n1, 127–29, 151; singing as, 148; texts, 151
preachers (*predicadores*), 96–97, 103–6; duties, 50, 96, 140; gender, 104; performance, 139–42, 183–84, 187–89; qualities, 108–9, 110, 113–15. *See also* authority, preachers; sermons, preachers
processions, 93n6, 129, 201–22 *passim*; effects of, 214–15, 219, 222; funding, 208–9; patron saint's day, 34–35, 51–52; preparations for, 206–11; sensorium of, 201–4; *visitas de hogares*, 209–10, 214–15. *See also* biers; Holy Week
Protestant Christians. *See* Evangélicos
Puebla. *See* CELAM

Q'eqchi' language, 5, 31, 83, 85, 123; and Catholicism, 8, 10–11, 13, 26, 41–42n4, 124–25, 132n9, 150, 164n13, 171 (*see also* code consistency), 228, 229; Ladinos' knowledge of, 31, 123n3
Q'eqchi'-Maya cultural concepts: community (*ch'utam*), 45; earth spirits (*Tzuultaq'a*), 62, 91; heart (*ch'ool*), 4n3, 83, 193; honorifics (*Qawa'* and *Qana'*), 53n1; household (*junkab'al*), 41; kinship categories, 138n11; respect, 5, 109, 125, 128, 194–95, 224; social maturity, 107n13. *See also* ancestors; elders; *mayejak*
Q'eqchi'-Maya ethnic identity, 60, 82–83, 85; and religion, 4–5, 7, 10–11, 24, 55–57, 60, 86, 225, 231–32

racism, 65–66, 125, 140n14
radio: Charismatics' use of, 115, 157, 164, 176–77; Hermandad de San Felipe's use of, 208, 211
Renacer en Cristo (band), 176–77, 187

Roman Catholic Church. *See* Catholic Church
Rosary. *See* prayer, Rosary
Rosell y Arellano, Mariano (archbishop), 63

San Felipe church, 41, 56, 89, 92n5, 176n2, 228
San Felipe parish, 8–11, 24–25, 41–51 *passim*, 82–87, 228–32; founding of, 41–42. *See also* Hermandad de San Felipe
San Juan Chamelco, Alta Verapaz, 150n3
San Pedro Carchá, Alta Verapaz, 48, 151, 153, 176
Santa Catalina La Tinta, Alta Verapaz, 151
Santa Cruz Verapaz, Alta Verapaz, 31, 122
Santa María Cahabón, Alta Verapaz, 151n4
Santiago Atitlán, Sololá, 61n4, 205
Santo Domingo (city). *See* CELAM
Santo Domingo de Guzmán (Saint Dominico of Osma), 34–35
santos (saints), 34–35, 37, 51–52, 55, 74, 127–29, 176n2, 208n3, 201–4, 206–11; carrying of, 213–15, 217–18, 221–22; in Costumbre: 62, 65, 80, 152n6. *See also* El Señor de Esquipulas; El Señor en Agonía; La Virgen del Rosario; Santo Domingo de Guzmán
Scheut, missionaries of. *See* CICM
Schmitt, Carl. *See* complexio oppositorum
Second Vatican Council. *See* Vatican II
sermons, 47, 95–96; catechists, 100–3, 107, 109, 110–11, 183; preachers, 103–6, 108, 109–10, 113–15, 161, 183–84. *See also* preaching

sign language, 185n7
Simon of Cyrene, 221
singing, 98, 106, 119, 154, 155, 164; embodied aspects, 195–99; evangelization and, 146–47; as point of contention between congregations, 7–8, 10, 125, 149, 173–74; as prayer, 148; and subjectivity, 169–71. *See also* hymns; music
sodalities. *See* cofradías; Hermandad de San Felipe
spontaneity, 109–10, 140–41, 188–89; rehearsed, 110n14
Suenens, Leo Jozef (cardinal), 77–78
suffering, 67, 215, 219, 222, 225
syncretism, 55. *See also* Costumbre

Tezulutlán, 35, 145–46. *See also* Alta Verapaz

Vatican II, 25, 41, 60–61, 67–68, 77, 96
Verapaz, 35, 145–46. *See also* Alta Verapaz; Diocese of Verapaz; Tezulutlán
Verbist, Theophile, 42n6
village (*aldea, k'aleb'aal*), 8, 38–40, 44
vigils (*vigilias*), 49, 175–78, 191
voice (grammatical construction), 160, 169–70
voice (sound), 149–50, 171–73, 190, 196, 197, 197n12. *See also* anthropology of, voice; singing
voicing, 21–23, 94, 124, 137, 169–70; of Catholicism, 24, 87–88, 95, 111–12, 190, 200, 227, 231–32; double-voicing, 23. *See also* animation of voices
Vološinov, V. N., 20, 23

ABOUT THE AUTHOR

Eric Hoenes del Pinal was born in Guatemala. He has earned a BA from Boston University, a PhD from the University of California, San Diego, and is currently an assistant professor of religious studies at the University of North Carolina at Charlotte. He is the co-editor of *Mediating Catholicism: Religion and Media in Global Catholic Imaginaries*, and his work has appeared in *Anthropological Quarterly*, *Contemporary Religion*, and the *Journal of Global Catholicism*.